pompom

READY -SET- SOCKS

SOCK DESIGNS FOR EVERY KNITTER

PATTERNS BY RACHEL COOPEY

Ready Set Socks
Published in 2022 by Pom Pom Press

ISBN: 978-1-9160295-9-0

A catalogue record for this book is available from the British Library.

Sock Pattern Designer: Rachel Coopey

Editors + Creative Directors: Lydia Gluck + Meghan Fernandes

Managing Editor: Amy Collins

Design + Layout: Bless

Pattern Photography: Kendra Bellamy

Tutorial Writing: Sophie Heathscott

Publisher + Marketing Director: Belinda Johnson

UK Wholesale Manager + Community Liaison: Sophie Heathscott

US Wholesale Manager: Jasmine Payne

Features Editor: Francesca Baldry

Production Coordinator + Retail Manager: Alice Sleight

Social Media + Digital Content Coordinator: Sofia Aatkar

Studio Managers: Anoushka Hartounian + Gayle Taliaferro Gilner

Technical Editors: Jemima Bicknell + Laura Chau + Chaitanya Muralidhara

Tutorial Illustrations: Lydia Gluck

Copy Editor: Annie Prime

Consultant: Emi Ito

Models: Lauren Nathan-Lane, Araba Olivia Ackon, Kit Aatkar, Anoushka Hartounian, Belinda Johnson, Lydia Gluck, Sofia Aatkar, Sophie Heathscott

Photographer's Assistant: Olivia Ezechukwu

Hair + Makeup: Jenny Green

Yarn Support: Black Elephant, Coop Knits, John Arbon Textiles, La Bien Aimée, Neighborhood Fiber Co., Opal, Purl Soho, Retrosaria Rosa Pomar, The Uncommon Thread, The Wandering Flock, Qing Fibre, The Wool Kitchen, Vicki Brown Designs

Sample Knitters: Alison Hellyer, Chonita Olivas, Lauren Shields, Rachel Coopey, Rebecca Yohe, Sofia Aatkar, Sophie Heathscott, Tanya Kirk

Test Knitters: Agnese Linarts, Alex Eloriaga, Alexandra Sébastien, Angela Espute, Anne-Marie Fairhurst, Ashley Little, Beth Leath, Cardner Babakitis, Catherine Boucher, Cheryl A Tan, Darlene Daigle, Eva Jonsson, Jade Kelley, Jessica Schons, Julie Keymolen, Katrien Hoes, Kellen Boucher, Kristin Irgens, Lauryl Fine, Libby Newhousek, Liz Barron, Liz Dunphy, Maddy Moe, Maria dooley, Marie-Elyse Dugal, Michaela, Michele Messenger, N.Santos, Nicola Nicholson, Orvietta Shannon, Raphi Tayvah, Rebecca Newman, Reiko, Sabine Prehn-Schuldt, Sabine Drachenherz, Sam Wu, Samantha Geary, Sarah Friend, Sarah Varnavides, Sigga, Silke Piehlig, Stacey McDonald, Suzanne Stallard, Tamara Bubalo, Veena Mosur

For pattern corrections, please visit: *pompommag.com/errata*

Printed sustainably in the UK by Pureprint Group Limited, a CarbonNeutral® Company with FSC® chain of custody and an ISO 14001 certified environmental management system recycling over 99% of all dry waste. The paper is Carbon Balanced with the World Land Trust™, an international conservation charity, who offset carbon emissions through the purchase and preservation of high conservation value land.

www.carbonbalancedpaper.com
CBP00019082504183028

POM POM PRESS
Hackney Downs Studios
Charcoal Hall
Amhurst Terrace
London E8 2BT
United Kingdom

Stay in Touch:
pompommag.com
ravelry.com/groups/pom-pom

@pompommag
@pompommag
@pompommag
@pompommag

CONTENTS

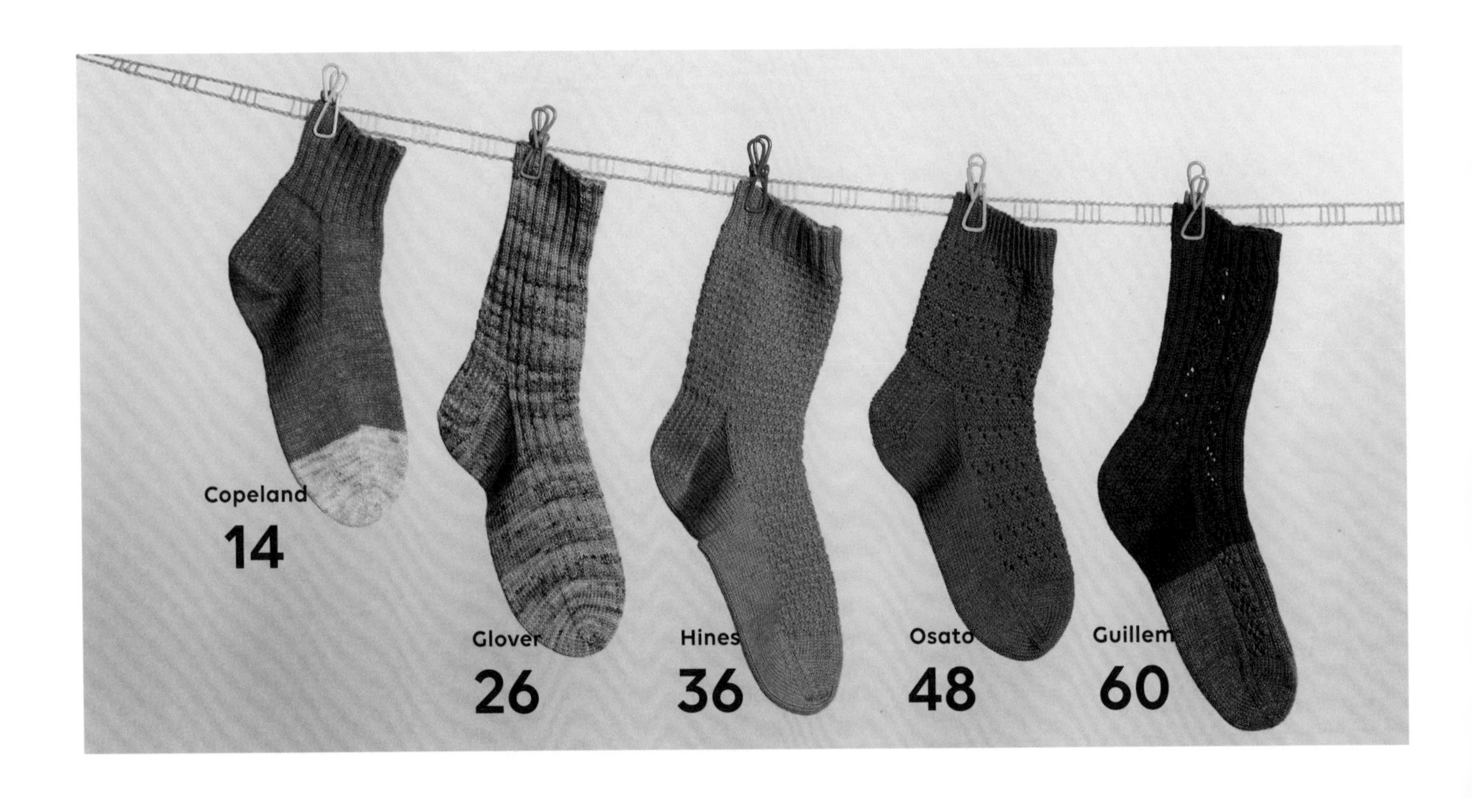

To download your free digital edition of this book, please see the download code printed on the inside of the back cover.

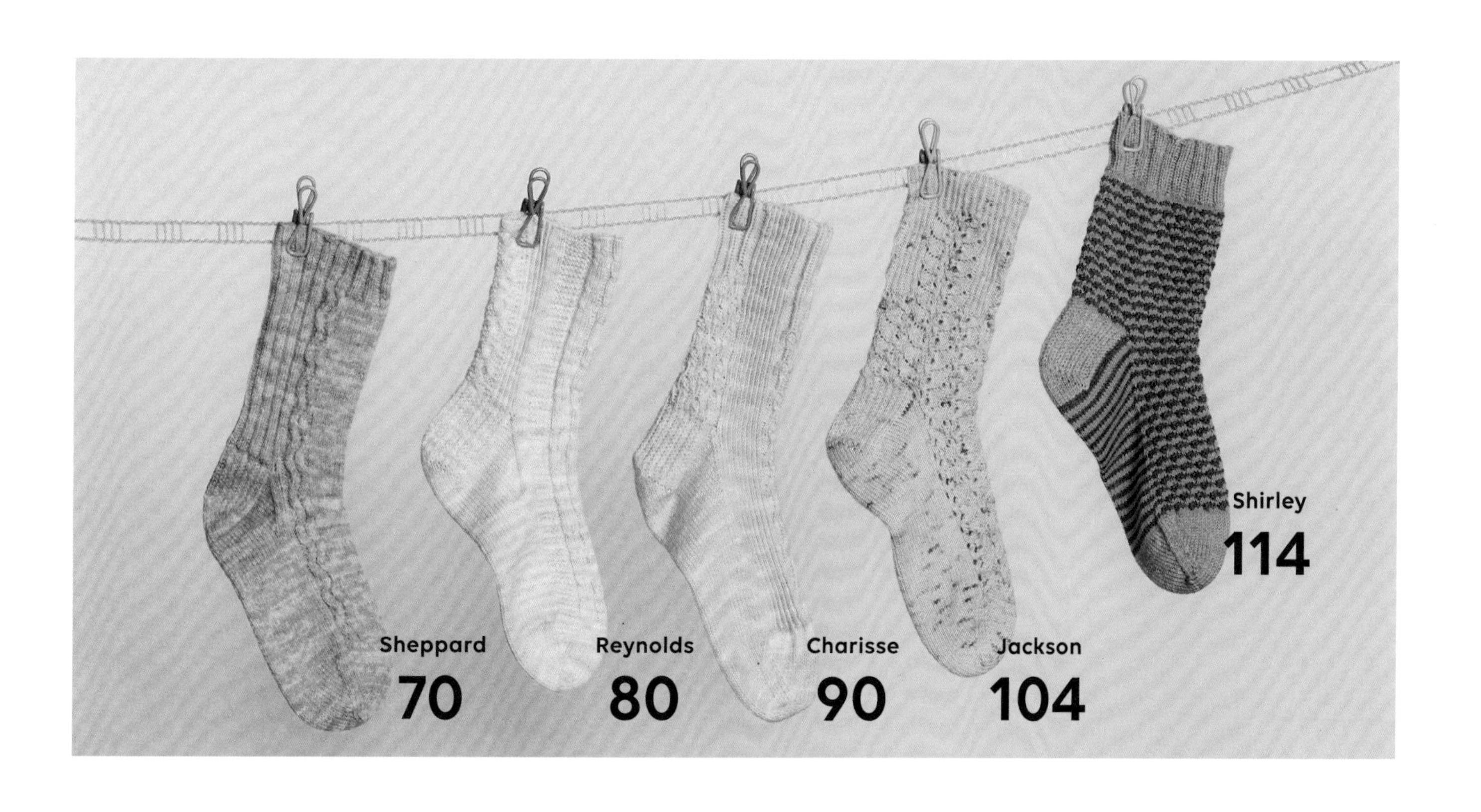

INTRODUCTION

Hello sock knitter!

That's you! You might know that already. You might be a Sock Knitter, with capitals because it's a part of your identity. One of those people who always has a pair on the go in their bag, ready to whip out while waiting around at the post office, able to stitch away without even looking. *Or* you might be new to socks, and thinking to yourself, "how on earth do you make that weird foot shape with just string and pointy sticks?!" Either way, now you have this book in your hands, you can knit socks, and you are well on your way to becoming a Sock Knitter, if you like.

You might be joining us on our knit book journey, starting with our beginner's guide, *Knit How,* followed by our pullover book, *Ready Set Raglan.* And if so, welcome back! Not to worry if that's not the case; we can pick up with socks from right here.

We've taught a lot of people to knit over the years, and socks are often the thing they want to knit most. There's nothing like the lush, cosy feeling of handknitted socks on what is often the most neglected, hard-worn part of our bodies. Knowing that this great desire to knit socks is out there, as is the need for a modern, inclusive compendium of patterns for new and seasoned sock knitters alike, we are proud to present *Ready Set Socks.*

Sock maven Rachel Coopey joins us on this leg (foot?!) of our journey and we couldn't be more excited to have her glorious designs as our map. We know that once you get started, you'll be as hooked on making socks as we are!

Lots of woolly love,
Meghan + Lydia
xoxo

LET'S TALK ABOUT SOCKS, BABY

Handknitted socks have a very long history. An early example of socks made with yarn date back to Egypt some time between the 3rd and 5th centuries AD, and can be found at the Victoria & Albert Museum in London. These were made using a technique known as 'nålbindning', thought to be a precursor to knitting. Since then, advances in technology mean that most people wear store-bought socks that are made by machine, often of cotton. Like many handcrafts today, there is no need financially or otherwise to knit one's own socks. Still, socks remain one of the most frequently handknit items today. Why is that?

The answer is much the same as why we'd choose to knit *anything* ourselves these days! It's partly for the enjoyment of the process and partly to create a finished product that is truly unique. In terms of the process, one of the reasons we love knitting socks in particular is because they are small and portable so you can always have a pair on the go in your bag. There's nothing like realising your train is late or that you have a long wait at the doctor's office and remembering you have some knitting you can work on to pass the time! Socks are also relatively quick to make - they make a great palette cleanser after working on a big pullover project, for example, because they are so much smaller. By the same token, they also don't require a lot of yarn, meaning you can use up scraps or that lonely single skein that has been hanging around for a while.

Handknitted socks can be simple and snuggly, or you can go all out with texture, lace, or cables (or all of the above!) without having to commit to any of those techniques on a large project like a pullover. Socks are compelling in that people are often happy to wear colourful socks even if the rest of their clothing style is not quite so loud. The colour and pattern can be a fun secret for the wearer alone to enjoy. Their unobtrusiveness in our outfits means that they are a safe bet as gifts too if you're even remotely unsure of the recipient's tastes - and a very lovely gift, at that!

More than anything, for us, the joy of handmade socks is that making them feels like a superpower. When we started knitting it didn't occur to us that we would want to make something that is so often hidden by shoes or only worn at home. But once we made our first socks, we were in love! Creating a heel shape is mind-blowing and the speed at which you can finish a sock is very satisfying. And when you put them on you will be amazed at how different they feel - so much better than regular socks, like a warm hug for your feet!

There are several ways to knit a sock. It might seem obvious, but it is much more preferable to knit a sock in the round - as a tube - than to knit a flat piece and seam it. Seams on socks can be uncomfortable, like having a tiny stone stuck in your shoe, and we wouldn't wish that on anyone! In this book, all the sock patterns start from the cuff and end with the toe. This is the easiest way to ensure a perfect fit for the intended recipient, as you can knit the foot portion until it reaches the exact length you need (as opposed to working from the toe upwards).

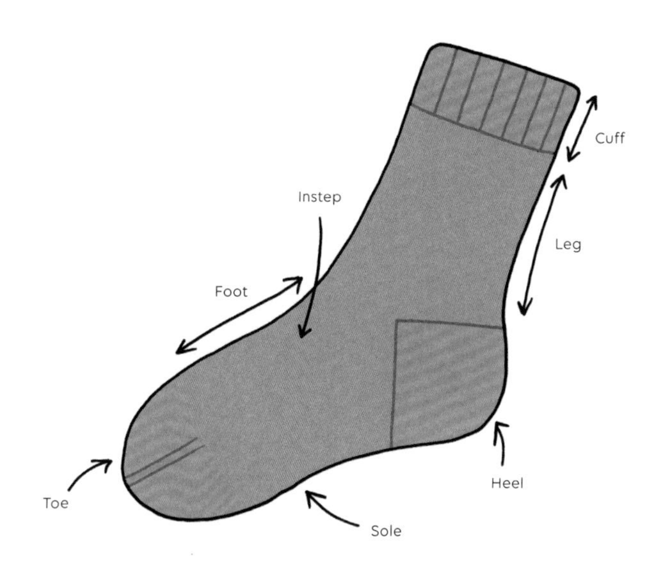

TOP-DOWN SOCK BASICS

- **Sock is worked down the leg, to create a knee-length, mid-calf, or ankle-length sock**
- **Then, the heel is worked**
- **Foot portion (instep and sole) is worked to desired length**
- **Stitches are decreased to shape the toe section**
- **Remaining stitches are grafted together to finish**

The socks in this book are knit in the round on circular or double-pointed needles, starting from the top of the sock and moving down to the heel. Working a heel is pure alchemy - the first few times you do it, it's a bit of a mystery (feet are such an odd shape!), but if you follow the instructions exactly and trust the pattern, you'll find you have 'turned a heel', as if by magic! We still haven't lost the wonder of turning a heel, even after knitting hundreds of socks between us.

Once you've turned the heel and knit the instep and sole of the foot, stitches are worked for the toe. This means decreasing stitches to shape the sock at the natural narrowing of the toes, followed, finally, by grafting the remaining stitches together to make a seamless pocket for the tip of your foot. In knitting terminology, the grafting technique used to close the opening at the toe is sometimes referred to as Kitchener stitch. The namesake for this eponymous stitch was Lord Kitchener, an official in the British army during multiple wars, including a number of imperialistic campaigns. In an effort to decolonise the language we use, we will refer to the technique simply as 'grafting' throughout the book.

We start with the simplest of the bunch: a plain stocking stitch sock with basic ribbing that works as a wonderful jumping-off point for learning the mechanics of sock knitting, *or* if you're already a pro, as a blank canvas for letting stripes or particularly interesting yarns shine. Following these are pairs with simple textures, followed by lacy, cabled, twisted stitch, and even mosaic stitch socks to keep you engrossed in your knitting as your confidence builds, sock by sock. Throughout the book, we show you each pattern in both 4-ply (fingering) and DK-weight yarns of all different colours to illustrate just how unique a small adjustment can make your pair. You might find it hard to believe they were all made from the same pattern! Such is the beauty of knitting your own socks.

For our guide on how to make modifications to your socks, see the Variations, Tutorials + Adjustments section on page 124.

Top Tip! Needle Know-How

Socks can be made using any method of working in the round over a small circumference. Double pointed needles (DPNs), magic loop with a long circular needle, two circular needles, or a small circular needle will all yield the same result. Everyone will find a favourite way of working and we encourage sock knitters to try all the methods to find the one which works for them! We've got tutorials on using DPNs or the magic loop method on page 150.

Needles are available in different materials and, again, personal preference will dictate the ones you choose. Wooden needles feel warmer and may have more give than metal needles; metal needles may have a sharper point (perhaps allowing you to knit faster but also increasing the likelihood of split stitches). Metal needles may also allow the stitches to slide over the needle tips more easily than on other materials - depending on which fibres you're using, this may or may not be a good thing! We recommend trying out your friends' needles or even asking your local yarn shop if you can try before you buy so you can get a feel for what you like.

Top Tip! The Classic Cast-On

Any cast-on used for socks has to stretch enough to be pulled on and off the foot easily and repeatedly. A cable cast-on is known for its firm and stable edge but will not stretch enough to fit over your heel. There are many variations of a long-tail cast-on that are commonly used for socks.

We used a standard long-tail cast-on for all the socks in this book; it is simple, stretchy enough, and looks very neat. See page 146 for instructions. It's our go-to!

Customisation Station: Substituting Yarns

You might not be interested in customising your socks and would like to stick to the pattern as written to avoid any unnecessary surprises that experimenting with yarns, colours, or fibres can sometimes bring. You do you! Once you've settled in and become more confident with socks, you may find yourself ready to explore the various ways in which you can customise.

The yarns featured in this book work brilliantly for their respective patterns and we love them, but they are not the only options! Substitutions can be daunting, but if you keep the following two things in mind, you'll be on the right track:

- The ratio of yarn ball length to the weight of the yarn. This means the number of metres/yards to grams/ounces. If your yarn's ratio is similar to that of the yarn called for in the pattern, your yarn will usually be the right thickness to get gauge.
- Yarn characteristics. Choose an alternative with similar features to the yarn listed in the pattern. Socks usually do not lend themselves to drapey fibres like silk or alpaca, and work best with more structured fibres like wool (sometimes blended with nylon) so that they keep their form-fitting shape. There are *many* yarns out there that are branded specifically as sock yarns - these are more than likely a very safe bet!

See page 142 of the Variations, Tutorials + Adjustments section for even more helpful information about choosing yarns for your socks!

Choose Your Own Adventure: Gauge + Heel Options

GAUGE

Each pattern in this book gives you some options. The first is the yarn weight (thickness) you want to use. The patterns are written for either 4-ply (fingering) or DK-weight yarns. 4-ply is the thinner yarn, so it takes more stitches (and therefore more time) to create a sock. *But* your sock fabric will also be closer to the thickness of typical socks you'd buy in a shop and generally easier to wear inside your shoes. DK yarn is the thicker option, so the converse is true: because the yarn is thicker, it makes bigger stitches, which means it takes less time to knit a sock. But squishy, cosy DK socks will be more for lounging around the house in or for wearing with boots, because they will be chunkier.

HEELS

The other choice you'll have to make in some patterns is whether you'd like to work a 'heel flap,' a 'short row heel', or an 'afterthought heel' for your socks. Everyone's foot shape is different and each type of heel has qualities that will fit some people better than others.

Any one of these heel options is perfectly acceptable and you will get much the same result regardless of which method you choose. It is mainly about the look and process *you* enjoy the most! We recommend experimenting with each option and seeing what you prefer. Each pattern in this book works with any of these heel types. Head to page 126 in the Variations, Tutorials + Adjustments section for a more in-depth look at each heel type and instructions on how to work each one.

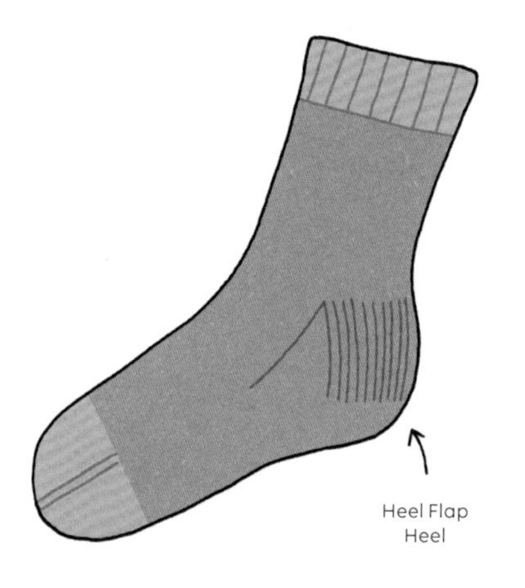

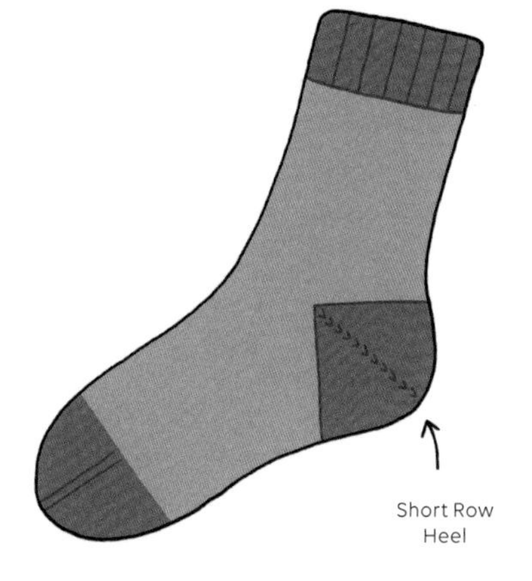

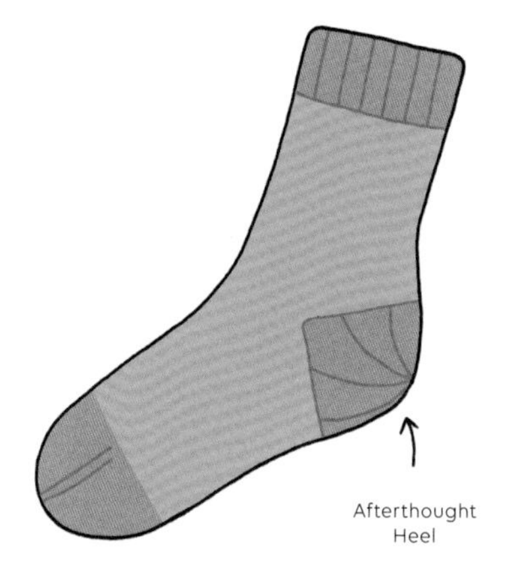

THE PATTERNS

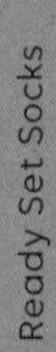

COPELAND

Stocking Stitch + Rib

This is our version of what is sometimes referred to as a 'vanilla sock' - no fuss, just simple stitches that are easy to work and can get you to grips with the basics of sock making. Copeland has three rib stitch pattern options for the cuff, so you can go classic, a bit sporty with a short length and wide ribs, or a bit more elegant with a slight twisted rib.

We love a vanilla sock for letting particularly special skeins of yarn sing! Equally it's great for making stripes with every last little scrap of yarn you have. Whatever you choose to do, these little garments for your feet are the place to start out and then experiment. After all, socks' diminutive size makes them particularly low stakes!

#CopelandSocks

Pattern: Copeland - Basic Stocking Stitch + Rib Socks 4-ply

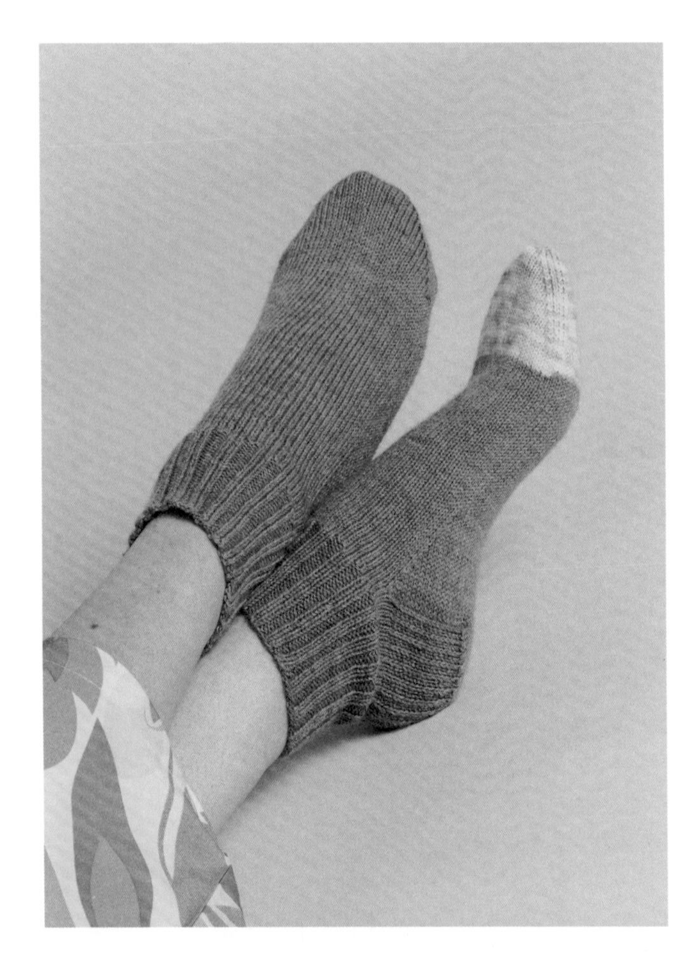

Sizes: 1 (2, 3)
To fit foot circumference: 20.5 (23, 25.5)cm / 8 (9, 10)" – to be worn with approx. 2.5cm / 1" negative ease
Foot length is fully adjustable within the pattern. Finished sock measures 0.5cm / ¼" less than actual foot length to ensure a good fit.
Yarn: Approximately 210 (250, 290)m / 229 (272, 316)yds of fingering / 4-ply-weight yarn for ankle sock with Heel Flap & Gusset.
OR approximately 245 (290, 340)m / 267 (316, 370)yds of fingering / 4-ply-weight yarn for mid-calf sock with Heel Flap & Gusset; Short row and Afterthought heels use slightly less yarn.

Sample 1 (Pink with contrast toe version, shown in Rib Option A here)
Model wears a UK 7 / US 9 and is shown wearing a size 2.
Coop Knits Socks Yeah! (fingering / 4-ply-weight; 75% superwash Merino wool, 25% nylon; 212m / 231yds per 50g skein)
Shade (Main): Ammolite (102); 2 skeins
Vicki Brown Designs Sock (fingering / 4-ply-weight; 75% superwash Merino wool, 25% nylon; 84m / 92yds per 20g skein)
Shade (Toe): Fizz; 5g (one toe)
Gauge: 36 sts & 50 rounds = 10cm / 4" over St st on 2.5mm needles, after blocking.
Needles: 2.5mm / US 1.5 needles suitable for working small circumferences in the round
Always use a needle size that will result in the correct gauge after blocking.
Notions: 2 stitch markers, tapestry needle
Notes: These socks are worked from the cuff down. There are three rib options and two length options provided for the cuff. The samples shown are worked using the Heel Flap & Gusset method (pink with contrast toe & dark purple), Short Row (blue), Afterthought (green).

Stitch Glossary
Rib Option A (in the round):
Round 1: *P2, k2; rep from * to end.
Rep round 1 for patt.

Rib Option B (in the round):
Round 1: *P4, k4; rep from * to end.
Rep round 1 for patt.

Rib Option C (in the round):
Round 1: *P3, k1tbl; rep from * to end.
Rep round 1 for patt.

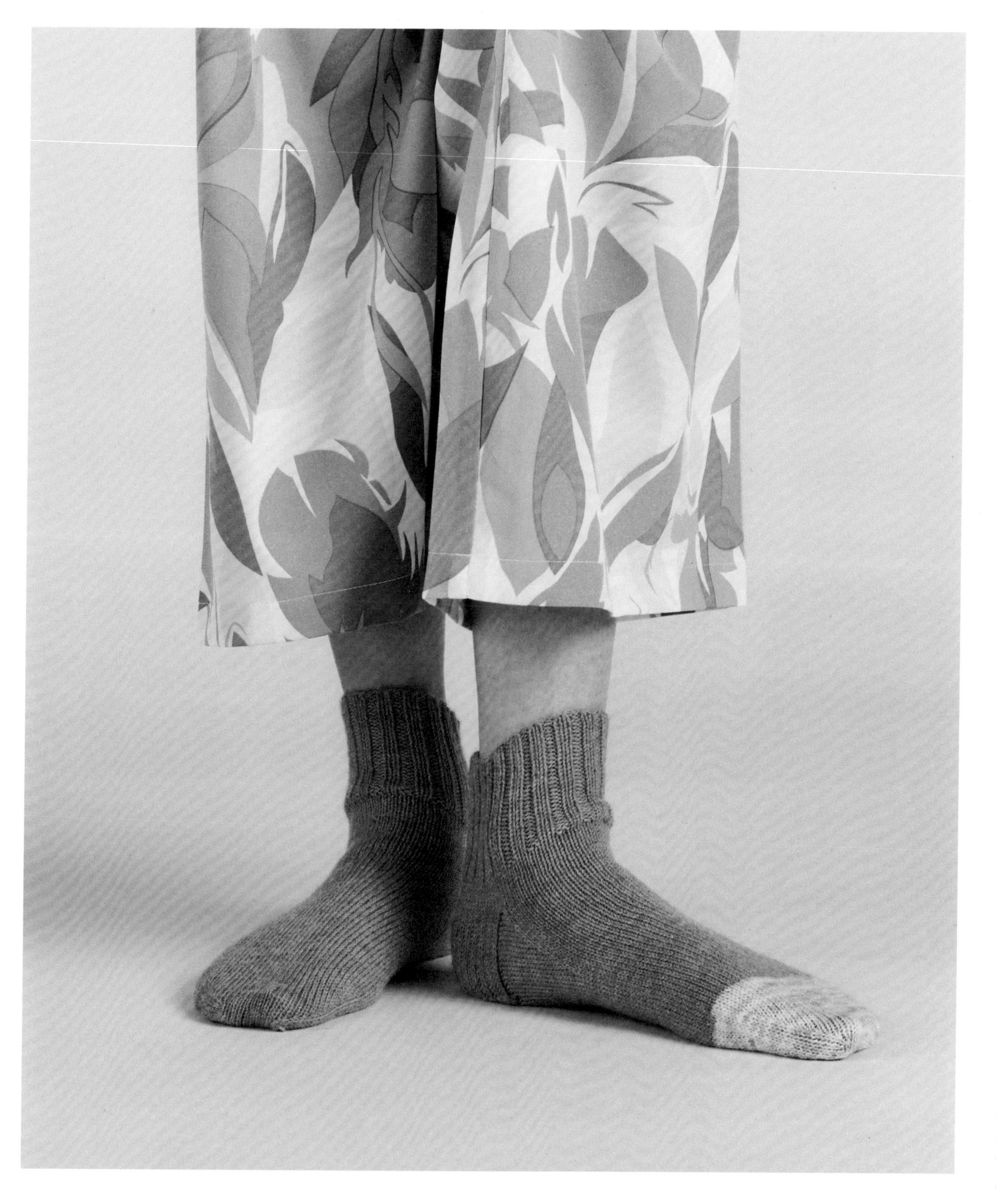

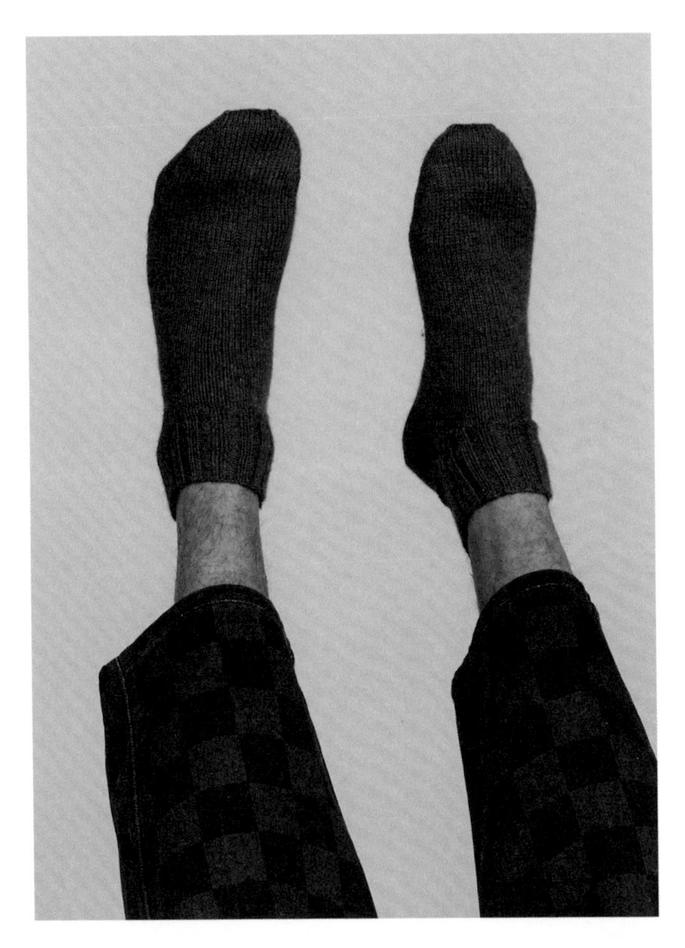

Sample 2 (Blue version, shown in Rib Option B above and on page 21)
Model wears a UK 9 / US 10 and is shown wearing a size 3.
Coop Knits Socks Yeah! (fingering / 4-ply-weight; 75% superwash Merino wool, 25% nylon; 212m / 231yds per 50g skein)
Shade: Azurite (120); 2 skeins

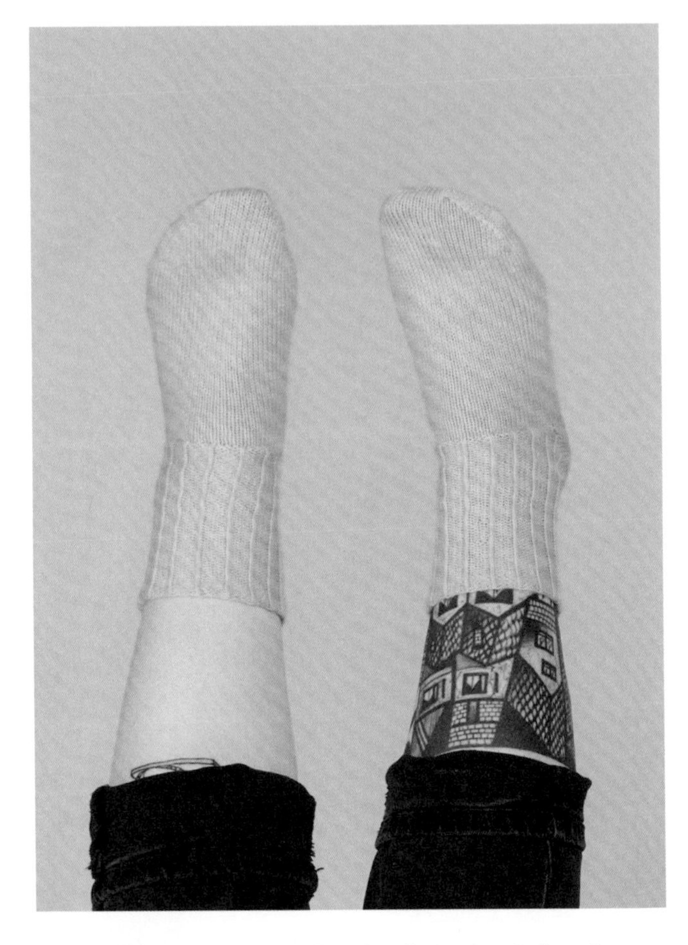

Sample 3 (Green version, show in Rib Option C above)
Model wears a UK 7 / US 9 and is shown wearing a size 2.
Coop Knits Socks Yeah! (fingering / 4-ply-weight; 75% superwash Merino wool, 25% nylon; 212m / 231yds per 50g skein)
Shade: Jadeite (115); 2 skeins

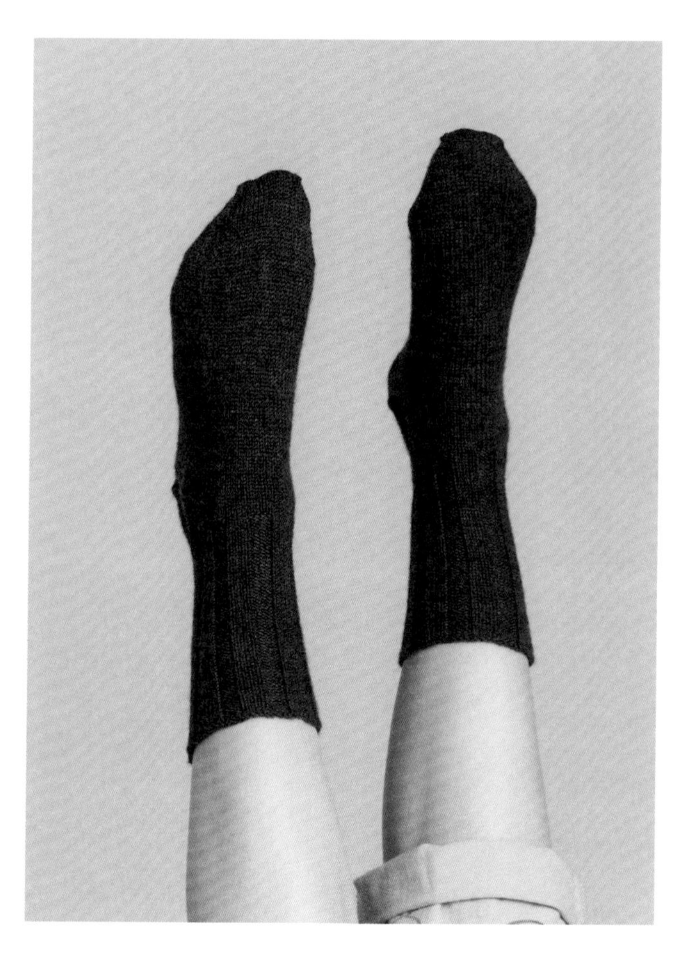

Sample 4 (Dark purple version, shown in Rib Option B above)
Model wears a UK 7 / US 9 and is shown wearing a size 2.
Coop Knits Socks Yeah! (fingering / 4-ply-weight;
75% superwash Merino wool, 25% nylon; 212m / 231yds per 50g skein)
Shade: Sugilite (112); 2 skeins

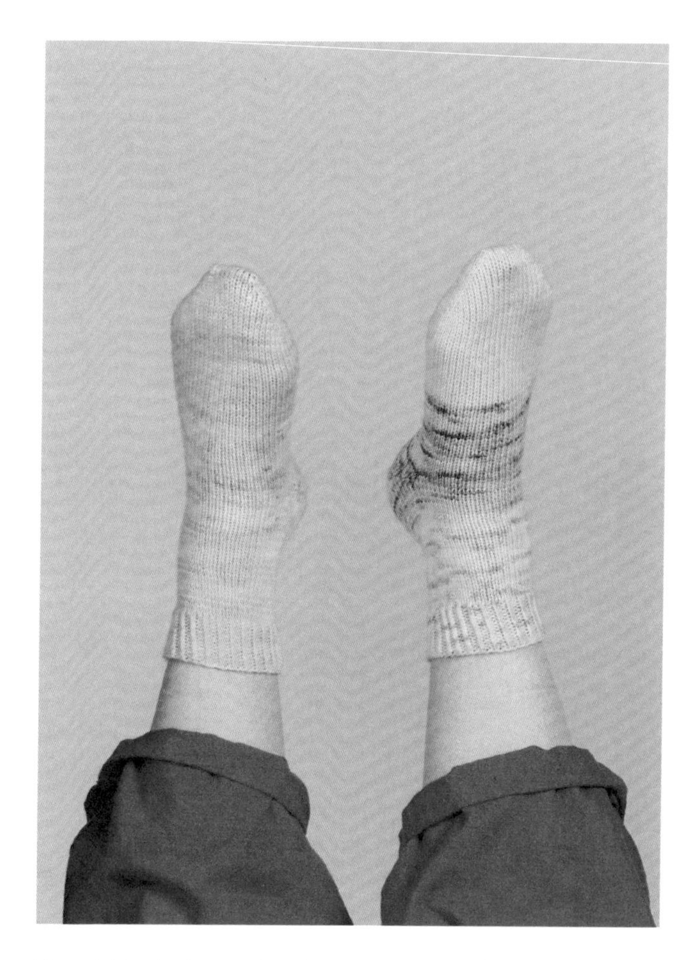

Note: This design is also shown in DK-weight yarn above and on page 23.
Please see page 22 for the pattern for the DK-weight version.

PATTERN BEGINS (both alike)

CUFF

Cast on 64 (72, 80) sts. Join to work in the round, being careful not to twist sts. PM for beg of round.
Round 1: Work round 1 of chosen Rib Option A, B or C.
Ankle Sock Length ONLY: Rep round 1 until cuff measures 6cm / 2½".
Mid-Calf Sock Length ONLY: Rep round 1 until cuff measures 12cm / 4¾".

HEEL

Work heel over 32 (36, 40) sts using preferred method: Heel Flap & Gusset (below or page 128) OR Short Row (page 132) OR Afterthought (page 138).

Heel Flap

Turn work so WS is facing. Heel flap will be worked back and forth on next 32 (36, 40) sts only, beg with a WS row. Keep rem 32 (36, 40) sts on needles for instep.
Row 1 (WS): Sl1 wyif, p31 (35, 39), turn.
Row 2 (RS): *Sl1 wyib, k1; rep from * to end.
Rep rows 1-2 a further 14 times, then work row 1 only once more.

Heel Turn

Row 1 (RS): Sl1 wyib, k18 (20, 22), ssk, k1, turn, leaving rem 10 (12, 14) sts unworked. *1 st dec*
Row 2 (WS): Sl1 wyif, p7, p2tog, p1, turn, leaving rem 10 (12, 14) sts unworked. *1 st dec*
Row 3: Sl1 wyib, k to 1 st before gap, ssk, k1, turn. *1 st dec*
Row 4: Sl1 wyif, p to 1 st before gap, p2tog, p1, turn. *1 st dec*
Rep rows 3-4 a further 4 (5, 6) times. All heel sts have now been worked. *20 (22, 24) heel sts rem*

Gusset

Begin working in the round again as foll:
Set-up round: Sl1 wyib, k19 (21, 23), pick up and knit 16 sts along edge of heel flap (1 st in each slipped st along edge of flap), knit across 32 (36, 40) instep sts, pick up and knit 16 sts along edge of heel flap, k36 (38, 40), PM for beg of round at beg of instep sts. *84 (90, 96) sts*
Round 1 (dec): K32 (36, 40), ssk, k to last 2 sts, k2tog. *2 sts dec*
Round 2: Knit.
Rep rounds 1-2 a further 9 (8, 7) times. *64 (72, 80) sts: 32 (36, 40) sts each for instep and sole*

FOOT

Work in St st in the round across all sts until sock measures 4.5 (5, 6)cm / 1¾ (2, 2¼)" less than desired foot length.

TOE

Round 1: Knit.
Round 2 (dec): K1, ssk, k26 (30, 34), k2tog, k1, PM, k1, ssk, k to last 3 sts, k2tog, k1. *60 (68, 76) sts*
Round 3: Knit.
Round 4 (dec): *K1, ssk, k to 3 sts before marker, k2tog, k1, SM; rep from * once more. *4 sts dec*
Rep rounds 3-4 a further 9 (10, 12) times. *20 (24, 24) sts*
Break yarn, leaving a 30cm / 12" tail. Graft sts together (page 147).

FINISHING

Weave in ends and block to measurements (page 25).

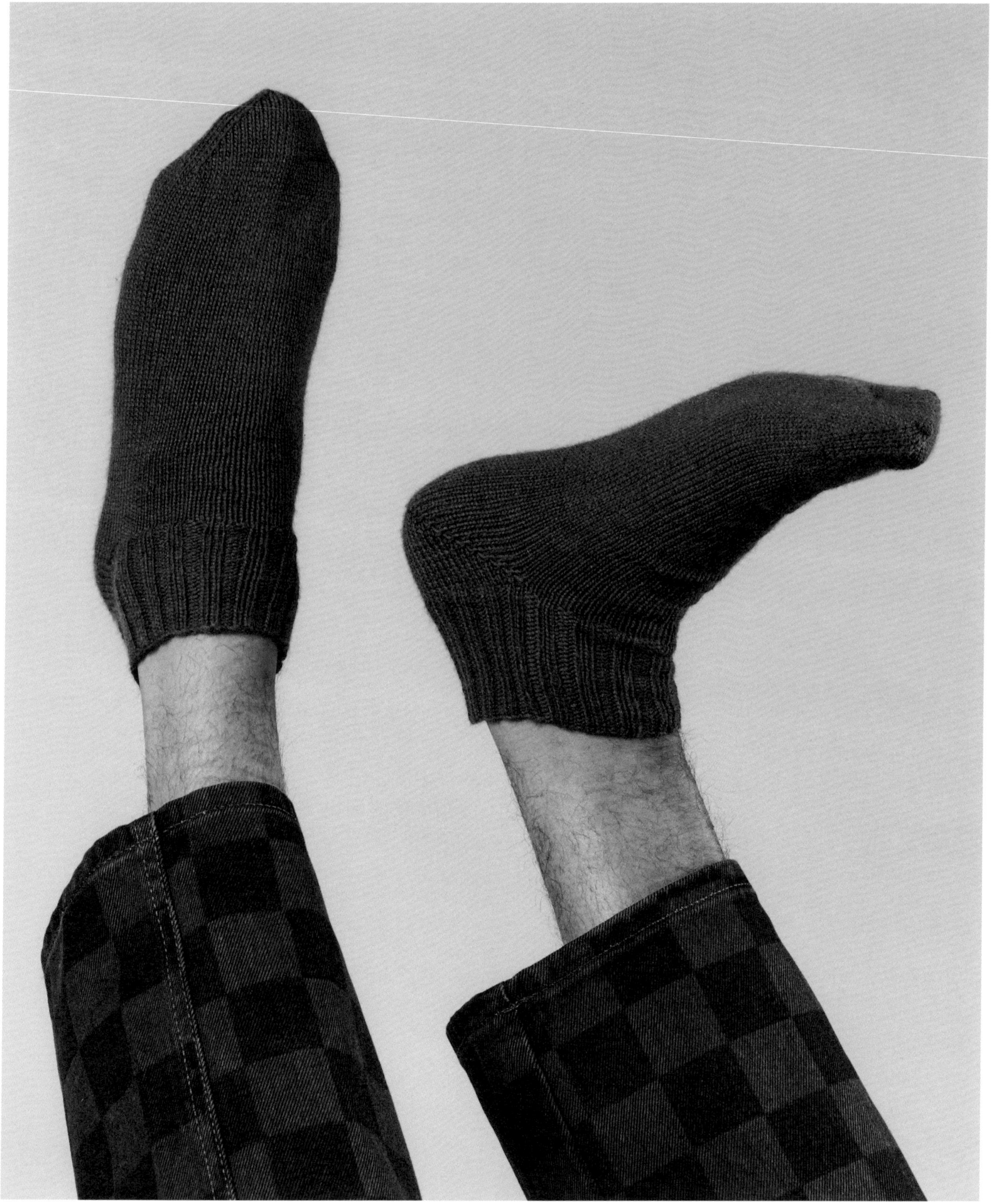

Pattern: Copeland - Basic Stocking Stitch + Rib Socks DK

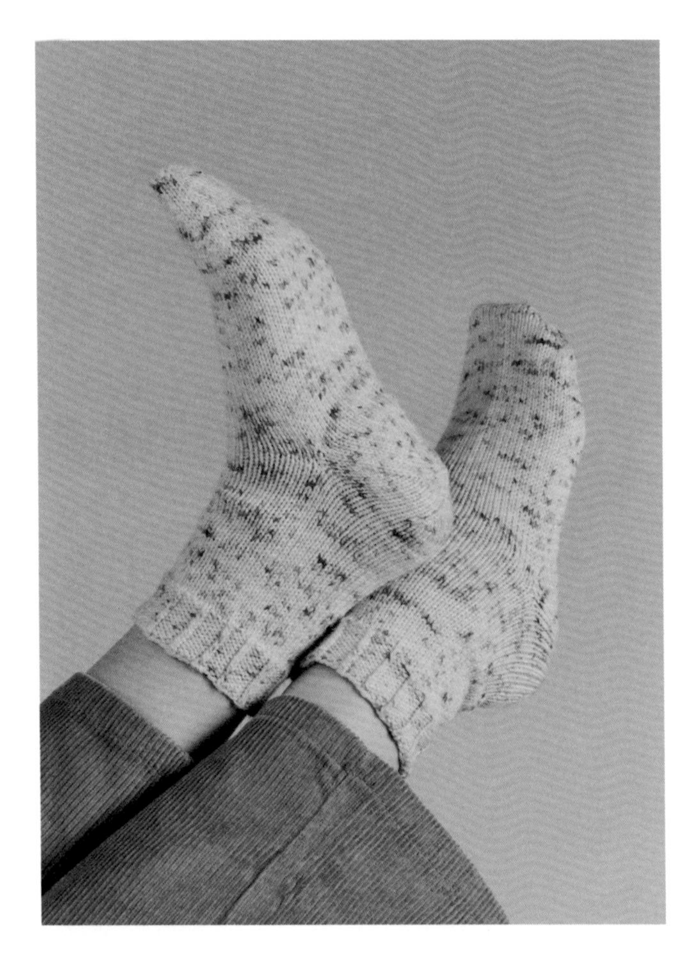

Sizes: 1 (2, 3, 4)
To fit foot circumference: 20.5 (21.5, 23, 24.5)cm / 8 (8½, 9, 9¾)" – to be worn with approx. 2.5cm / 1" negative ease
Foot length is fully adjustable within the pattern. Finished sock measures 0.5cm / ¼" less than actual foot length to ensure a good fit.
Yarn: approximately 220 (250, 280, 305)m / 240 (272, 305, 332)yds of DK-weight yarn for socks with Heel Flap & Gusset; Short row and Afterthought heels use slightly less yarn.

Sample 1 (Speckle version, shown in Rib Option C on this page)
Model wears a UK 7 / US 9 and is shown wearing a size 2.
Vicki Brown Designs DK (DK-weight; 75% superwash Merino wool, 25% nylon; 225m / 246yds per 100g skein)
Shade: Funfetti; 1 (2, 2, 2) balls/skeins
Gauge: 28 sts & 40 rounds = 10cm / 4" over St st on 3mm needles, after blocking
Needles: 3mm / US 2.5 needles suitable for working small circumferences in the round
Always use a needle size that will result in the correct gauge after blocking.
Notions: 2 stitch markers, tapestry needle
Notes: These socks are worked from the cuff down.
There are three rib options provided for the cuff.
The samples shown are worked using the Heel Flap & Gusset method (orange), Short Row (sorbet stripes), Afterthought (speckled).

Stitch Glossary
Rib Option A (in the round):
Round 1: *P2, k2; rep from * to end.
Rep round 1 for patt.

Rib Option B (in the round):
Round 1: *P1, k1tbl; rep from * to end.
Rep round 1 for patt.

Rib Option C (in the round):
Round 1: *P3, k1tbl; rep from * to end.
Rep round 1 for patt.

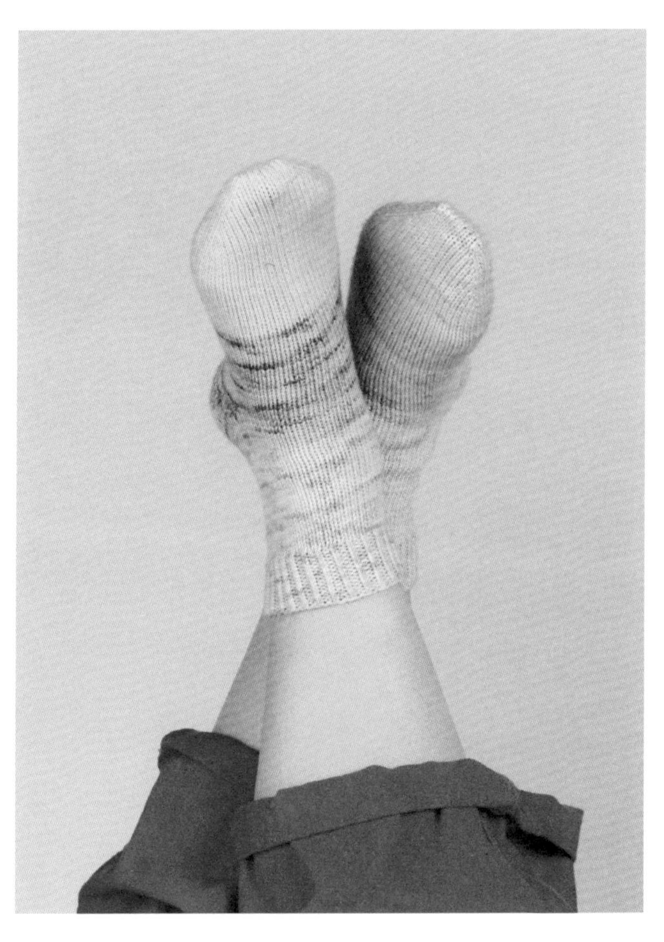

Sample 2 (Sorbet Stripes version, shown in Rib Option B above and on page 19)
Model wears a UK 7 / US 9 and is shown wearing a size 2.
Vicki Brown Designs DK Minis (DK-weight; 75% superwash Merino wool, 25% nylon; 44m / 48yds per 20g skein)
Shade: Assorted; 6 (6, 7, 7) skeins

Sample 3 (Orange version, shown in Rib Option A above)
Model wears a UK 7 / US 9 and is shown wearing a size 2.
Opal Uni 4ply (held double) (fingering / 4-ply-weight; 75% virgin wool, 25% polyamide; 425m / 465yds per 100g skein)
Shades:
Yarn A: Orange (5181); 1 skein
Yarn B: Feenrosa (9940); 1 skein
Note: Yarns A and B are held together throughout

Note: This design is also shown in fingering / 4-ply-weight yarn held as a single strand from page 16.

PATTERN BEGINS

CUFF

Cast on 48 (52, 56, 60) sts. Join to work in the round, being careful not to twist sts. PM for beg of round.
Round 1: Work round 1 of chosen Rib Option A, B or C.
Rep round 1 a further 11 times.

LEG

Next round: Knit.
Rep last round a further 37 times or desired leg length.

HEEL

Work heel over 24 (26, 28, 30) sts using preferred method: Heel Flap & Gusset (below or page 128) OR Short Row (page 132) OR Afterthought (page 138).

Heel Flap

Turn work so WS is facing. Heel flap will be worked back and forth on next 24 (26, 28, 30) sts only, beg with a WS row. Keep rem 24 (26, 28, 30) sts on needles for instep.
Row 1 (WS): Sl1 wyif, p23 (25, 27, 29), turn.
Row 2 (RS): *Sl1 wyib, k1; rep from * to end.
Rep rows 1-2 a further 10 times, then work row 1 only once more.

Heel Turn

Row 1 (RS): Sl1 wyib, k14 (14, 16, 16), ssk, k1, turn, leaving rem 6 (8, 8, 10) sts unworked. *1 st dec*
Row 2 (WS): Sl1 wyif, p7 (5, 7, 5), p2tog, p1, turn, leaving rem 6 (8, 8, 10) sts unworked. *1 st dec*
Row 3: Sl1 wyib, k to 1 st before gap, ssk, k1, turn. *1 st dec*
Row 4: Sl1 wyif, p to 1 st before gap, p2tog, p1, turn. *1 st dec*
Rep rows 3-4 a further 2 (3, 3, 4) times. All heel sts have now been worked. *16 (16, 18, 18) heel sts rem*

Gusset

Begin working in the round again as foll:
Set-up round: Sl1 wyib, k15 (15, 17, 17), pick up and knit 12 sts along edge of heel flap (1 st in each slipped st along edge of flap), knit across 24 (26, 28, 30) instep sts, pick up and knit 12 sts along edge of heel flap, k28 (28, 30, 30), PM for beg of round at beg of instep sts. *64 (66, 70, 72) sts*
Round 1 (dec): K24 (26, 28, 30), ssk, k to last 2 sts, k2tog. *2 sts dec*
Round 2: Knit.
Rep rounds 1-2 a further 7 (6, 6, 5) times. *48 (52, 56, 60) sts: 24 (26, 28, 30) sts each for instep and sole*

FOOT

Work in St st in the round across all sts until sock measures 4.5 (5, 5, 5.5)cm / 1¾ (2, 2, 2¼)" less than desired foot length.

TOE

Round 1: Knit.
Round 2 (dec): K1, ssk, k18 (20, 22, 24), k2tog, k1, PM, k1, ssk, k to last 3 sts, k2tog, k1. *44 (48, 52, 56) sts*
Round 3: Knit.
Round 4 (dec): *K1, ssk, k to 3 sts before marker, k2tog, k1, SM; rep from * once more. *4 sts dec*
Rep rounds 3-4 a further 6 (7, 7, 8) times. *16 (16, 20, 20) sts*
Break yarn, leaving a 30cm / 12" tail. Graft sts together (page 147).

FINISHING

Weave in ends and block to measurements.

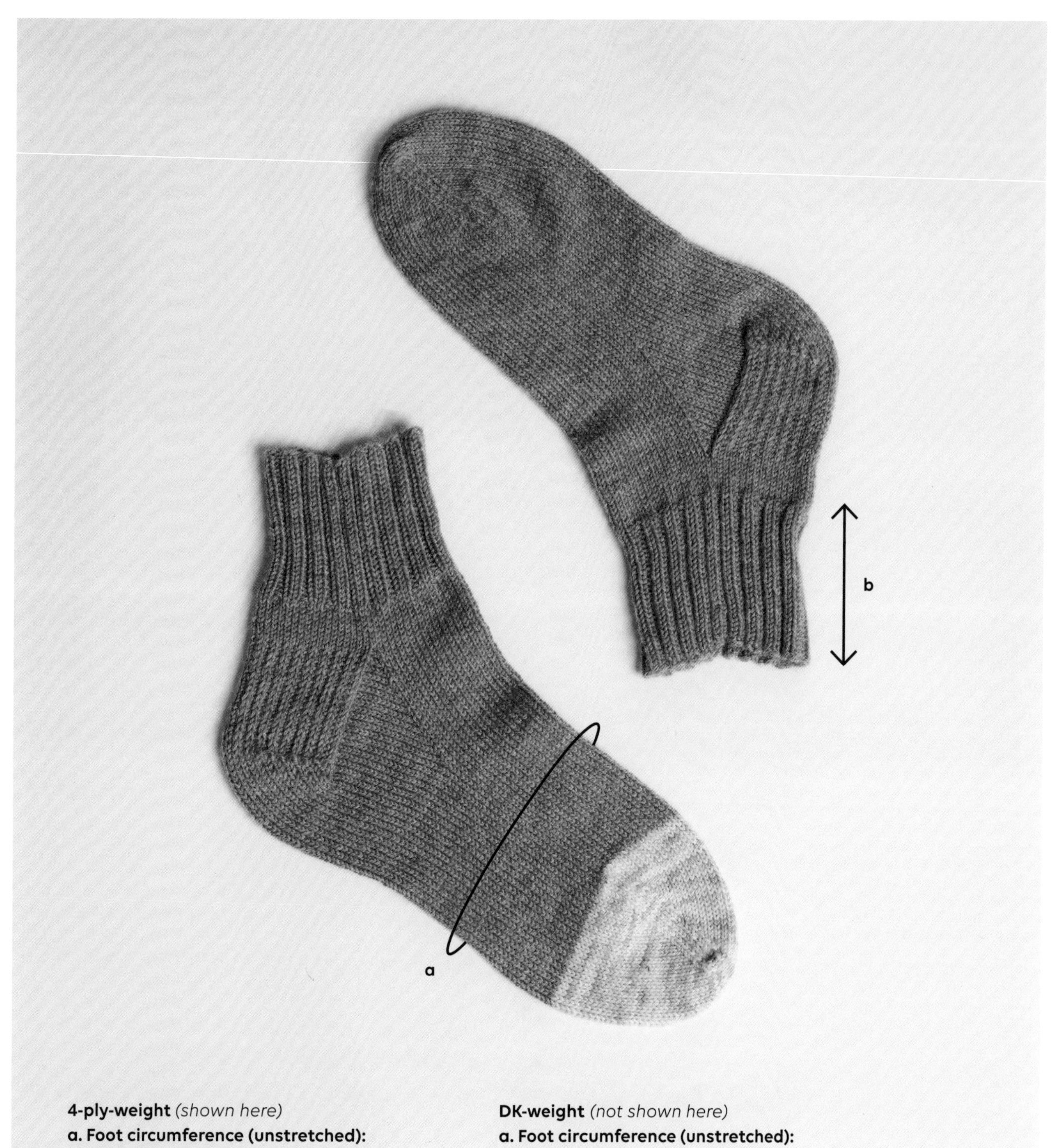

4-ply-weight *(shown here)*
a. Foot circumference (unstretched):
18 (20.5, 22.5)cm / 7¼ (8, 8¾)"
b. Leg length (Ankle Sock): 6cm / 2½"
c. Leg length (Mid-Calf Sock): 12cm / 4¾"

DK-weight *(not shown here)*
a. Foot circumference (unstretched):
17.5 (19, 20, 22)cm / 7 (7½, 8, 8¾)"
b. Leg length: 12.5cm / 5"

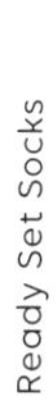

GLOVER

Simple Textured Socks

Long or short, colour-blocked or variegated, mismatched or perfectly symmetrical, the Glover socks are a wonderful first departure from the basic sock. Just a touch of texture thrown into the mix adds an abundance of interest that's satisfying and easy-going to both make and wear!

If you're new to sock knitting, once you've got to grips with the method and structure of the Copeland socks, this pair will be a big confidence booster that will have you marvelling at your own super sock skills in no time.

#GloverSocks

Pattern: Glover - Simple Textured Socks 4-ply

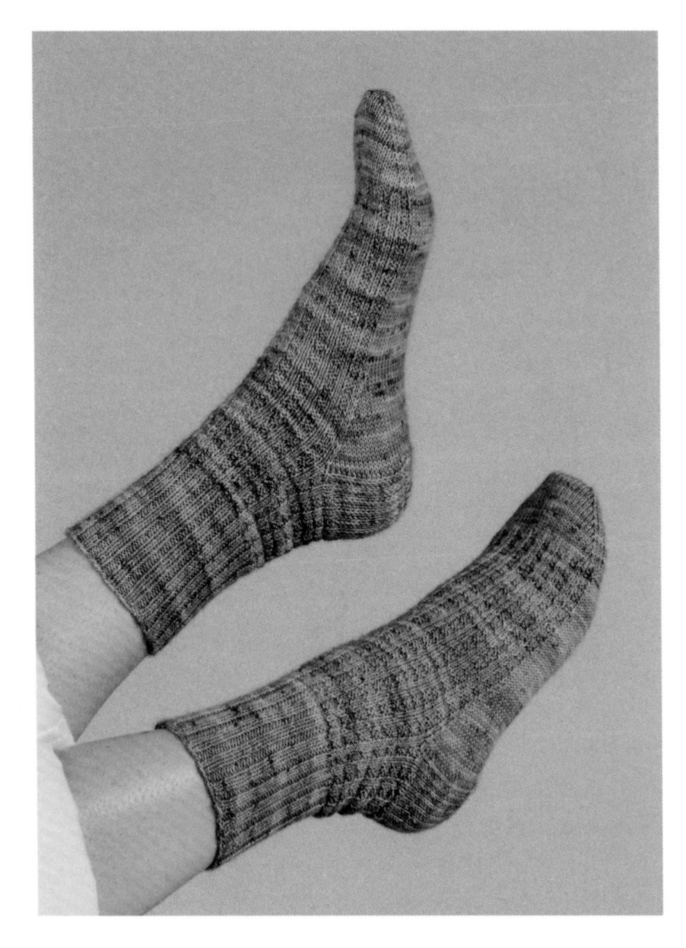

Sizes: 1 (2, 3)
To fit foot circumference: 20.5 (23, 25.5)cm / 8 (9, 10)" – to be worn with approx. 2.5cm / 1" negative ease
Foot length is fully adjustable within the pattern. Finished sock measures 0.5cm / ¼" less than actual foot length to ensure a good fit.
Yarn: approximately 275 (325, 375)m / 300 (354, 409)yds of fingering / 4-ply-weight yarn for Heel Flap & Gusset version; Short row and Afterthought heels use slightly less yarn.

Sample 1 (Grey speckled version, shown on this page)
Model wears a UK 7 / US 9 and is shown wearing a size 2.
La Bien Aimée Merino Super Sock (fingering / 4-ply-weight; 75% superwash Merino wool, 25% nylon; 425m / 465yds per 100g skein)
Shade: Totoro & Mei; 1 skein
Gauge: 36 sts & 50 rounds = 10cm / 4" over St st on 2.5mm needles, after blocking
Needles: 2.5mm / US 1.5 needles suitable for working small circumferences in the round
Always use a needle size that will result in the correct gauge after blocking.
Notions: 2 stitch markers, tapestry needle
Notes: These socks are worked from the cuff down, with a ribbed cuff. The leg is worked in a textured pattern which continues on the top of the foot, and the samples shown are worked using the Heel Flap & Gusset method.

Stitch Glossary
Texture Pattern (in the round):
Worked over a multiple of 4 sts
Rounds 1-2: Knit.
Rounds 3-4: *K1, p2, k1; rep from * to end.
Rep rounds 1-4 for patt.

Sample 2 (Mint & Brown version, shown on pages 29 and 33)
Model wears a UK 7 / US 9 and is shown wearing a size 2.
John Arbon Textiles Exmoor Sock (fingering / 4-ply-weight; 60% Exmoor Blueface, 20% Corriedale, 10% Zwartbles, 10% Nylon; 200m / 219yds per 50g skein)
Shades:
A: Mackerel-Sky (Mint): 1 skein
B: Bibble Bug (Brown): 1 skein

Note: This design is also shown in DK-weight yarn from page 32.

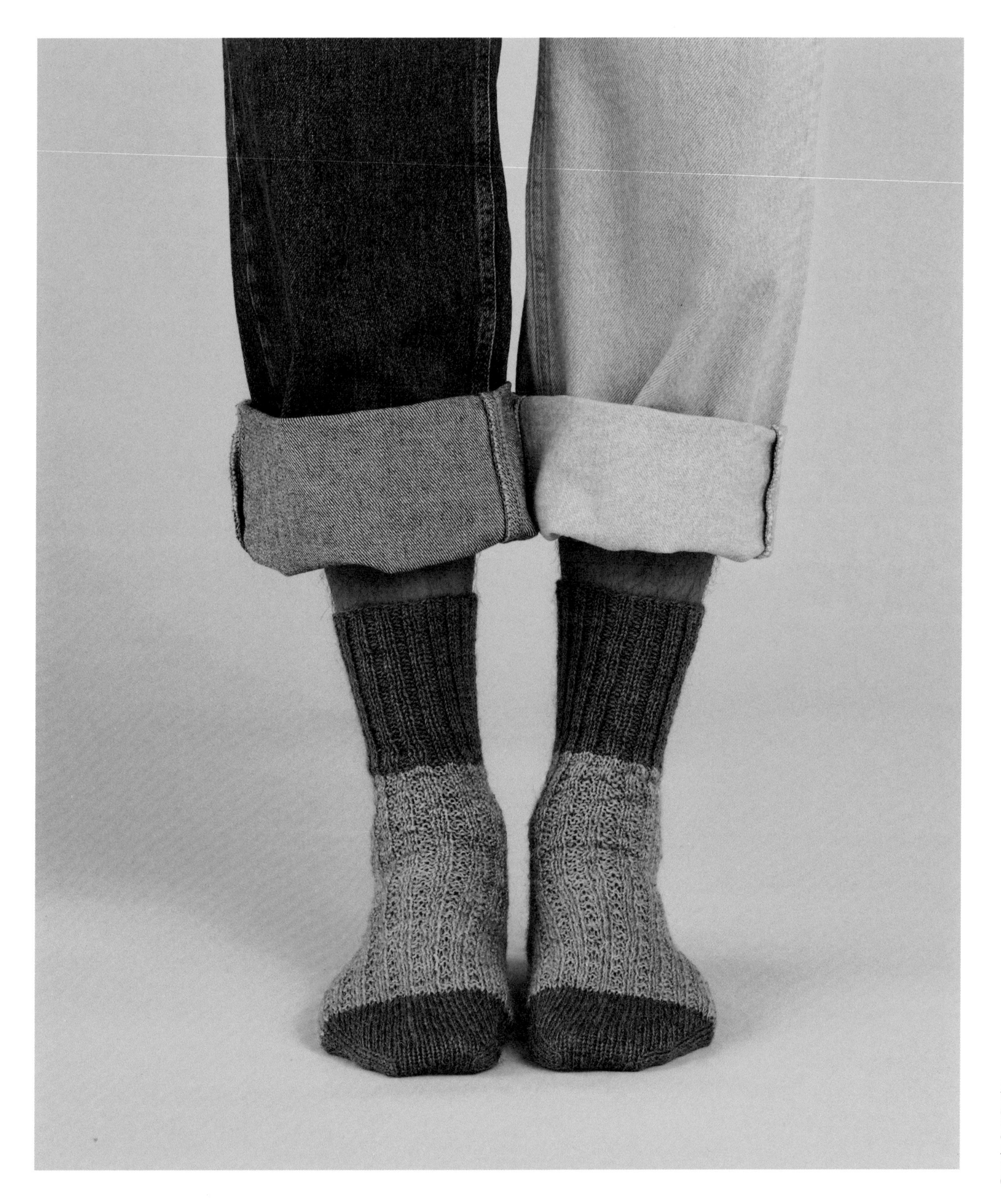

PATTERN BEGINS (both alike)

CUFF

Cast on 64 (72, 80) sts. Join to work in the round, being careful not to twist sts. PM for beg of round.
Rib round: *K1, p2, k1; rep from * to end.
Rep last round a further 39 times.

LEG

Beg working in Texture Pattern as foll:
Rounds 1-2: Knit.
Rounds 3-4: *K1, p2, k1; rep from * to end.
Rep rounds 1-4 of Texture Pattern a further 7 times.

HEEL

Work heel over 32 (36, 40) sts using preferred method: Heel Flap & Gusset (below or page 128) OR Short Row (page 132) OR Afterthought (page 138).

Heel Flap

Turn work so WS is facing. Heel flap will be worked back and forth on next 32 (36, 40) sts only, beg with a WS row. Keep rem 32 (36, 40) sts on needles for instep.
Row 1 (WS): Sl1 wyif, p31 (35, 39), turn.
Row 2 (RS): *Sl1 wyib, k1; rep from * to end.
Rep rows 1-2 a further 14 times, then work row 1 only once more.

Heel Turn

Row 1 (RS): Sl1 wyib, k18 (20, 22), ssk, k1, turn, leaving rem 10 (12, 14) sts unworked. *1 st dec*
Row 2 (WS): Sl1 wyif, p7, p2tog, p1, turn, leaving rem 10 (12, 14) sts unworked. *1 st dec*
Row 3: Sl1 wyib, k to 1 st before gap, ssk, k1, turn. *1 st dec*
Row 4: Sl1 wyif, p to 1 st before gap, p2tog, p1, turn. *1 st dec*
Rep rows 3-4 a further 4 (5, 6) times. All heel sts have now been worked. *20 (22, 24) heel sts rem*

Gusset

Begin working in the round again as foll:
Set-up round: Sl1 wyib, k19 (21, 23), pick up and knit 16 sts along edge of heel flap (1 st in each slipped st along edge of flap), work in patt across 32 (36, 40) instep sts, pick up and knit 16 sts along edge of heel flap, k36 (38, 40), PM for beg of round at beg of instep sts. *84 (90, 96) sts*
Round 1 (dec): Patt across 32 (36, 40) sts, ssk, k to last 2 sts, k2tog. *2 sts dec*
Round 2: Patt across 24 (26, 28, 30) sts, k to end.
Working next round of patt each time, rep rounds 1-2 a further 9 (8, 7) times. *64 (72, 80) sts: 32 (36, 40) sts each for instep and sole*

FOOT

Work straight in Texture Pattern and St st as set until sock measures 4.5 (5, 6)cm / 1¾ (2, 2¼)" less than desired foot length.

TOE

Round 1: Knit.
Round 2 (dec): K1, ssk, k26 (30, 34), k2tog, k1, PM, k1, ssk, k to last 3 sts, k2tog, k1. *60 (68, 76) sts*
Round 3: Knit.
Round 4 (dec): *K1, ssk, k to 3 sts before marker, k2tog, k1, SM; rep from * once more. *4 sts dec*
Rep rounds 3-4 a further 9 (10, 12) times. *20 (24, 24) sts*
Break yarn, leaving a 30cm / 12" tail. Graft sts together (page 147).

FINISHING

Weave in ends and block to measurements (page 35).

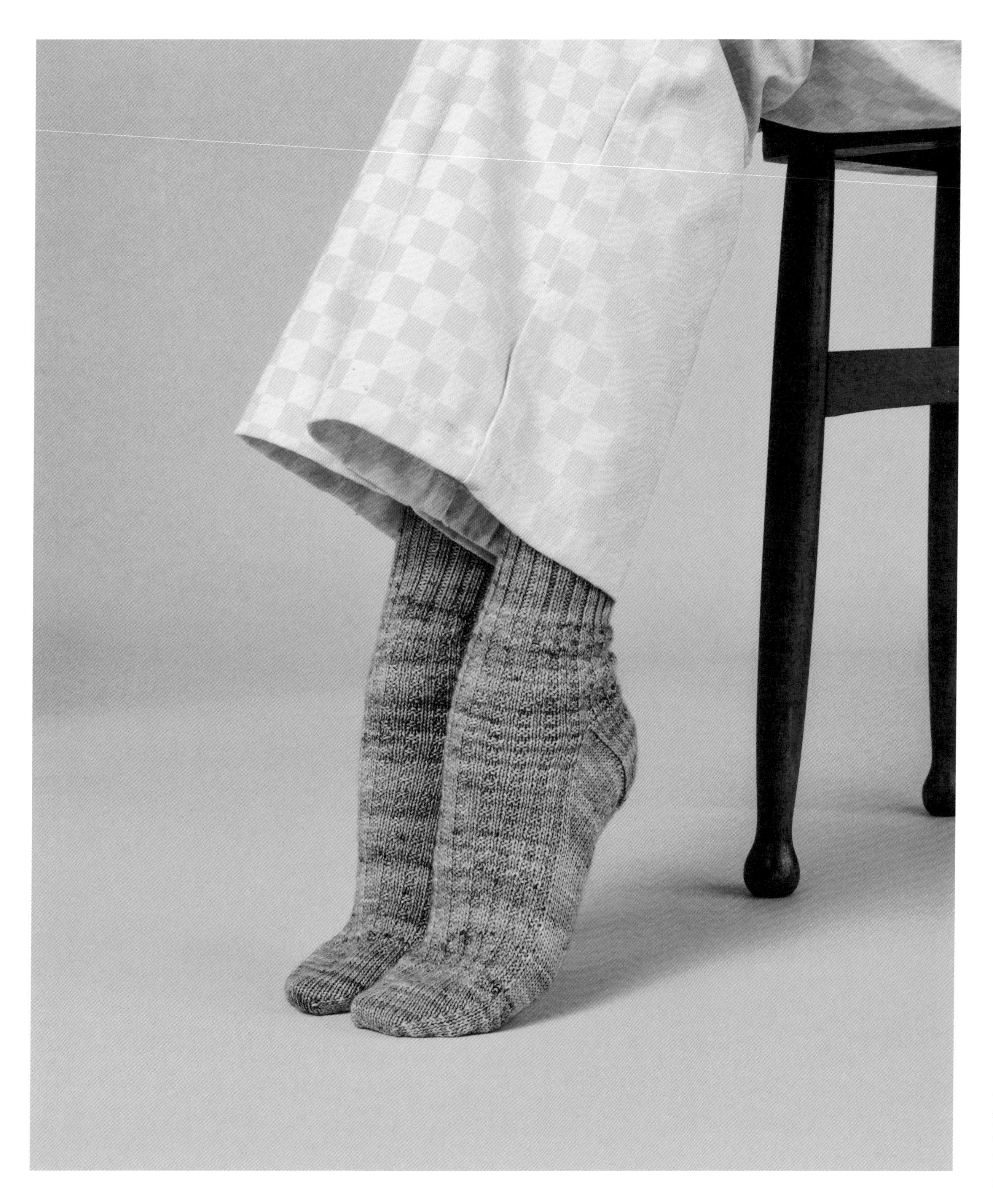

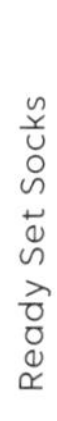

Pattern: Glover - Simple Textured Socks DK

Sizes: 1 (2, 3, 4)
To fit foot circumference: 20.5 (21.5, 23, 24.5)cm / 8 (8½, 9, 9¾)" – to be worn with approx. 2.5cm / 1" negative ease
Foot length is fully adjustable within the pattern. Finished sock measures 0.5cm / ¼" less than actual foot length to ensure a good fit.
Yarn: Approximately 220 (256, 285, 310)m / 240 (280, 310, 338)yds of DK-weight yarn for Heel Flap & Gusset version; Short row and Afterthought heels use slightly less yarn.
Sample 1 (Mustard & Burgundy version, shown above and on page 33)
Model wears a UK 7 / US 9 and is shown wearing a size 2.
Coop Knits Socks Yeah! DK (DK-weight; 75% superwash Merino wool, 25% nylon; 112m / 122yds per 50g skein)

Shades:
Yarn A: Moselle (Burgundy, 213); 1 (2, 2, 2) skeins
Yarn B: Sphene (Mustard, 215); 1 (2, 2, 2) skeins
Note: If working both feet in the same colour you will need: 2 (3, 3, 3) skeins
Gauge: 28 sts & 40 rounds = 10cm / 4" over St st on 3mm needles, after blocking
Needles: 3mm / US 2.5 needles suitable for working small circumferences in the round
Always use a needle size that will result in the correct gauge after blocking.
Notions: 2 stitch markers, tapestry needle
Notes: These socks are worked from the cuff down, with a ribbed cuff. The leg is worked in a textured pattern which continues on the top of the foot, and the sample shown is worked using the Short Row heel method.

Stitch Glossary
Texture pattern (in the round):
Worked over a multiple of 4 sts
Sizes 1 & 3 ONLY:
Rounds 1-2: Knit.
Rounds 3-4: *K1, p2, k1; rep from * to end.
Rep rounds 1-4 for patt.

Sizes 2 & 4 ONLY:
Rounds 1-2: Knit.
Rounds 3-4: *P2, k2; rep from * to end.
Rep rounds 1-4 for patt.

Note: This design is also shown in fingering / 4-ply-weight yarn from page 28.

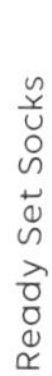

PATTERN BEGINS

SOCK ONE

CUFF

With Yarn A, cast on 48 (52, 56, 60) sts. Join to work in the round, being careful not to twist sts. PM for beg of round.

Sizes 1 & 3 ONLY:
Rib round: *K1, p2, k1; rep from * to end.

Sizes 2 & 4 ONLY:
Rib round: *P2, k2; rep from * to end.

ALL sizes again:
Rep last round a further 24 times.

LEG

Beg working in Texture Pattern as foll:
Sizes 1 & 3 ONLY:
Rounds 1-2: Knit.
Rounds 3-4: *K1, p2, k1; rep from * to end.

Sizes 2 & 4 ONLY:
Rounds 1-2: Knit.
Rounds 3-4: *P2, k2; rep from * to end.

ALL sizes again:
Rep rounds 1-4 of Texture Pattern as set a further 4 times.

HEEL

Work heel over 24 (26, 28, 30) sts using preferred method: Heel Flap & Gusset (page 128) OR Short Row (below or page 132) OR Afterthought (page 138)

Short Row Heel

The heel will be worked back and forth over the first 24 (26, 28, 30) sts only. Keep rem 24 (26, 28, 30) sts on needles for instep.
Row 1 (RS): K23 (25, 27, 29), w&t.
Row 2 (WS): P22 (24, 26, 28), w&t.
Row 3: K to 1 st before next 'wrapped' st, w&t.
Row 4: P to 1 st before next 'wrapped' st, w&t.
Rep rows 3-4 until there are 8 (8, 10, 10) unwrapped central sts with 8 (9, 9, 10) wrapped sts on either side.
Row 1 (RS): K to first wrapped st, pick up the wrap and k the st tog with the wrap tbl, w&t the next st (this st is now wrapped twice).
Row 2 (WS): P to first wrapped st, pick up the wrap and p the st tog with the wrap, w&t the next st (this st is now wrapped twice).
Row 3: K to first wrapped st (which now has 2 wraps), pick up the wraps and k the st tog with the wraps tbl, w&t the next st (this st is now wrapped twice).
Row 4: P to first wrapped st (which now has 2 wraps), pick up the wraps and p the st tog with the wraps, w&t the next st (this st is now wrapped twice).
Rep rows 3-4 a further 5 (6, 6, 7) times, then work row 3 only once more but do not w&t at end of row, PM for new beg of round, k across 24 (26, 28, 30) held instep sts, k the next st tog with its wraps, k to end.

FOOT

Work straight in Texture Pattern and St st as set until sock measures 4.5 (5, 5, 5.5)cm / 1¾ (2, 2, 2¼)" less than desired foot length.

TOE

Round 1: Knit.
Round 2 (dec): K1, ssk, k18 (20, 22, 24), k2tog, k1, PM, k1, ssk, k to last 3 sts, k2tog, k1. *44 (48, 52, 56) sts*
Round 3: Knit.
Round 4 (dec): *K1, ssk, k to 3 sts before marker, k2tog, k1, SM; rep from * once more. *4 sts dec*
Rep rounds 3-4 a further 6 (7, 7, 8) times. *16 (16, 20, 20) sts*
Break yarn, leaving a 30cm / 12" tail. Graft sts together (page 147)

SOCK TWO

With Yarn B, work as for Sock One.

FINISHING

Weave in ends and block to measurements.

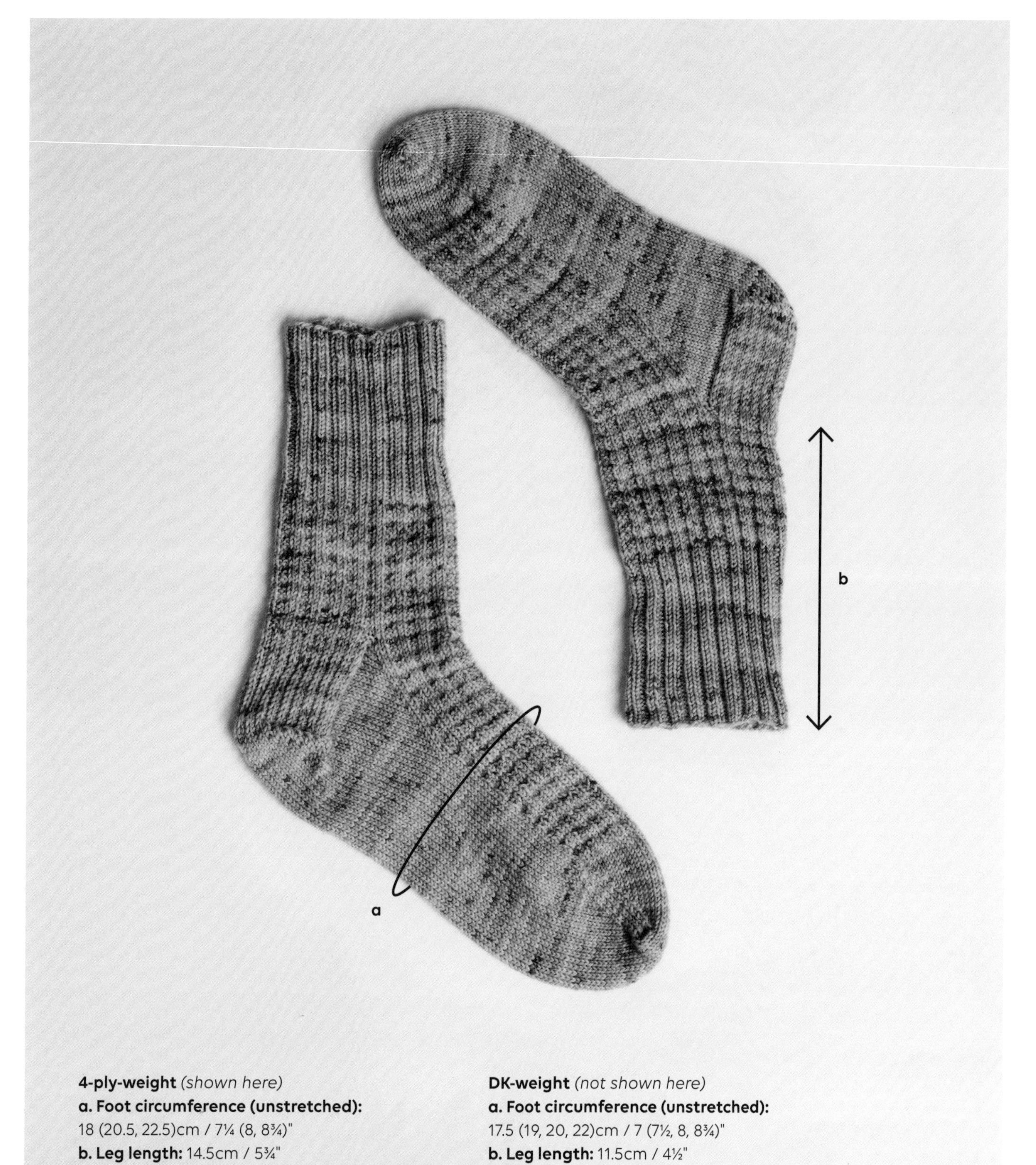

4-ply-weight *(shown here)*
a. Foot circumference (unstretched):
18 (20.5, 22.5)cm / 7¼ (8, 8¾)"
b. Leg length: 14.5cm / 5¾"

DK-weight *(not shown here)*
a. Foot circumference (unstretched):
17.5 (19, 20, 22)cm / 7 (7½, 8, 8¾)"
b. Leg length: 11.5cm / 4½"

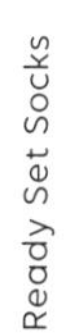

HINES

Simple Knit Purl Socks

The advanced-beginner stitch pattern featured on the Hines socks are just the jazzy upgrade your feet need! A hop, skip, and a jump away from the simple texture of the Glover socks, this pair will flex your pattern-reading muscles a little bit more, and you may just learn a new skill along the way - chart reading! For extra credit, throw some colour-blocking in. Our top tip is to make sure you swap colours just before you start a plain knit stitch-only round; this will ensure a smooth transition between shades.

#HinesSocks

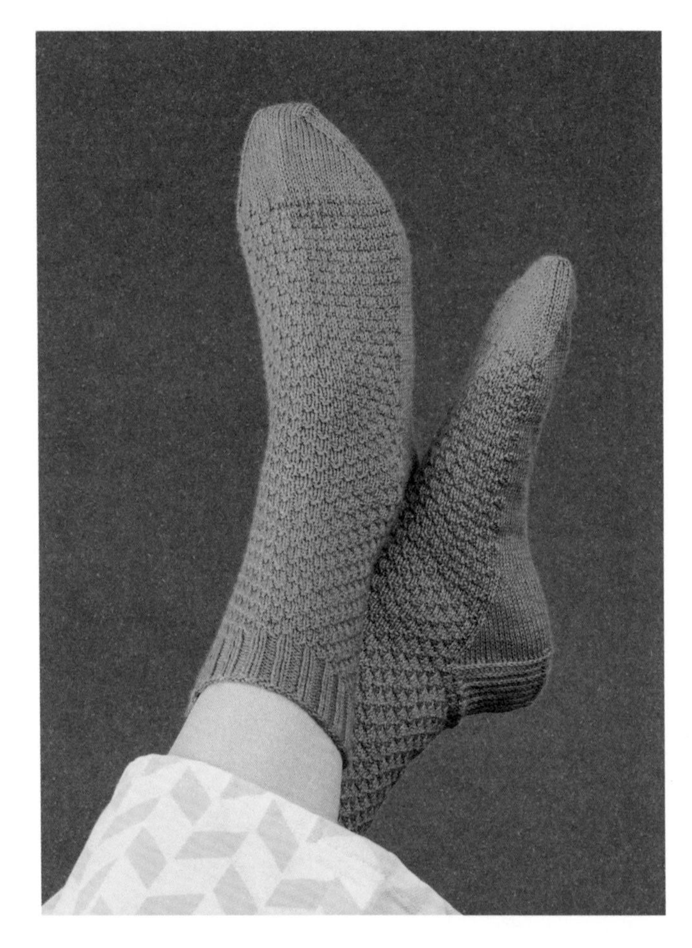

Sizes: 1 (2, 3)
To fit foot circumference: 20.5 (23, 25.5)cm / 8 (9, 10)" – to be worn with approx. 2.5cm / 1" negative ease
Foot length is fully adjustable within the pattern. Finished sock measures 0.5cm / ¼" less than actual foot length to ensure a good fit.
Yarn: Approximately 280 (330, 385)m / 305 (360, 420)yds of fingering / 4-ply-weight yarn for Heel Flap & Gusset version; Short row and Afterthought heels use slightly less yarn.
Sample 1 (Mustard version, shown above)
Model wears a UK 9 / US 10 and is shown wearing a size 3.
Coop Knits Socks Yeah! (fingering / 4-ply-weight; 75% superwash Merino wool, 25% nylon; 212m / 231yds per 50g skein)
Shade: Sphene (104); 2 skeins

Gauge: 36 sts & 50 rounds = 10cm / 4" over St st on 2.5mm needles, after blocking
Needles: 2.5mm / US 1.5 needles suitable for working small circumferences in the round
Always use a needle size that will result in the correct gauge after blocking.
Notions: 2 stitch markers, tapestry needle
Notes: These socks are worked from the cuff down, with a ribbed cuff and a textured pattern on the leg and foot. The samples shown are worked using the Heel Flap & Gusset method. If using multiple colours, the best time to change colour for stripes or colour blocking is directly prior to a knit round. Read all chart rounds from right to left.

WRITTEN INSTRUCTIONS FOR CHARTS

Chart A
Worked over a multiple of 4 sts
Round 1: Knit.
Round 2: [K2, p2] to end.
Round 3: [K3, p1] to end.
Round 4: Knit.
Round 5: [P2, k2] to end.
Round 6: [K1, p1, k2] to end.
Rep rounds 1-6 for patt.

Chart B
Worked over a multiple of 4 sts
Round 1: Knit.
Round 2: [K2, p2] to end.
Round 3: [K2, p1, k1] to end.
Round 4: Knit.
Round 5: [P2, k2] to end.
Round 6: [P1, k3] to end.
Rep rounds 1-6 for patt.

Sample 2 (Grey version, shown above)
Model wears a UK 7 / US 9 and is shown wearing a size 2.
The Uncommon Thread Tough Sock (fingering / 4-ply-weight; 80% superwash Blue Faced Leicester wool, 20% Nylon; 365m / 400yds per 100g skein)
Shade: Space Oddity; 1 (1, 2) skeins

Note: This design is also shown in DK-weight yarn from page 42.

PATTERN BEGINS
SOCK ONE
CUFF
Cast on 64 (72, 80) sts. Join to work in the round, being careful not to twist sts. PM for beg of round.
Rib round: *P2, k2; rep from * to end.
Rep last round a further 15 times.

LEG
Round 1: Work round 1 of Chart A to end, working 4-st rep 16 (18, 20) times across the round.
Working next round of Chart A each time, continue in patt as set until rounds 1-6 of Chart A have been completed 10 times in total.

HEEL
Work heel over 32 (36, 40) sts using preferred method: Heel Flap & Gusset (below or page 128) OR Short Row (page 132) OR Afterthought (page 138).

Heel Flap:
Turn work so WS is facing. Heel flap will be worked back and forth on the next 32 (36, 40) sts, beg with a WS row. Keep rem 32 (36, 40) sts on needles for instep.

Row 1 (WS): Sl1 wyif, p31 (35, 39).
Row 2 (RS): *Sl1 wyib, k1; rep from * to end.
Rep rows 1-2 a further 14 times, then work row 1 only once more.

Heel Turn:
Row 1 (RS): Sl1 wyib, k18 (20, 22), ssk, k1, turn, leaving rem 10 (12, 14) sts unworked. *1 st dec*
Row 2 (WS): Sl1 wyif, p7, p2tog, p1, turn, leaving rem 10 (12, 14) sts unworked. *1 st dec*
Row 3: Sl1 wyib, k to 1 st before gap, ssk, k1, turn. *1 st dec*
Row 4: Sl1 wyif, p to 1 st before gap, p2tog, p1, turn. *1 st dec*
Rep rows 3-4 a further 4 (5, 6) times. All heel sts have now been worked. *20 (22, 24) heel sts rem*

Gusset:
Begin working in the round again as foll:
Set-up round: Sl1 wyib, k19 (21, 23), pick up and knit 16 sts along edge of heel flap (1 st in each slipped st along edge of flap), change back to main yarn if necessary, work round 1 of Chart A 8 (9, 10) times across 32 (36, 40) instep sts, pick up and knit 16 sts along edge of heel flap, k36 (38, 40), PM for beg of round at beg of instep sts. *84 (90, 96) sts*

Round 1 (dec): Work next round of Chart A across 32 (36, 40) sts, ssk, k to last 2 sts, k2tog. *2 sts dec*
Round 2: Work next round of Chart A across 32 (36, 40) sts, k to end.
Working next round of Chart A each time, rep rounds 1-2 a further 9 (8, 7) times. *64 (72, 80) sts: 32 (36, 40) sts each on instep and sole*

FOOT
Work straight in pattern as set, working Chart A on instep and St st on sole, until sock measures 4.5 (5, 6)cm / 1¾ (2, 2¼)" less than desired foot length.

TOE
Round 1: Knit.
Round 2 (dec): K1, ssk, k26 (30, 34), k2tog, k1, PM, k1, ssk, k to last 3 sts, k2tog, k1. *60 (68, 76) sts*
Round 3: Knit.
Round 4 (dec): *K1, ssk, k to 3 sts before marker, k2tog, k1, SM; rep from * once more. *4 sts dec*
Rep rounds 3-4 a further 9 (10, 12) times. *20 (24, 24) sts*
Break yarn, leaving a 30cm / 12" tail. Graft sts together (page 147).

SOCK TWO
CUFF
Work as for Sock One.

LEG
Round 1: Work round 1 of Chart B to end, working 4-st rep 16 (18, 20) times across the round.
Working next row of Chart B each time, continue in patt as set until rounds 1-6 of Chart B have been completed 10 times in total.

HEEL
Work Heel Flap & Turn as for Sock One.

Gusset:
Begin working in the round again as foll:
Set-up round: Sl1 wyib, k19 (21, 23), pick up and knit 16 sts along edge of heel flap (1 st in each slipped st along edge of flap), work round 1 of Chart B 8 (9, 10) times across 32 (36, 40) instep sts, pick up and knit 16 sts along edge of heel flap, k36 (38, 40), PM for beg of round at beg of instep sts. *84 (90, 96) sts*

Round 1 (dec): Work next round of Chart B across 32 (36, 40) sts, ssk, k to last 2 sts, k2tog. *2 sts dec*
Round 2: Work next round of Chart B across 32 (36, 40) sts, k to end.
Working next round of Chart B each time, rep rounds 1-2 a further 9 (8, 7) times. *64 (72, 80) sts: 32 (36, 40) sts each on instep and sole*

FOOT
Work straight in pattern as set, working Chart B on instep and St st on sole, until sock measures 4.5 (5, 6)cm / 1¾ (2, 2¼)" less than desired foot length.

TOE
Work as for Sock One.

FINISHING
Weave in ends and block to measurements (page 47).

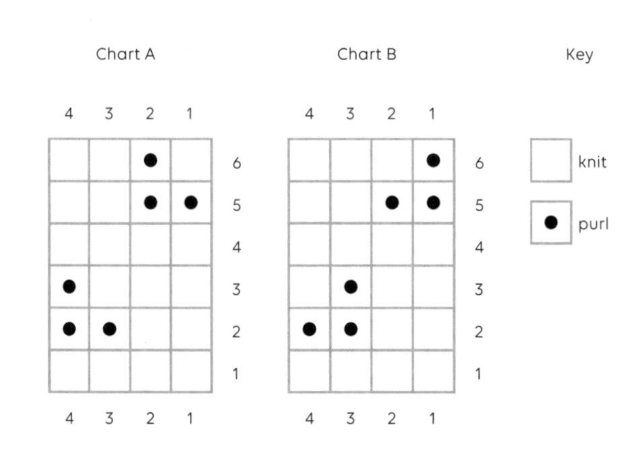

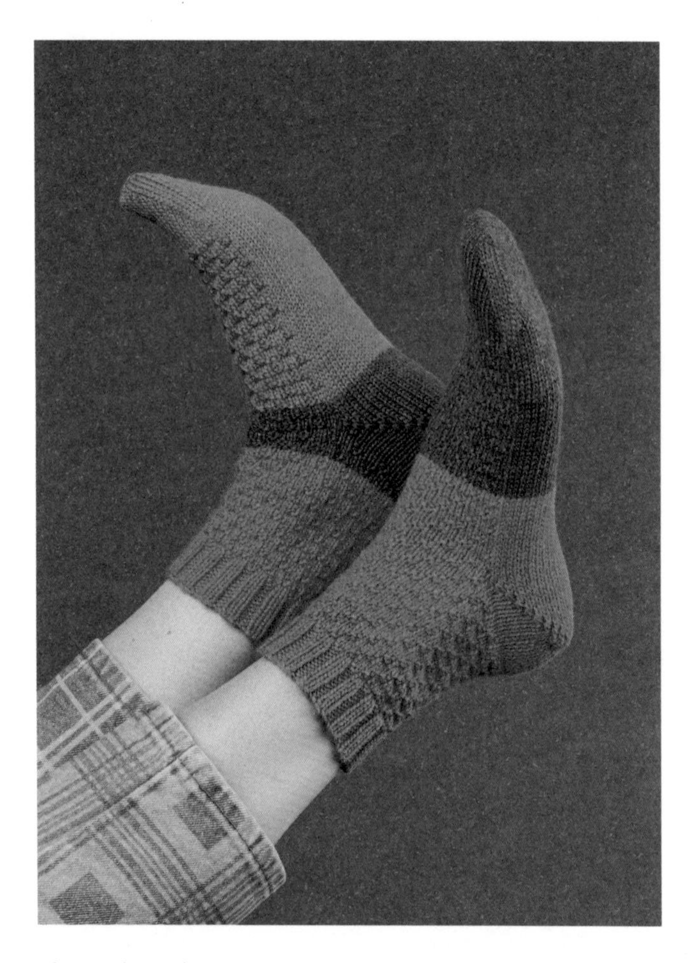

Sizes: 1 (2, 3, 4)
To fit foot circumference: 20.5 (21.5, 23, 24.5)cm / 8 (8½, 9, 9¾)" – to be worn with approx. 2.5cm / 1" negative ease
Foot length is fully adjustable within the pattern. Finished sock measures 0.5cm / ¼" less than actual foot length to ensure a good fit.
Yarn: Approximately 200 (230, 255, 280)m / 218 (250, 277, 305)yds of DK-weight yarn for Heel Flap & Gusset version; Short row and Afterthought heels use slightly less yarn.

Sample 1 (Pink & Purple Colourblock version, shown on this page)
Model wears a UK 7 / US 9 and is shown wearing a size 2.
Coop Knits Socks Yeah! DK (DK-weight; 75% superwash Merino wool, 25% nylon; 112m / 122yds per 50g skein)
Shades:
Yarn A: Morpheus (coral, 206); 1 skein
Yarn B: Xenon (pink, 217); 1 skein
Yarn C: Moselle (burgundy, 213); 1 skein
Note: Pattern does not include instructions for colourblock pattern - change colours as desired.
Gauge: 28 sts & 40 rounds = 10cm / 4" over St st on 3mm needles, after blocking
Needles: 3mm / US 2.5 needles suitable for working small circumferences in the round
Always use a needle size that will result in the correct gauge after blocking.
Notions: 2 stitch markers, tapestry needle
Notes: These socks are worked from the cuff down, with a ribbed cuff and a textured pattern on the leg and foot that is mirrored between the two socks. The samples shown are worked using the Short Row method (pink & purple colourblock) and Heel Flap & Turn method (grey speckles). If using multiple colours, the best time to change colour for stripes or colour blocking is directly prior to a knit round. Read all chart rounds from right to left.

WRITTEN INSTRUCTIONS FOR CHARTS

Chart A

Worked over a multiple of 4 sts
Round 1: Knit.
Round 2: [K2, p2] to end.
Round 3: [K3, p1] to end.
Round 4: Knit.
Round 5: [P2, k2] to end.
Round 6: [K1, p1, k2] to end.
Rep rounds 1-6 for patt.

Chart B

Worked over a multiple of 4 sts
Round 1: Knit.
Round 2: [K2, p2] to end.
Round 3: [K2, p1, k1] to end.
Round 4: Knit.
Round 5: [P2, k2] to end.
Round 6: [P1, k3] to end.
Rep rounds 1-6 for patt.

Chart C

Worked over a multiple of 4 sts + 2
Round 1: Knit.
Round 2: [K2, p2] to last 2 sts, k2.
Round 3: [K3, p1] to last 2 sts, k2.
Round 4: Knit.
Round 5: [P2, k2] to last 2 sts, p2.
Round 6: [K1, p1, k2] to last 2 sts, k1, p1.
Rep rounds 1-6 for patt.

Chart D

Worked over a multiple of 4 sts + 2
Round 1: Knit.
Round 2: [K2, p2] to last 2 sts, k2.
Round 3: [K2, p1, k1] to last 2 sts, k2.
Round 4: Knit.
Round 5: [P2, k2] to last 2 sts, p2.
Round 6: [P1, k3] to last 2 sts, p1, k1.
Rep rounds 1-6 for patt.

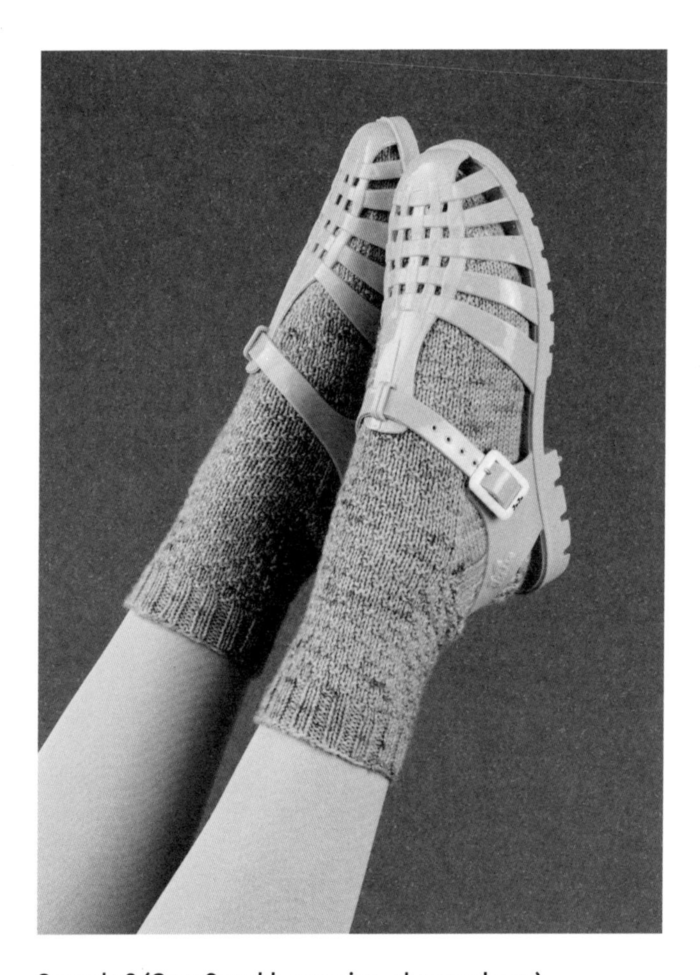

Sample 2 (Grey Speckles version, shown above)
Model wears a UK 7 / US 9 and is shown wearing a size 2.
The Wool Kitchen BFL DK (DK-weight; 100% Superwash BFL; 225m / 246yds per 100g skein)
Shade: Space Jam; 1 skein

Note: This design is also shown in fingering / 4-ply-weight yarn from page 38.

PATTERN BEGINS

SOCK ONE

CUFF

With desired colour, cast on 48 (52, 56, 60) sts. Join to work in the round, being careful not to twist sts. PM for beg of round.
Rib round: *P2, k2; rep from * to end.
Rep last round a further 11 times.

LEG

Round 1: Work round 1 of Chart A to end, working 4-st rep 12 (13, 14, 15) times across the round.
Working next round of Chart A each time, continue in patt as set until rounds 1-6 of Chart A have been completed 6 times in total.

HEEL

Work heel over 24 (26, 28, 30) sts using preferred method: Heel Flap & Gusset (page 128) OR Short Row (below or page 132) OR Afterthought (page 138).

Short Row Heel

The heel will be worked back and forth over the first 24 (26, 28, 30) sts only. Keep rem 24 (26, 28, 30) sts on needles for instep.
Row 1 (RS): K23 (25, 27, 29), w&t.
Row 2 (WS): P22 (24, 26, 28), w&t.
Row 3: K to 1 st before next 'wrapped' st, w&t.
Row 4: P to 1 st before next 'wrapped' st, w&t.
Rep rows 3-4 until there are 8 (8, 10, 10) unwrapped central sts with 8 (9, 9, 10) wrapped sts on either side.

Row 1 (RS): K to first wrapped st, pick up the wrap and k the st tog with the wrap tbl, w&t the next st (this st is now wrapped twice).
Row 2: (WS): P to first wrapped st, pick up the wrap and p the st tog with the wrap, w&t the next st (this st is now wrapped twice).
Row 3: K to first wrapped st (which now has 2 wraps), pick up the wraps and k the st tog with the wraps tbl, w&t the next st (this st is now wrapped twice).
Row 4: P to first wrapped st (which now has 2 wraps), pick up the wraps and p the st tog with the wraps, w&t the next st (this st is now wrapped twice).
Rep rows 3-4 a further 5 (6, 6, 7) times, then work row 3 only once more but do not w&t at end of row, PM for new beg of round, patt across 24 (26, 28, 30) held instep sts, k the next st tog with its wraps, k to end.

FOOT

Next round: Work next round of Chart A (C, A, C) across 24 (26, 28, 30) sts, working 4-st rep 6 (6, 7, 7) times, k to end.

Work straight in pattern as set, working next round of chart each time on instep and St st on sole, until sock measures 4.5 (5, 5, 5.5)cm / 1¾ (2, 2, 2¼)" less than desired foot length.

TOE

Round 1: Knit.
Round 2 (dec): K1, ssk, k18 (20, 22, 24), k2tog, k1, PM, k1, ssk, k to last 3 sts, k2tog, k1. *44 (48, 52, 56) sts*
Round 3: Knit.
Round 4 (dec): *K1, ssk, k to 3 sts before marker, k2tog, k1, SM; rep from * once more. *4 sts dec*
Rep rounds 3-4 a further 6 (7, 7, 8) times. *16 (16, 20, 20) sts*
Break yarn, leaving a 30cm / 12" tail. Graft sts together (page 147).

SOCK TWO

CUFF

Work as for Sock One.

LEG

Round 1: Work round 1 of Chart B to end, working 4-st rep 12 (13, 14, 15) times across the round.
Working next round of Chart B each time, continue in patt as set until rounds 1-6 of Chart B have been completed 6 times in total.

HEEL

Work heel as for Sock One.

FOOT

Next round: Work next round of Chart B (D, B, D) across 24 (26, 28, 30) sts, working 4-st rep 6 (6, 7, 7) times, k to end.
Work straight in pattern as set, working chart patt on instep and St st on sole, until sock measures 4.5 (5, 5, 5.5)cm / 1¾ (2, 2, 2¼)" less than desired foot length.

TOE

Work as for Sock One.

FINISHING

Weave in ends and block to measurements.

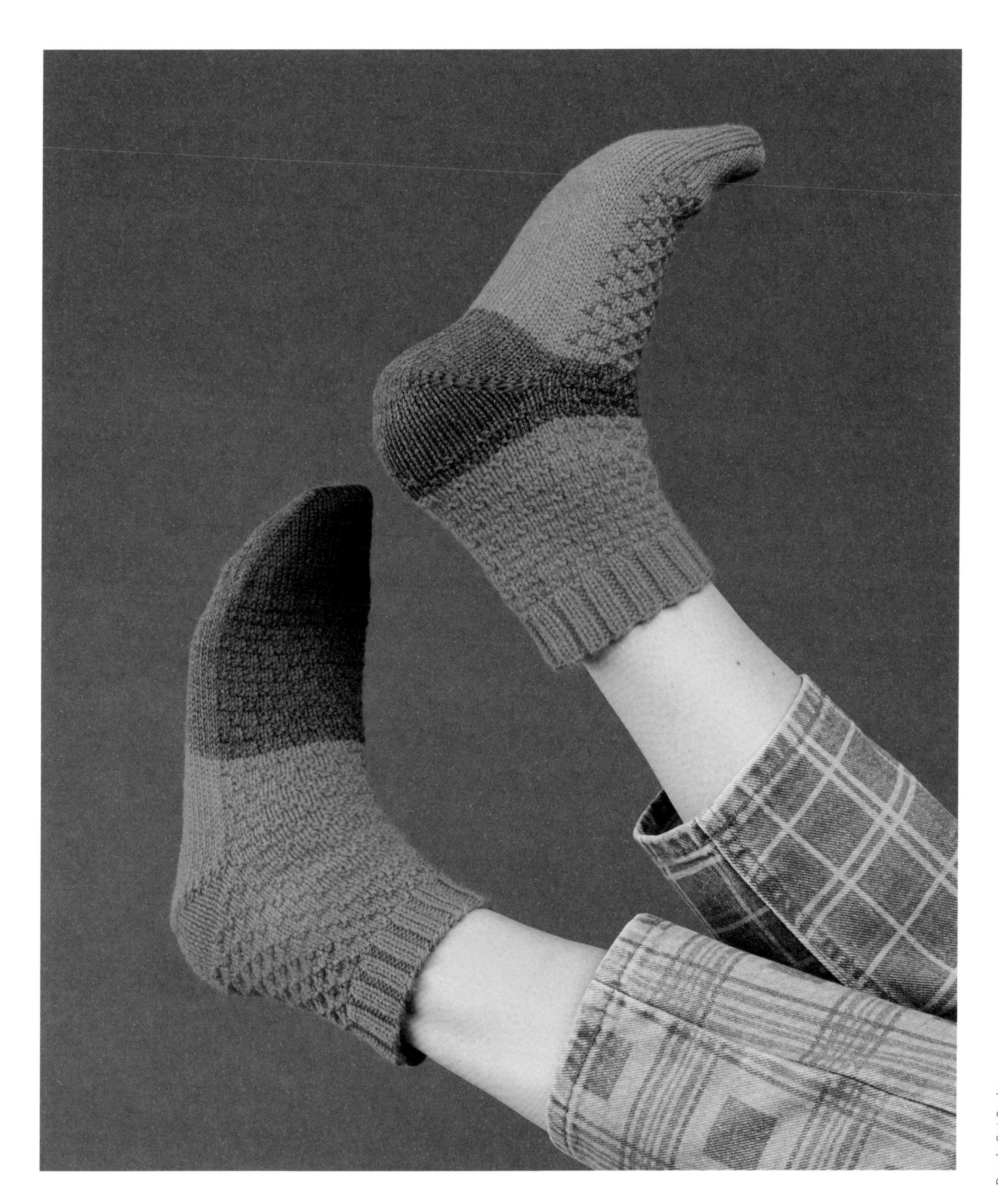

Pattern: Hines - Simple Knit Purl Socks DK

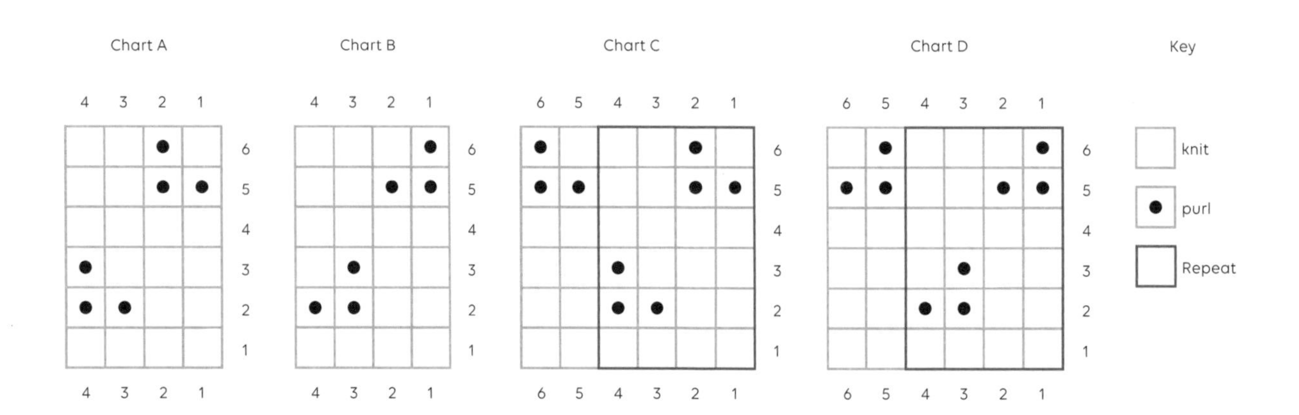

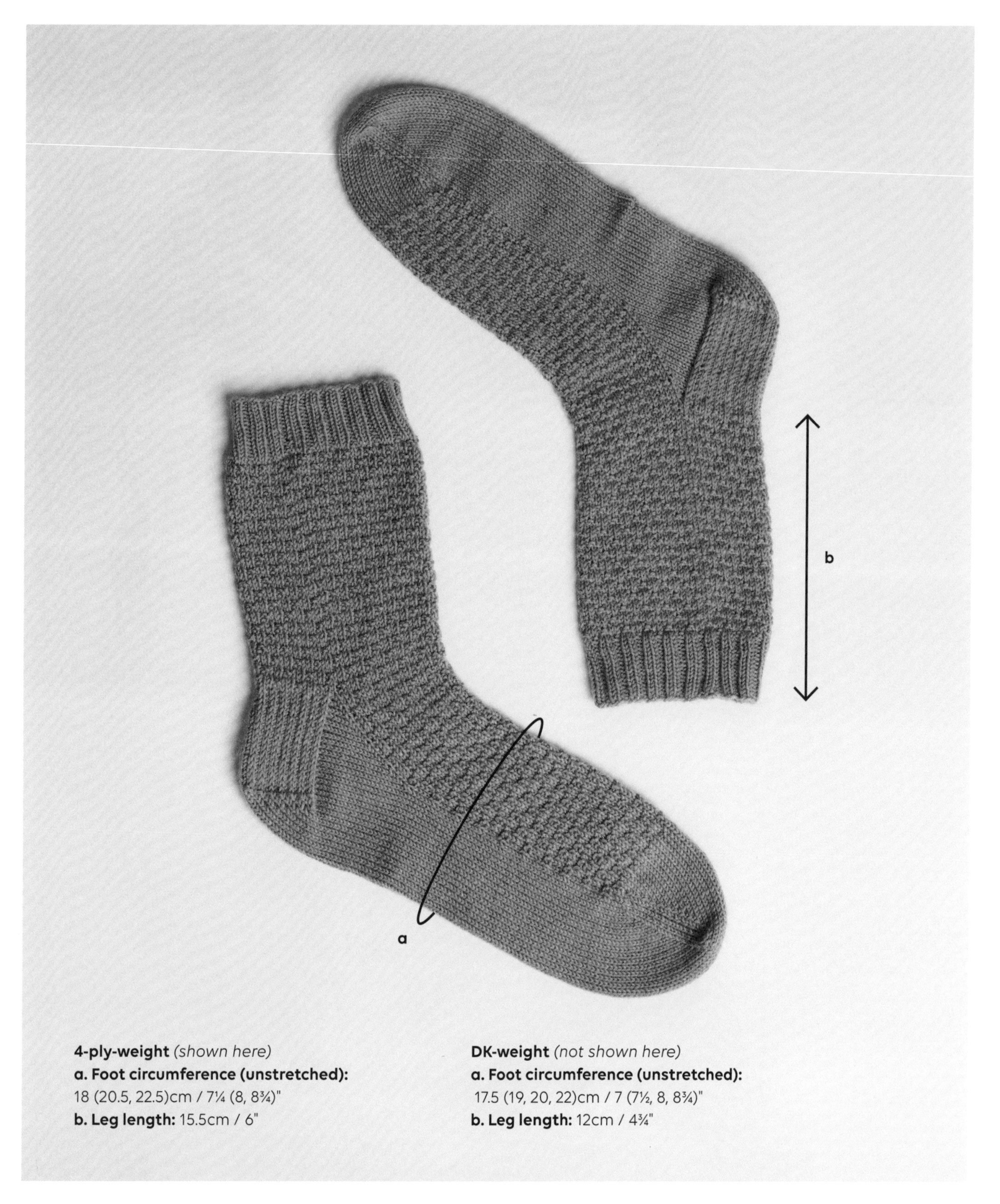

4-ply-weight *(shown here)*
a. Foot circumference (unstretched):
18 (20.5, 22.5)cm / 7¼ (8, 8¾)"
b. Leg length: 15.5cm / 6"

DK-weight *(not shown here)*
a. Foot circumference (unstretched):
17.5 (19, 20, 22)cm / 7 (7½, 8, 8¾)"
b. Leg length: 12cm / 4¾"

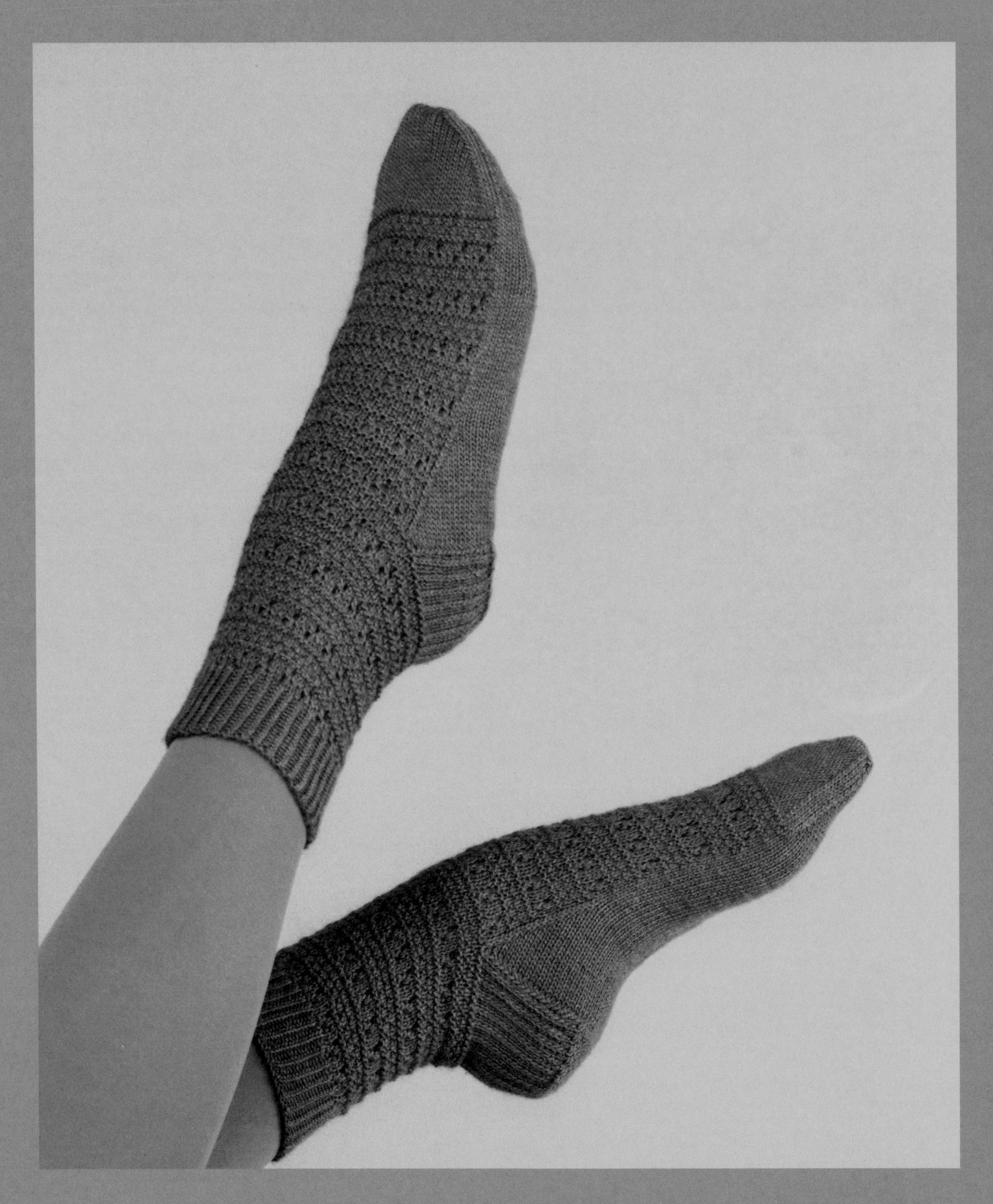

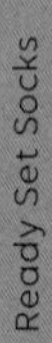
Ready Set Socks

OSATO

Eyelet Stripe Socks

Two contrasting stitch patterns make for textured stripes on this cosy, characterful pair of socks. We find it hard to choose whether we like the solid-colour or two-colour version best, but we can all agree that the subtle plain stocking stitch on the sole of the foot is an excellent touch.

#OsatoSocks

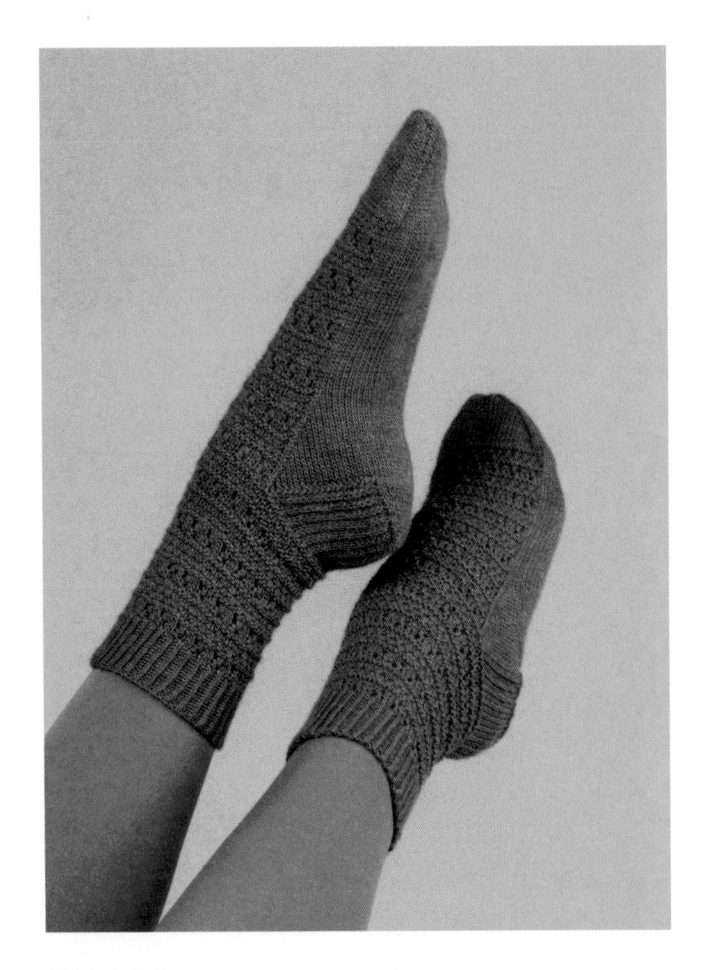

Sizes: 1 (2, 3)
To fit foot circumference: 20.5 (23, 25.5)cm / 8 (9, 10)" – to be worn with approx. 2.5cm / 1" negative ease
Foot length is fully adjustable within the pattern. Finished sock measures 0.5cm / ¼" less than actual foot length to ensure a good fit.
Yarn: Approximately 255 (300, 350)m / 278 (327, 382)yds of fingering / 4-ply-weight yarn for Heel Flap & Gusset version; Short row and Afterthought heels use slightly less yarn.

Sample 1 (Purple version, shown here)
Model wears a UK 7 / US 9 and is shown wearing a size 2.
Coop Knits Socks Yeah! (fingering / 4-ply-weight; 75% superwash Merino wool, 25% nylon; 212m / 231yds per 50g skein)
Shade: Amethyst (129); 2 skeins
Gauge: 36 sts & 50 rounds = 10cm / 4" over St st on 2.5mm needles after blocking.
Needles: 2.5mm / US 1.5 needles suitable for working small circumferences in the round
Always use a needle size that will result in the correct gauge after blocking.
Notions: 2 stitch markers, tapestry needle
Notes: These socks are worked from the cuff down, with a ribbed cuff and a textured pattern on the leg and foot. The sample shown is worked using the Heel Flap & Gusset method. Read all chart rounds from right to left.

WRITTEN INSTRUCTIONS FOR CHARTS
Chart A
Worked over a multiple of 4 sts
Round 1 and all odd-numbered rounds: Knit.
Round 2: [K1, yo, ssk, k1] to end.
Round 4: [K1, k2tog, yo, k1] to end.
Round 6: Purl.
Round 8: [K1, p1] to end.
Round 10: [P1, k1] to end.
Round 12: Purl.
Rep rounds 1-12 for patt.

Chart B
Worked over a multiple of 4 sts
Round 1 and all odd-numbered rounds: Knit.
Round 2: [K1, k2tog, yo, k1] to end.
Round 4: [K1, yo, ssk, k1] to end.
Round 6: Purl.
Round 8: [P1, k1] to end.
Round 10: [K1, p1] to end.
Round 12: Purl.
Rep rounds 1-12 for patt.

Note: This design is also shown in DK-weight yarn from page 54.

PATTERN BEGINS

SOCK ONE

CUFF

With yarn A, cast on 64 (72, 80) sts. Join to work in the round, being careful not to twist sts. PM for beg of round.
Rib round: *P1, k1tbl; rep from * to end.
Rep last round a further 15 times.

LEG

Solid Leg ONLY

Round 1: Work round 1 of Chart A to end, working 4-st rep 16 (18, 20) times across the round.
Working next round of Chart A each time, continue in patt as set until rounds 1-12 of Chart A have been completed 4 times in total.

Striped Leg ONLY:

Work rounds 1-4 of Chart A with yarn B.
Work rounds 5-12 of Chart A with yarn C.
Rep last 12 rounds a further 3 times.

HEEL

Work heel over 32 (36, 40) sts using preferred method: Heel Flap & Gusset (below or page 128) OR Short Row (page 132) OR Afterthought (page 138).

Heel Flap:

Turn work so WS is facing. Change to yarn A. Heel flap will be worked back and forth on the next 32 (36, 40) sts with yarn A, beg with a WS row. Keep rem 32 (36, 40) sts on needles for instep.
Row 1 (WS): Sl1 wyif, p31 (35, 39).
Row 2 (RS): *Sl1 wyib, k1; rep from * to end.
Rep rows 1-2 a further 14 times, then work row 1 only once more.

Heel Turn:

Row 1 (RS): Sl1 wyib, k18 (20, 22), ssk, k1, turn, leaving rem 10 (12, 14) sts unworked. *1 st dec*
Row 2 (WS): Sl1 wyif, p7, p2tog, p1, turn, leaving rem 10 (12, 14) sts unworked. *1 st dec*
Row 3: Sl1 wyib, k to 1 st before gap, ssk, k1, turn. *1 st dec*
Row 4: Sl1 wyif, p to 1 st before gap, p2tog, p1, turn. *1 st dec*
Rep rows 3-4 a further 4 (5, 6) times. All heel sts have now been worked. *20 (22, 24) heel sts rem*

Gusset:

Change to yarn B. Begin working in the round again as foll:
Set-up round: Sl1 wyib, k19 (21, 23), pick up and knit 16 sts along edge of heel flap (1 st in each slipped st along edge of flap), work round 1 of Chart A across 32 (36, 40) instep sts working 4-st rep 8 (9, 10) times, pick up and knit 16 sts along edge of heel flap, k36 (38, 40), PM for beg of round at beg of instep sts. *84 (90, 96) sts*
Round 1 (dec): Work next round of Chart A across 32 (36, 40) sts, ssk, k to last 2 sts, k2tog. *2 sts dec*
Round 2: Work next round of Chart A across 32 (36, 40) sts, k to end.
Working next row of Chart A each time and changing colour in stripe sequence as set on Leg, rep rounds 1-2 a further 9 (8, 7) times. *64 (72, 80) sts: 32 (36, 40) sts each on instep and sole*

FOOT

Work straight in pattern and stripe sequence as set, working Chart A on instep and St st on sole, until sock measures 4.5 (5, 6)cm / 1¾ (2, 2¼)" less than desired foot length.

TOE

Change to yarn A.
Round 1: Knit.
Round 2 (dec): K1, ssk, k26 (30, 34), k2tog, k1, PM, k1, ssk, k to last 3 sts, k2tog, k1. *60 (68, 76) sts*
Round 3: Knit.
Round 4 (dec): *K1, ssk, k to 3 sts before marker, k2tog, k1, SM; rep from * once more. *4 sts dec*
Rep rounds 3-4 a further 9 (10, 12) times. *20 (24, 24) sts*
Break yarn, leaving a 30cm / 12" tail. Graft sts together page (147).

SOCK TWO

CUFF

Work as for Sock One.

LEG

Solid Leg ONLY

Round 1: Work round 1 of Chart B to end, working 4-st rep 16 (18, 20) times across the round.
Working next round of Chart B each time, continue in patt as set until rounds 1-12 of Chart B have been completed 4 times in total.

Striped Leg ONLY:
Work rounds 1-4 of Chart B with yarn B.
Work rounds 5-12 of Chart B with yarn C.
Rep last 12 rounds a further 3 times.

HEEL

Work Heel Flap and Heel Turn as for Sock One.

Gusset:

Change to yarn B. Begin working in the round again as foll:
Set-up round: Sl1 wyib, k19 (21, 23), pick up and knit 16 sts along edge of heel flap (1 st in each slipped st along edge of flap), work round 1 of Chart B across 32 (36, 40) instep sts working 4-st rep 8 (9, 10) times, pick up and knit 16 sts along edge of heel flap, k36 (38, 40), PM for beg of round at beg of instep sts. *84 (90, 96) sts*
Round 1 (dec): Work next round of Chart B across 32 (36, 40) sts, ssk, k to last 2 sts, k2tog. *2 sts dec*
Round 2: Work next round of Chart B across 32 (36, 40) sts, k to end.

Working next row of Chart B each time and changing colour in stripe sequence as set on Leg, rep rounds 1-2 a further 9 (8, 7) times. *64 (72, 80) sts: 32 (36, 40) sts each on instep and sole*

FOOT

Work straight in pattern and stripe sequence as set, working Chart B on instep and St st on sole, until sock measures 4.5 (5, 6)cm / 1¾ (2, 2¼)" less than desired foot length.

TOE

Work as for Sock One.

FINISHING

Weave in ends and block to measurements (page 59)

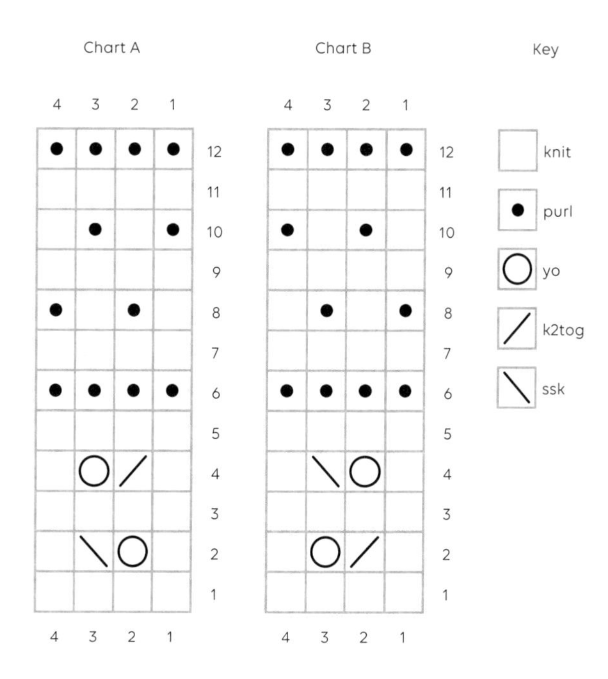

Sizes: 1 (2, 3, 4)
To fit foot circumference: 20.5 (21.5, 23, 24.5)cm / 8 (8½, 9, 9¾)" – to be worn with approx. 2.5cm / 1" negative ease
Foot length is fully adjustable within the pattern. Finished sock measures 0.5cm / ¼" less than actual foot length to ensure a good fit.
Yarn: Approximately 225 (260, 285, 310)m / 245 (283, 310, 338)yds of DK-weight yarn for Heel Flap & Gusset version; Short Row and Afterthought heels use slightly less yarn.
Sample 1 (Striped version, shown here)
Model wears a UK 9 / US 10 and is shown wearing a size 3.
Coop Knits Socks Yeah! DK (DK-weight; 75% superwash Merino wool, 25% nylon; 112m / 122yds per 50g skein)

Shades:
Yarn A: Minos (202); 1 skein
Yarn B: Beryl (219); 1 (2, 2, 2) skeins
Yarn C: Wandle (221); 1 skein
Or approximately:
A: 50 (56, 62, 70)m / 55 (61, 68, 77)yds of DK-weight yarn
B: 97 (112, 125, 135)m / 105 (122, 136, 148)yds of DK-weight yarn
C: 48 (57, 63, 70)m / 52 (62, 68, 76)yds of DK-weight yarn
Gauge: 28 sts & 40 rounds = 10cm / 4" over St st on 3mm needles, after blocking.
Needles: 3mm / US 2.5 needles suitable for working small circumferences in the round
Always use a needle size that will result in the correct gauge after blocking.
Notions: 2 stitch markers, tapestry needle
Notes: These socks are worked from the cuff down, with a ribbed cuff and a textured pattern on the leg and foot. The sample shown is worked using the Short Row heel method. Read all chart rounds from right to left.

WRITTEN INSTRUCTIONS FOR CHARTS

Chart A
Worked over a multiple of 4 sts
Round 1 and all odd-numbered rounds: Knit.
Round 2: [K1, yo, ssk, k1] to end.
Round 4: [K1, k2tog, yo, k1] to end.
Round 6: Purl.
Round 8: [K1, p1] to end.
Round 10: [P1, k1] to end.
Round 12: Purl.
Rep rounds 1-12 for patt.

Chart B
Worked over a multiple of 4 sts
Round 1 and all odd-numbered rounds: Knit.
Round 2: [K1, k2tog, yo, k1] to end.
Round 4: [K1, yo, ssk, k1] to end.
Round 6: Purl.
Round 8: [P1, k1] to end.
Round 10: [K1, p1] to end.
Round 12: Purl.
Rep rounds 1-12 for patt.

Chart C

Worked over a multiple of 4 sts + 2

Round 1 and all odd-numbered rounds: Knit.

Round 2: K1, [k1, yo, ssk, k1] to last st, k1.

Round 4: K1, [k1, k2tog, yo, k1], to last st, k1.

Round 6: Purl.

Round 8: [P1, k1] to end.

Round 10: [K1, p1] to end.

Round 12: Purl.

Rep rounds 1-12 for patt.

Chart D

Worked over a multiple of 4 sts + 2

Round 1 and all odd-numbered rounds: Knit.

Round 2: K1, [k1, k2tog, yo, k1] to last st, k1.

Round 4: K1, [k1, yo, ssk, k1] to last st, k1.

Round 6: Purl.

Round 8: [K1, p1] to end.

Round 10: [P1, k1] to end.

Round 12: Purl.

Rep rounds 1-12 for patt.

Note: This design is also shown in fingering / 4-ply-weight yarn from page 50.

PATTERN BEGINS

SOCK ONE

CUFF

Cast on 48 (52, 56, 60) sts. Join to work in the round, being careful not to twist sts. PM for beg of round.

Rib round: *P2, k2; rep from * to end.

Rep last round a further 11 times.

LEG

Solid Leg ONLY:

Round 1: Work round 1 of Chart A to end, working 4-st rep 12 (13, 14, 15) times across the round.

Working next round of Chart A each time, continue in patt as set until rounds 1-12 of Chart A have been completed 4 times in total.

Striped Leg ONLY:

Work rounds 1-4 of Chart A with yarn B.

Work rounds 5-12 of Chart A with yarn C.

Rep last 12 rounds a further 3 times.

NOTE: For sizes 2 & 4 ONLY, do not work last st of final round; this st is now the first st of instep, adjust the arrangement of sts on the needles as necessary.

HEEL

Work heel over 24 (26, 28, 30) sts using preferred method: Heel Flap & Gusset (page 128) OR Short Row (below or page 132) OR Afterthought (page 138).

Short Row Heel

Change to yarn A if necessary. The heel will be worked back and forth on the first 24 (26, 28, 30) sts only. Keep rem 24 (26, 28, 30) sts on needles for instep.

Row 1 (RS): K23 (25, 27, 29), w&t.

Row 2 (WS): P22 (24, 26, 28), w&t.

Row 3: K to 1 st before next 'wrapped' st, w&t.

Row 4: P to 1 st before next 'wrapped' st, w&t.

Rep rows 3-4 until there are 8 (8, 10, 10) unwrapped central sts with 8 (9, 9, 10) wrapped sts on either side.

Row 1 (RS): K to first wrapped st, pick up the wrap and k the st tog with the wrap tbl, w&t the next st (this st is now wrapped twice).

Row 2 (WS): P to first wrapped st, pick up the wrap and p the st tog with the wrap, w&t the next st (this st is now wrapped twice).

Row 3: K to first wrapped st (which now has 2 wraps), pick up the wraps and k the st tog with the wraps tbl, w&t the next st (this st is now wrapped twice).

Row 4: P to first wrapped st (which now has 2 wraps), pick up the wraps and p the st tog with the wraps, w&t the next st (this st is now wrapped twice).

Rep rows 3-4 a further 5 (6, 6, 7) times and then work row 3 only once more but do not w&t at end of row, PM for new beg of round, patt across 24 (26, 28, 30) held instep sts, k the next st tog with its wraps, k to end.

FOOT

Note: If working striped socks, continue in stripe sequence as set on Leg throughout Foot.

Sizes 1 & 3 ONLY

Next round: Work round 1 of Chart A across 24 (28) sts, working 4-st rep 6 (7) times, k to end.

Sizes 2 & 4 ONLY

Next round: Work round 1 of Chart C across 26 (30) sts as foll: work first st of Chart C, rep 4-st rep 6 (7) times, work last st of Chart C; k to end.

ALL Sizes again

Work straight in pattern as set, working next round of chart each time on instep and St st on sole, until sock measures 4.5 (5, 5, 5.5)cm / 1¾ (2, 2, 2¼)" less than desired foot length.

TOE

Round 1: Knit.

Round 2 (dec): K1, ssk, k18 (20, 22, 24), k2tog, k1, PM, k1, ssk, k to last 3 sts, k2tog, k1. *44 (48, 52, 56) sts*

Round 3: Knit.

Round 4 (dec): *K1, ssk, k to 3 sts before marker, k2tog, k1, SM; rep from * once more. *4 sts dec*

Rep rounds 3-4 a further 6 (7, 7, 8) times. *16 (16, 20, 20) sts*

Break yarn, leaving a 30cm / 12" tail. Graft sts together (page 147)

SOCK TWO
CUFF
Work as for Sock One.

LEG
Solid Leg ONLY:
Round 1: Work round 1 of Chart B to end, working 4-st rep 12 (13, 14, 15) times across the round.
Working next round of Chart B each time, continue in patt as set until rounds 1-12 of Chart B have been completed 4 times in total.

Striped Leg ONLY:
Work rounds 1-4 of Chart B with yarn B.
Work rounds 5-12 of Chart B with yarn C.
Rep last 12 rounds a further 3 times.

NOTE: For sizes 2 & 4 ONLY, do not work last st of final round; this st is now the first st of instep, adjust the arrangement of sts on the needles as necessary.

HEEL
Work as for Sock One.

FOOT
Note: If working striped socks, continue in stripe sequence as set on Leg throughout Foot.

Sizes 1 & 3 ONLY
Next round: Work round 1 of Chart B across 24 (28) sts, working 4-st rep 6 (7) times, k to end.
Sizes 2 & 4 ONLY
Next round: Work round 1 of Chart D across 26 (30) sts as foll: work first st of Chart D, rep 4-st rep 6 (7) times, work last st of Chart D; k to end.

ALL Sizes again
Work straight in pattern as set, working chart patt on instep and St st on sole, until sock measures 4.5 (5, 5, 5.5) cm / 1¾ (2, 2, 2¼)" less than desired foot length.

TOE
Work as for Sock One.

FINISHING
Weave in ends and block to measurements.

Pattern: Osato - Eyelet Stripe Socks DK

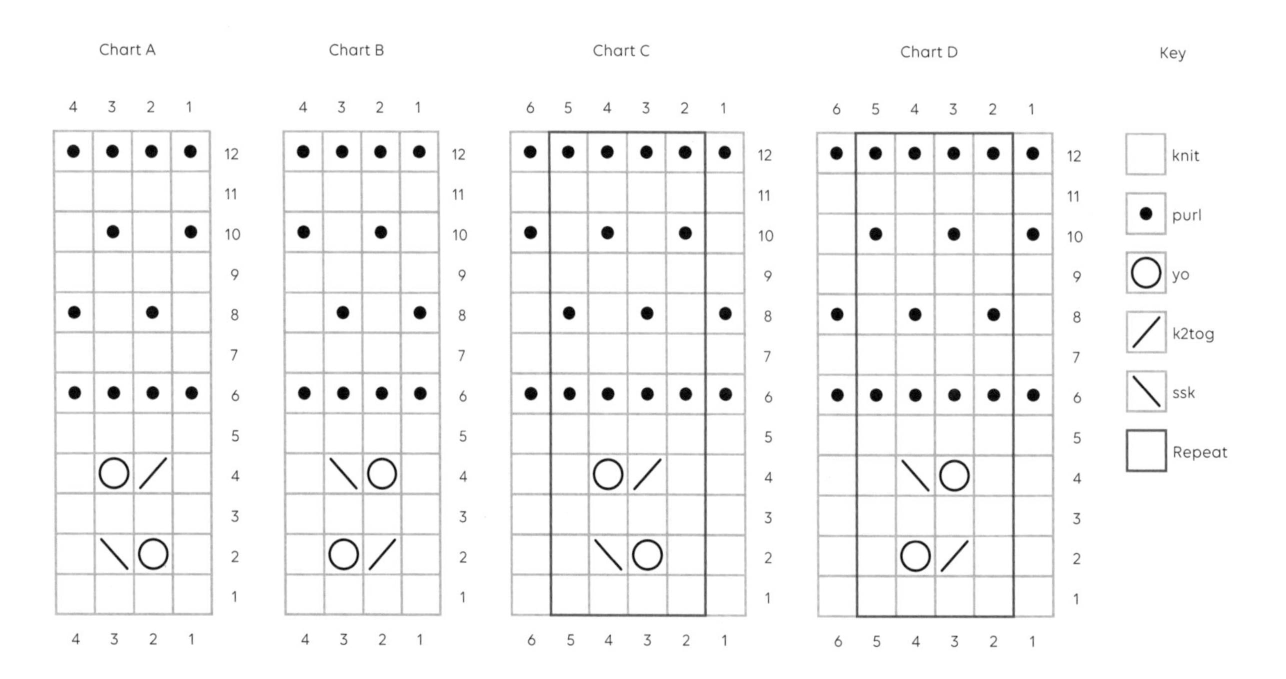

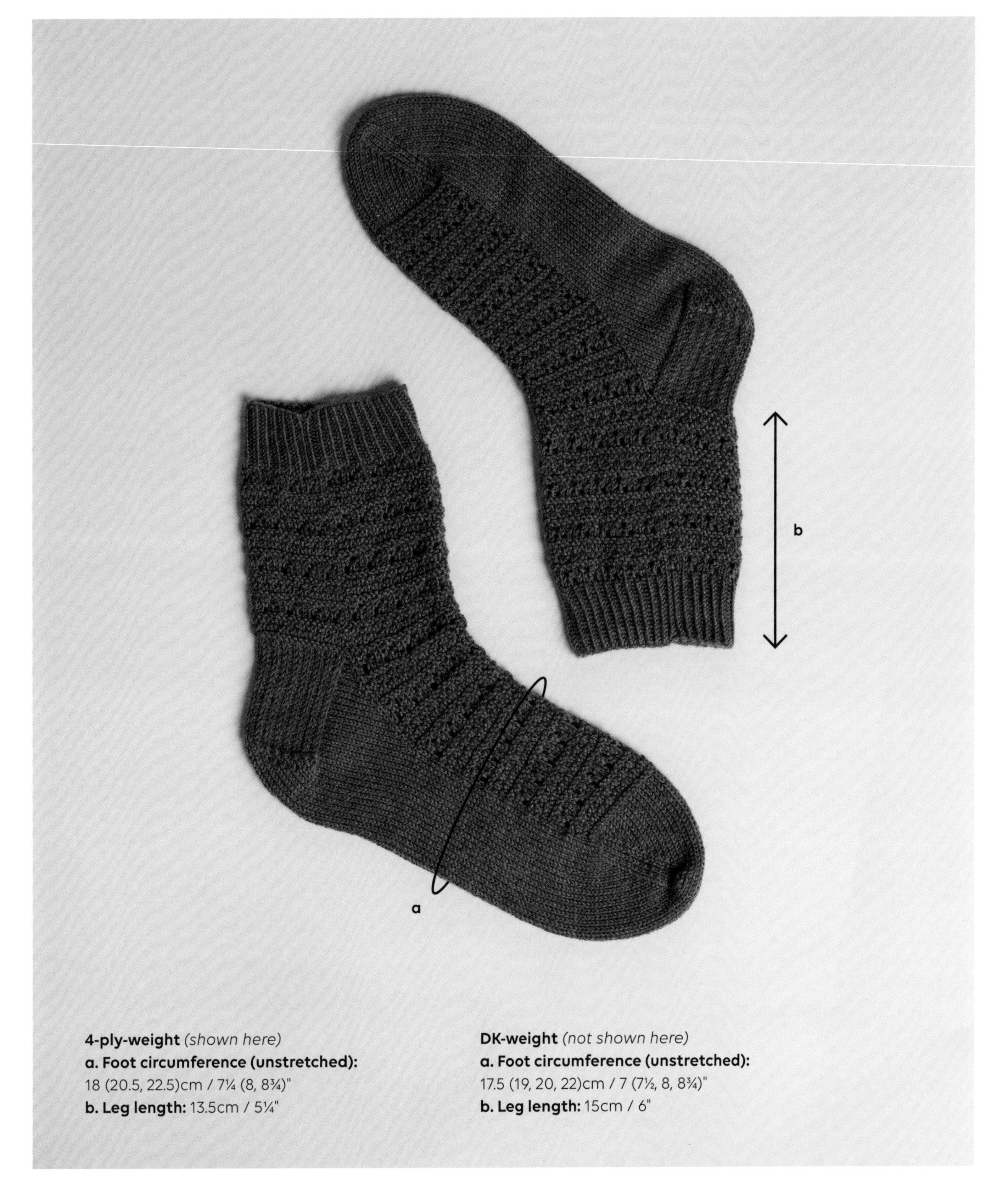

4-ply-weight *(shown here)*
a. Foot circumference (unstretched):
18 (20.5, 22.5)cm / 7¼ (8, 8¾)"
b. Leg length: 13.5cm / 5¼"

DK-weight *(not shown here)*
a. Foot circumference (unstretched):
17.5 (19, 20, 22)cm / 7 (7½, 8, 8¾)"
b. Leg length: 15cm / 6"

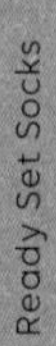

GUILLEM

Rib + Lace Socks

While most commercially available socks don't involve lace,
there's no reason why handknitted socks shouldn't!
These elegant socks incorporate columns of relatively
simple lace that elevate the humble sock to a work of art.

Feeling elegant *and* bold? Add some statement
colour-blocking to your pair. Either way, the Guillem
socks are guaranteed to put a spring in your step
(even if only metaphorically)!

#GuillemSocks

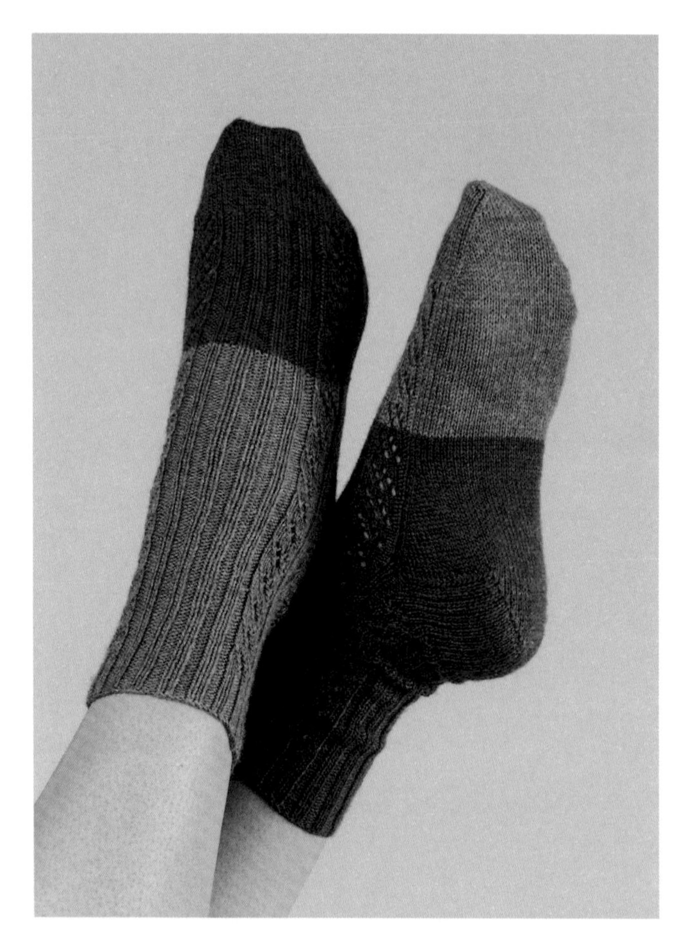

Sizes: 1 (2, 3)
To fit foot circumference: 20.5 (23, 25.5)cm / 8 (9, 10)" – to be worn with approx. 2.5cm / 1" negative ease
Foot length is fully adjustable within the pattern. Finished sock measures 0.5cm / ¼" less than actual foot length to ensure a good fit.
Yarn: Approximately 260 (310, 360)m / 283 (338, 392)yds of DK-weight yarn for Heel Flap & Gusset version; Short Row and Afterthought heels use slightly less yarn.

Sample 1 (Green version, shown on this page)
Model wears a UK 7 / US 9 and is shown wearing a size 2.
Coop Knits Socks Yeah (fingering / 4-ply-weight; 75% superwash Merino wool, 25% nylon; 212m / 231yds per 50g skein)
Shades:
Yarn A: Labradorite (124); 1 skein
Yarn B: Malachite (110); 1 skein
Gauge: 36 sts & 50 rounds = 10cm / 4" over St st on 2.5mm needles after blocking.
Needles: 2.5mm / US 1.5 needles suitable for working small circumferences in the round
Always use a needle size that will result in the correct gauge after blocking.
Notions: 2 stitch markers, tapestry needle
Notes: These socks are worked from the cuff down, with a ribbed cuff and a lace and rib pattern on the leg and foot. The samples shown are worked using the Heel Flap & Gusset method. Read all chart rounds from right to left.

WRITTEN INSTRUCTIONS FOR CHARTS
Chart A
Worked over 6 sts
Round 1: K2, [k2tog, yo] twice.
Round 2 and all even-numbered rounds: Knit.
Round 3: K1, [k2tog, yo] twice, k1.
Round 5: [K2tog, yo] twice, k2.
Rounds 7-8: Knit.
Rep rounds 1-8 for patt.

Chart B
Worked over 6 sts
Round 1: [Yo, ssk] twice, k2.
Round 2 and all even-numbered rounds: Knit.
Round 3: K1, [yo, ssk] twice, k1.
Round 5: K2, [yo, ssk] twice.
Rounds 7-8: Knit.
Rep rounds 1-8 for patt.

Sample 2 (Blue version, shown above)
Model wears a UK 7 / US 9 and is shown wearing a size 3.
Purl Soho Posy (fingering / 4-ply-weight; 75% superwash Merino wool, 15% cashmere, 10% nylon; 145m / 159yds per 50g skein)
Shade: Bellflower Blue; 2 (3, 3) balls/skeins

Note: This design is also shown in DK-weight yarn from page 66.

PATTERN BEGINS (both alike)
CUFF
Cast on 64 (72, 80) sts. Join to work in the round, being careful not to twist sts. PM for beg of round.
Rib round: *K1, p2, k1; rep from * to end.
Rep last round a further 15 times.

LEG
Round 1: *K1, p2, work round 1 of Chart A once, [p2, k2] 3 (4, 5) times, p2, work round 1 of Chart B once, p2, k1; rep from * once more.
NOTE: For a different look, swap the positions of Charts A and B (as worked in blue version).
Last round sets patt. Working next round of Chart A and B each time, continue in patt as set until rounds 1-8 of charts have been completed 7 times in total.

HEEL
Work heel over 32 (36, 40) sts using preferred method: Heel Flap & Gusset (below or page 128) OR Short Row (page 132) OR Afterthought (page 138).

Heel Flap:
Turn work so WS is facing. Heel flap will be worked back and forth on the next 32 (36, 40) sts, beg with a WS row. Keep rem 32 (36, 40) sts on needles for instep.
Row 1 (WS): Sl1 wyif, p31 (35, 39).
Row 2 (RS): *Sl1 wyib, k1; rep from * to end.
Rep rows 1-2 a further 14 times, then work row 1 only once more.

Heel Turn:
Row 1 (RS): Sl1 wyib, k18 (20, 22), ssk, k1, turn, leaving rem 10 (12, 14) sts unworked. *1 st dec*
Row 2 (WS): Sl1 wyif, p7, p2tog, p1, turn, leaving rem 10 (12, 14) sts unworked. *1 st dec*
Row 3: Sl1 wyib, k to 1 st before gap, ssk, k1, turn. *1 st dec*
Row 4: Sl1 wyif, p to 1 st before gap, p2tog, p1, turn. *1 st dec*
Rep rows 3-4 a further 4 (5, 6) times. All heel sts have now been worked. *20 (22, 24) heel sts rem*

Gusset:

Begin working in the round again as foll:

Set-up round: Sl1 wyib, k19 (21, 23), pick up and knit 16 sts along edge of heel flap (1 st in each slipped st along edge of flap); work across 32 (36, 40) instep sts as foll:
k1, p2, work round 1 of Chart A once, [p2, k2] 3 (4, 5) times, p2, work round 1 of Chart B once, p2, k1; pick up and knit 16 sts along edge of heel flap, k36 (38, 40), PM for beg of round at beg of instep sts. *84 (90, 96) sts*

Round 1 (dec): K1, p2, work next round of Chart A, [p2, k2] 3 (4, 5) times, p2, work next round of Chart B, p2, k1, ssk, k to last 2 sts, k2tog. *2 sts dec*

Round 2: K1, p2, work next round of Chart A, [p2, k2] 3 (4, 5) times, p2, work next round of Chart B, p2, k1, k to end.
Working next round of Chart A and B each time, rep rounds 1-2 a further 9 (8, 7) times. *64 (72, 80) sts: 32 (36, 40) sts each on instep and sole*

FOOT

Work straight in pattern as set, working charts and rib on instep and St st on sole, until sock measures 4.5 (5, 5, 6)cm / 1¾ (2, 2, 2¼)" less than desired foot length.

TOE

Round 1: Knit.

Round 2 (dec): K1, ssk, k26 (30, 34), k2tog, k1, PM, k1, ssk, k to last 3 sts, k2tog, k1. *60 (68, 76) sts*

Round 3: Knit.

Round 4 (dec): *K1, ssk, k to 3 sts before marker, k2tog, k1, SM; rep from * once more. *4 sts dec*

Rep rounds 3-4 a further 9 (10, 12) times. *20 (24, 24) sts*

Break yarn, leaving a 30cm / 12" tail. Graft sts together (page 147).

FINISHING

Weave in ends and block to measurements (page 69).

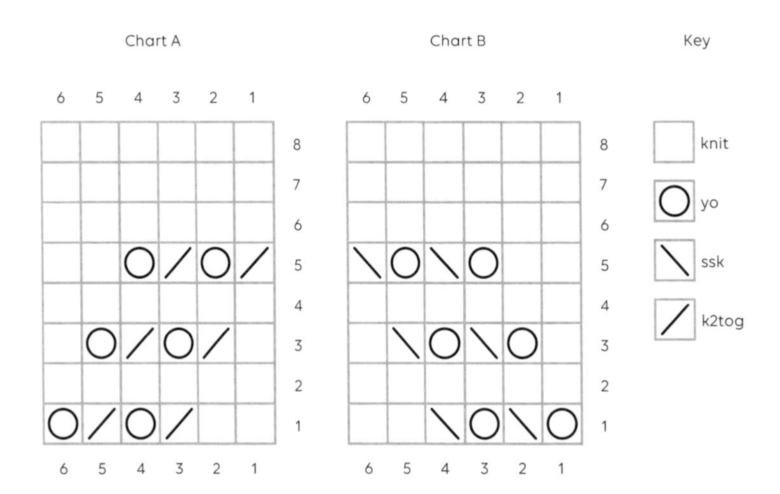

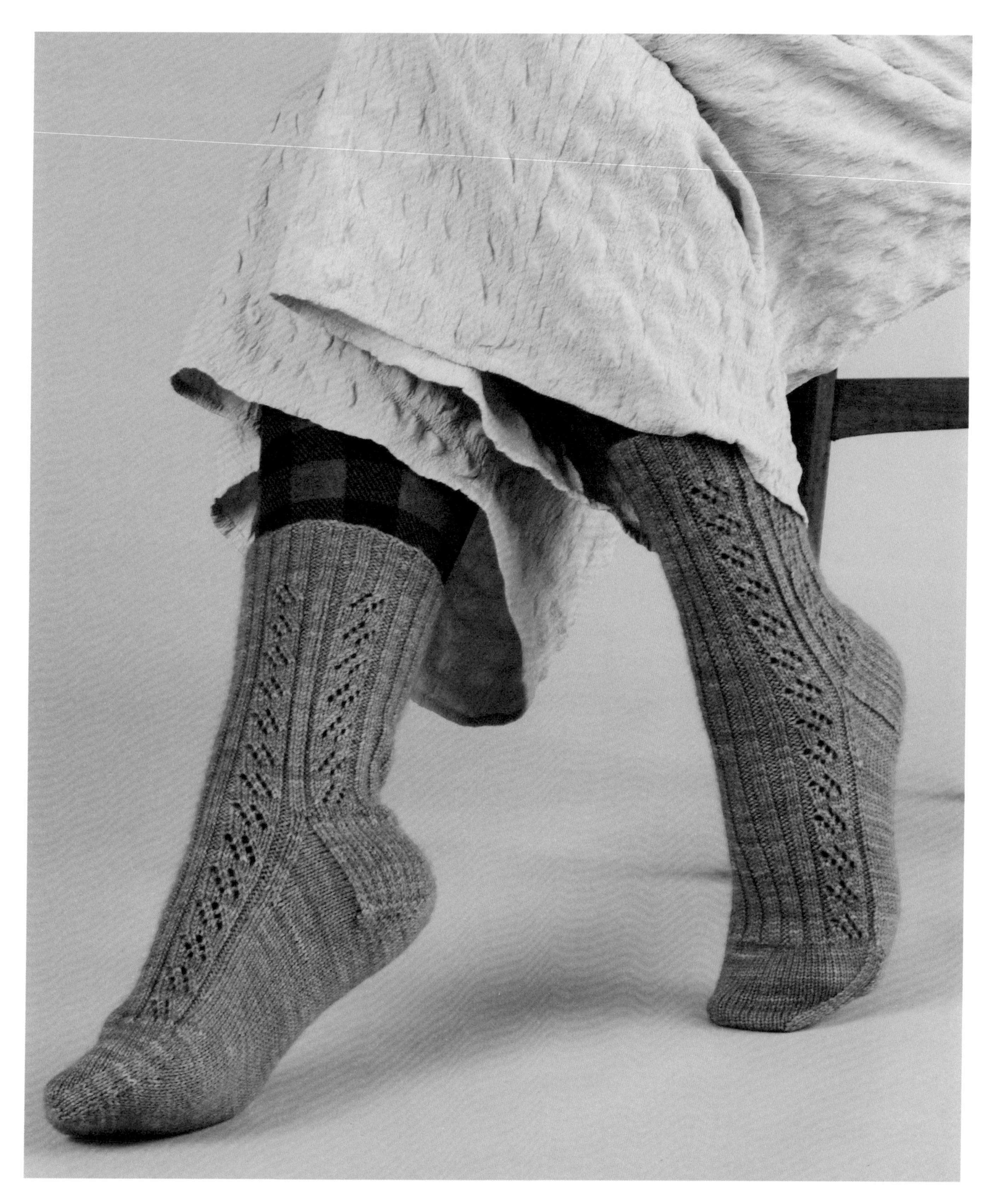

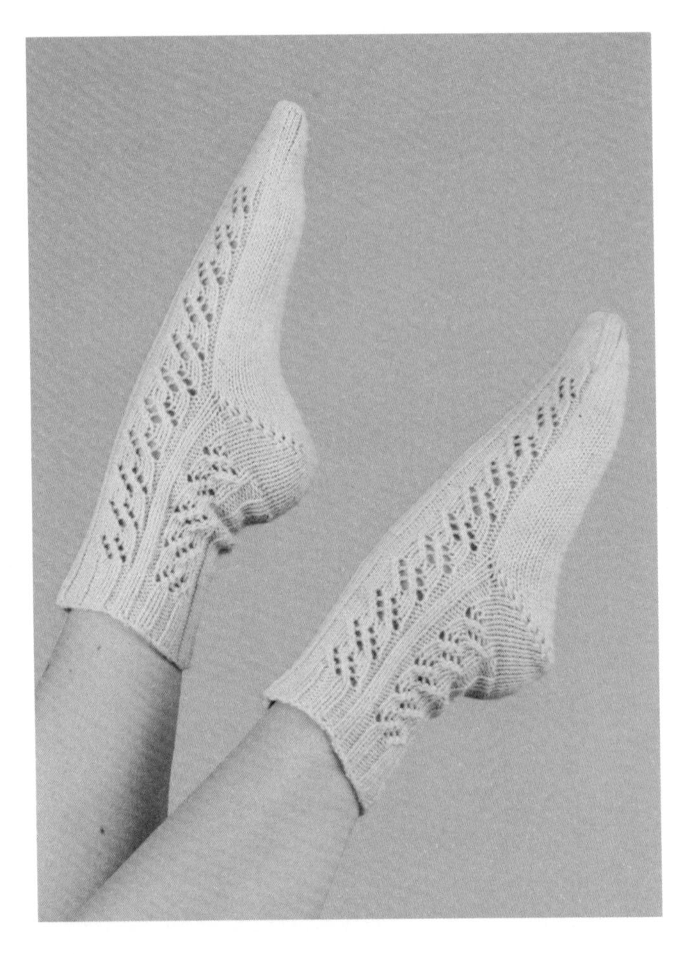

Sizes: 1 (2, 3, 4)
To fit foot circumference: 20.5 (21.5, 23, 24.5)cm / 8 (8½, 9, 9¾)" – to be worn with approx. 2.5cm / 1" negative ease
Foot length is fully adjustable within the pattern. Finished sock measures 0.5cm / ¼" less than actual foot length to ensure a good fit.
Yarn: Approximately 195 (225, 250, 275)m / 212 (245, 272, 300)yds of DK-weight yarn for Heel Flap & Gusset version; Short Row and Afterthought heels use slightly less yarn.

Sample 1 (Peach version, shown here)
Model wears a UK 7 / US 9 and is shown wearing a size 2.
Vicki Brown Designs Double Knit (DK-weight; 75% superwash Merino wool, 25% nylon; 225m / 244yds per 100g skein).
Shade: Boulangerie; 1 (1, 2, 2) skeins
Gauge: 28 sts & 40 rounds = 10cm / 4" over St st on 3mm needles, after blocking.
Needles: 3mm / US 2.5 needles suitable for working small circumferences in the round
Always use a needle size that will result in the correct gauge after blocking.
Notions: 2 stitch markers, tapestry needle
Notes: These socks are worked from the cuff down, with a ribbed cuff and a lace and rib pattern on the leg and foot. The sample shown is worked using the Short Row heel method. Read all chart rounds from right to left.

WRITTEN INSTRUCTIONS FOR CHARTS
Chart A
Worked over 6 sts
Round 1: K2, [k2tog, yo] twice.
Round 2 and all even-numbered rounds: Knit.
Round 3: K1, [k2tog, yo] twice, k1.
Round 5: [K2tog, yo] twice, k2.
Rounds 7-8: Knit.
Rep rounds 1-8 for patt.

Chart B
Worked over 6 sts
Round 1: [Yo, ssk] twice, k2.
Round 2 and all even-numbered rounds: Knit.
Round 3: K1, [yo, ssk] twice, k1.
Round 5: K2, [yo, ssk] twice.
Rounds 7-8: Knit.
Rep rounds 1-8 for patt.

Note: This design is also shown in fingering / 4-ply-weight yarn from page 62.

PATTERN BEGINS (both alike)

CUFF

Cast on 48 (52, 56, 60) sts. Join to work in the round, being careful not to twist sts. PM for beg of round.

Sizes 1 & 3 ONLY:

Rib round: *K1, p2, k1; rep from * to end.

Sizes 2 & 4 ONLY:

Rib round: *P2, k2; rep from * to end.

ALL sizes again:

Rep last round a further 11 times.

LEG

Sizes 1 & 3 ONLY:

Round 1: *K1, p2, work round 1 of Chart A once, [p2, k2] 1 (2) times, p2, work round 1 of Chart B once, p2, k1; rep from * once more.

Sizes 2 & 4 ONLY:

Round 1: P2, work round 1 of Chart A once, [p2, k2] 2 (3) times, p2, work round 1 of Chart B once, p2, work round 1 of Chart A once, [p2, k2] 3 (4) times, p2, work round 1 of Chart B once.

ALL sizes again:

Last round sets patt. Working next round of Chart A and B each time, continue in patt as set until rounds 1-8 of charts have been completed 5 times in total.

HEEL

Work heel over 24 (26, 28, 30) sts using preferred method: Heel Flap & Gusset (page 128) OR Short Row (below or page 132) OR Afterthought (page 138).

Short Row Heel

The heel will be worked back and forth over the first 24 (26, 28, 30) sts only.

Row 1 (RS): K23 (25, 27, 29), w&t.

Row 2 (WS): P22 (24, 26, 28), w&t.

Row 3: K to 1 st before next 'wrapped' st, w&t.

Row 4: P to 1 st before next 'wrapped' st, w&t.

Rep rows 3-4 until there are 8 (8, 10, 10) unwrapped central sts with 8 (9, 9, 10) wrapped sts on either side.

Row 1 (RS): K to first wrapped st, pick up the wrap and k the st tog with the wrap tbl, w&t the next st (this st is now wrapped twice).

Row 2 (WS): P to first wrapped st, pick up the wrap and p the st tog with the wrap, w&t the next st (this st is now wrapped twice).

Row 3: K to first wrapped st (which now has 2 wraps), pick up the wraps and k the st tog with the wraps tbl, w&t the next st (this st is now wrapped twice).

Row 4: P to first wrapped st (which now has 2 wraps), pick up the wraps and p the st tog with the wraps, w&t the next st (this st is now wrapped twice).

Rep rows 3-4 a further 5 (6, 6, 7) times, then work row 3 only once more but do not w&t at end of row, PM for new beg of round.

Sizes 1 & 3 ONLY:
Next round: Work across 24 (28) instep sts as foll: K1, p2, work round 1 of Chart A once, [p2, k2] 1 (2) times, p2, work round 1 of Chart B once, p2, k1, k the next st tog with its wraps, k to end.

Sizes 2 & 4 ONLY:
Next round: Work across 26 (30) instep sts as foll: P2, work round 1 of Chart A once, [p2, k2] 2 (3) times, p2, work round 1 of Chart B once, p2, k the next st tog with its wraps, k to end.

ALL Sizes again
FOOT
Work straight in pattern as set, working charts and rib on instep and St st on sole, until sock measures 4.5 (5, 6)cm / 1¾ (2, 2¼)" less than desired foot length.

TOE
Round 1: Knit.
Round 2 (dec): K1, ssk, k18 (20, 22, 24), k2tog, k1, PM, k1, ssk, k to last 3 sts, k2tog, k1. *44 (48, 52, 56) sts*
Round 3: Knit.
Round 4 (dec): *K1, ssk, knit to 3 sts before marker, k2tog, k1, SM; rep from * once more. *4 sts dec*
Rep rounds 3-4 a further 6 (7, 7, 8) times. *16 (16, 20, 20) sts*
Break yarn, leaving a 30cm / 12" tail. Graft sts together (page 147).

FINISHING
Weave in ends and block to measurements.

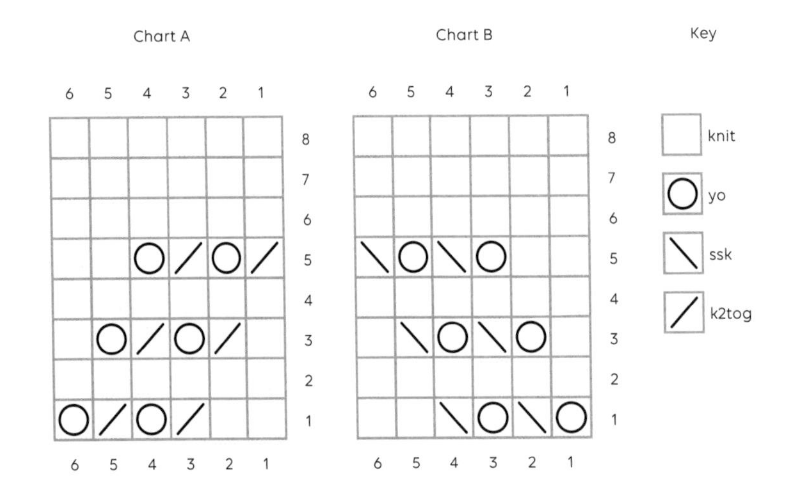

4-ply-weight *(shown here)*
a. Foot circumference (unstretched):
18 (20.5, 22.5)cm / 7¼ (8, 8¾)"
b. Leg length: 14.5cm / 5¾"

DK-weight *(not shown)*
a. Foot circumference (unstretched):
17.5 (19, 20, 22)cm / 7 (7½, 8, 8¾)"
b. Leg length: 13.5cm / 5¼"

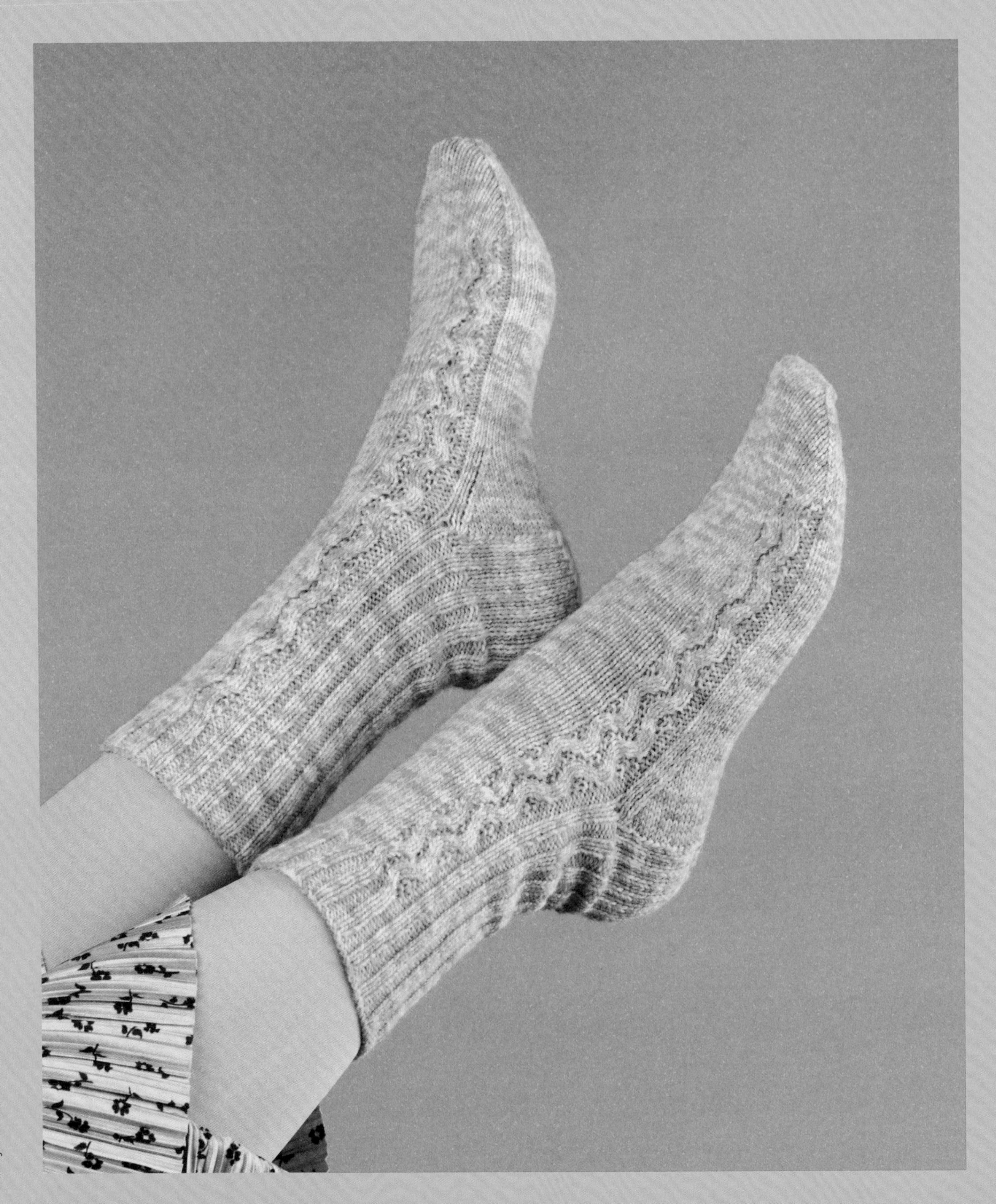

SHEPPARD

Cable Wave Socks

This design is all about texture, mixing rib and cables for a surprisingly rich fabric that allows subtle semi-solid or speckled yarns to shine.

Our top two cabled sock knitting tips: use removable tape (like washi tape) to mark your round on the pattern and remember to always work the chart from right to left when knitting in the round!

#SheppardSocks

Pattern: Sheppard - Cable Wave Socks (4-ply)

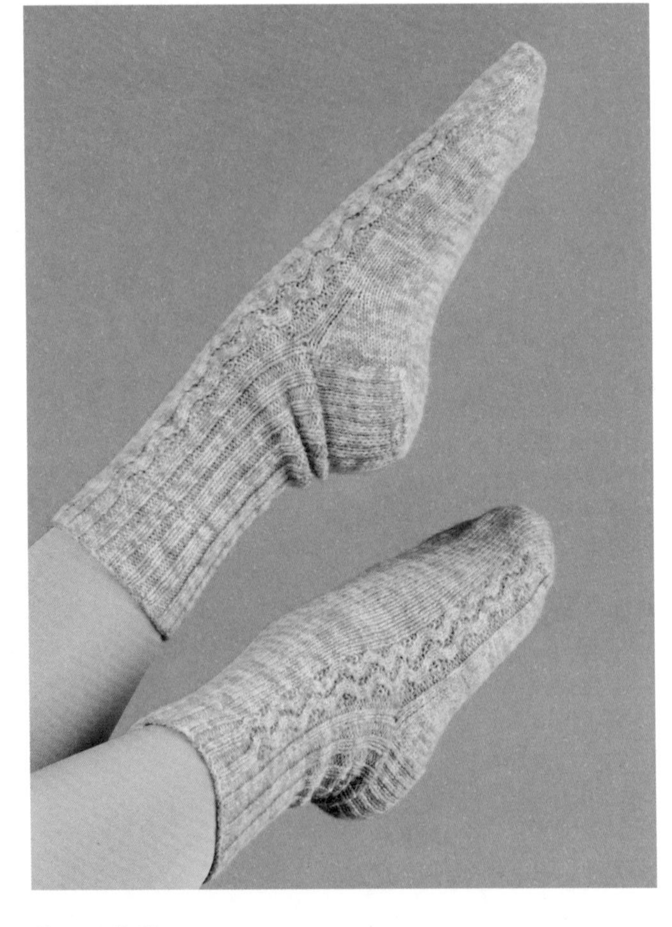

Sizes: 1 (2, 3)
To fit foot circumference: 20.5 (23, 25.5)cm / 8 (9, 10)" – to be worn with approx. 2.5cm / 1" negative ease
Foot length is fully adjustable within the pattern. Finished sock measures 0.5cm / ¼" less than actual foot length to ensure a good fit.
Yarn: Approximately 250 (300, 340)m / 272 (327, 370)yds of fingering / 4-ply-weight yarn for Heel Flap & Gusset version; Short Row and Afterthought heels use slightly less yarn.
Sample 1 (Yellow version, shown here)
Model wears a UK 7 / US 9 and is shown wearing a size 2.
Rosa Pomar Mondim (fingering / 4-ply-weight; 100% Fine Portuguese Wool; 385m / 421yds per 100g ball/skein)
Shade: 211; 1 skein

Gauge: 36 sts & 50 rounds = 10cm / 4" over St st on 2.5mm needles after blocking.
Needles: 2.5mm / US 1.5 needles suitable for working small circumferences in the round
Always use a needle size that will result in the correct gauge after blocking.
Notions: 2 stitch markers, cable needle, tapestry needle
Notes: These socks are worked from the cuff down, with a ribbed cuff and a cable pattern on the leg and foot. The samples shown are worked using the Heel Flap & Gusset method (yellow) and Short Row method (peach). Read all chart rounds from right to left.

Stitch Glossary
2/1 LPC: Slip 2 sts to cable needle and hold at front, p1, k2 from cable needle
2/1 RPC: Slip 2 sts to cable needle and hold at back, p1, k2 from cable needle

WRITTEN INSTRUCTIONS FOR CHARTS
Chart A
Worked over 8 sts
Round 1: [2/1 LPC, k1] twice.
Round 2 and all even-numbered rounds: Knit.
Round 3: [P1, 2/1 LPC] twice.
Round 5: [P2, k2] twice.
Round 7: [P1, 2/1 RPC] twice.
Round 9: [2/1 RPC, p1] twice.
Round 11: [K2, p2] twice.
Round 12: Knit.
Rep rounds 1-12 for patt.

Chart B
Worked over 8 sts
Round 1: [P1, 2/1 RPC] twice.
Round 2 and all even-numbered rounds: Knit.
Round 3: [2/1 RPC, p1] twice.
Round 5: [K2, p2] twice.
Round 7: [2/1 LPC, p1] twice.
Round 9: [P1, 2/1 LPC] twice.
Round 11: [P2, k2] twice.
Round 12: Knit.
Rep rounds 1-12 for patt.

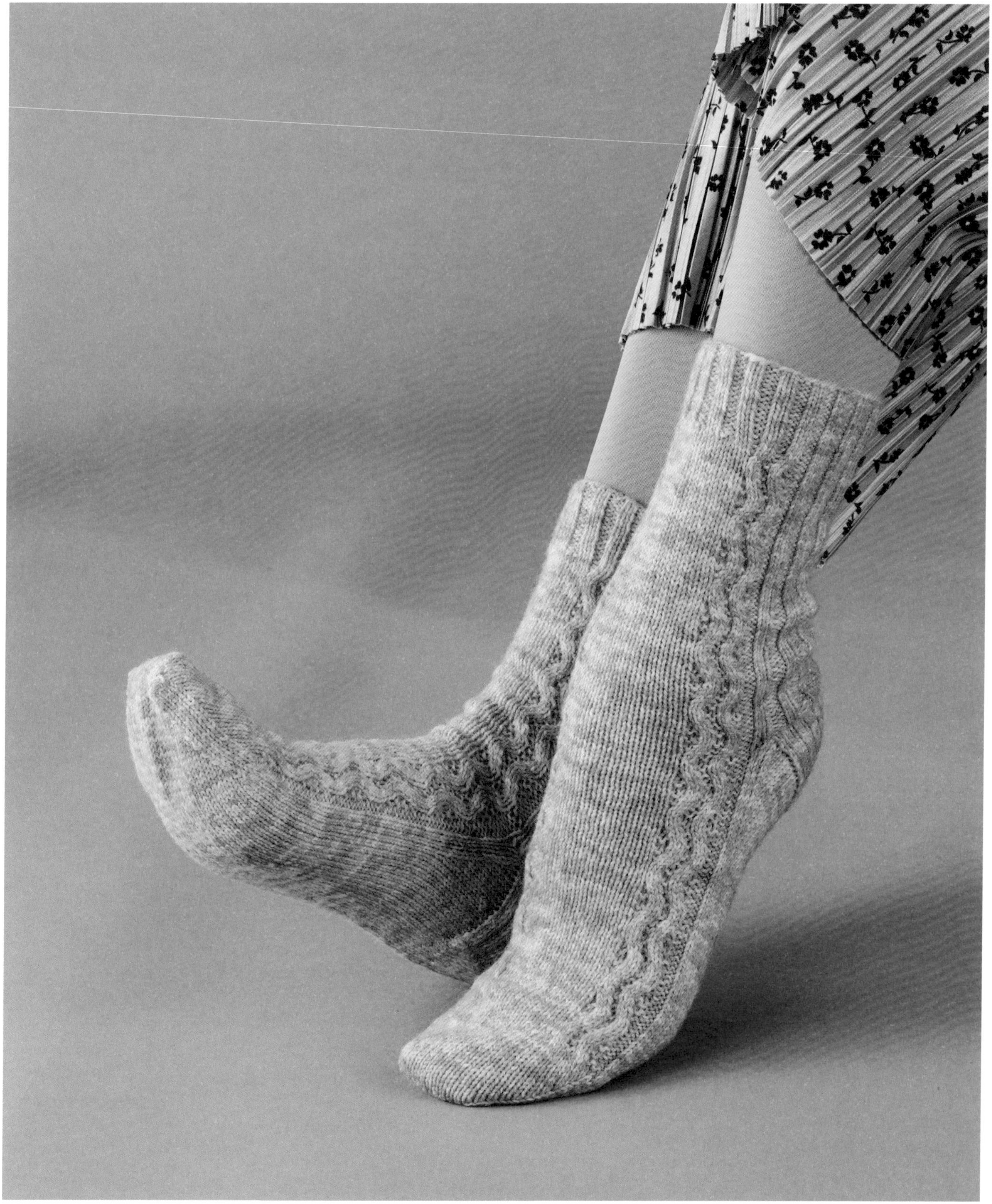

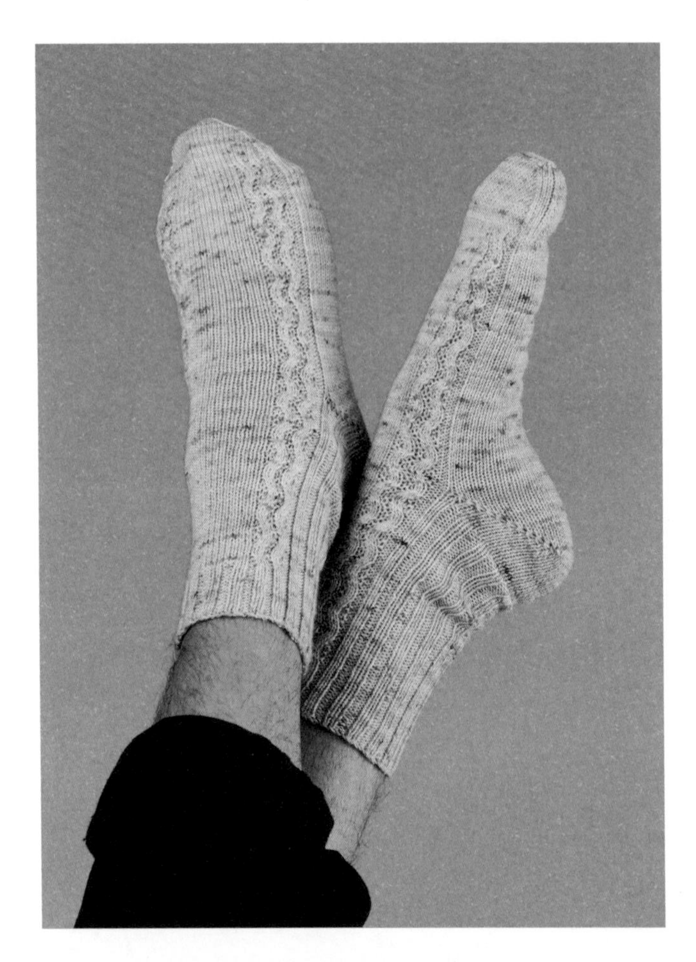

Sample 2 (Peach version, shown above)
Model wears a UK 9 / US 10 and is shown wearing a size 3.
Black Elephant Sock (fingering / 4-ply-weight; 75% superwash Merino wool, 25% nylon; 425m / 465yds per 100g skein)
Shade: Flower Moon; 1 skein

Note: This design is also shown in DK-weight yarn from page 76.

PATTERN BEGINS (both alike)

CUFF

Cast on 64 (72, 80) sts. Join to work in the round, being careful not to twist sts. PM for beg of round.
Rib round: *K1, p2, k1; rep from * to end.
Rep last round a further 15 times.

LEG

Round 1: K1, p2, work round 1 of Chart A once, k10 (14, 18), work round 1 of Chart B once, [p2, k2] 8 (9, 10) times, p2, k1.
Last round sets patt. Working next round of Chart A and B each time, continue in patt as set until rounds 1-12 of charts have been completed 5 times in total.

HEEL

Work heel over 32 (36, 40) sts using preferred method: Heel Flap & Gusset (below or page 128) OR Short Row (page 132) OR Afterthought (page 138). The samples shown are worked using the Heel Flap & Gusset method (yellow) and Short Row method (peach).

Heel Flap:

Turn work so WS is facing. Heel flap will be worked back and forth on the next 32 (36, 40) sts, beg with a WS row.
Keep rem 32 (36, 40) sts on needles for instep.
Row 1 (WS): Sl1 wyif, p31 (35, 39).
Row 2 (RS): *Sl1 wyib, k1; rep from * to end.
Rep rows 1-2 a further 14 times, then work row 1 only once more.

Heel Turn:

Row 1 (RS): Sl1 wyib, k18 (20, 22), ssk, k1, turn, leaving rem 10 (12, 14) sts unworked. *1 st dec*
Row 2 (WS): Sl1 wyif, p7, p2tog, p1, turn, leaving rem 10 (12, 14) sts unworked. *1 st dec*
Row 3: Sl1 wyib, k to 1 st before gap, ssk, k1, turn. *1 st dec*
Row 4: Sl1 wyif, p to 1 st before gap, p2tog, p1, turn. *1 st dec*
Rep rows 3-4 a further 4 (5, 6) times. All heel sts have now been worked. *20 (22, 24) heel sts rem*

Gusset:
Begin working in the round again as foll:
Set-up round: Sl1 wyib, k19 (21, 23), pick up and knit 16 sts along edge of heel flap (1 st in each slipped st along edge of flap); work across 32 (36, 40) instep sts as foll: k1, p2, work round 1 of Chart A once, k10 (14, 18), work round 1 of Chart B once, p2, k1; pick up and knit 16 sts along edge of heel flap, k36 (38, 40), PM for beg of round at beg of instep sts. *84 (90, 96) sts*
Next round (dec): K1, p2, work next round of Chart A, k10 (14, 18), work next round of Chart B, p2, k1, ssk, k to last 2 sts, k2tog. *2 sts dec*
Next round: K1, p2, work next round of Chart A, k10 (14, 18), work next round of Chart B, p2, k1, k to end.
Working next round of Chart A and B each time, rep last 2 rounds a further 9 (8, 7) times. *64 (72, 80) sts: 32 (36, 40) sts each on instep and sole*

FOOT
Work straight in pattern as set, working charts and St st on instep and St st on sole, until sock measures 4.5 (5, 6)cm / 1¾ (2, 2¼)" less than desired foot length.

TOE
Round 1: Knit.
Round 2 (dec): K1, ssk, k26 (30, 34), k2tog, k1, PM, k1, ssk, k to last 3 sts, k2tog, k1. *60 (68, 76) sts*
Round 3: Knit.
Round 4 (dec): *K1, ssk, k to 3 sts before marker, k2tog, k1, SM; rep from * once more. *4 sts dec*
Rep rounds 3-4 a further 9 (10, 12) times. *20 (24, 24) sts*
Break yarn, leaving a 30cm / 12" tail. Graft sts together (page 147).

FINISHING
Weave in ends and block to measurements (page 79).

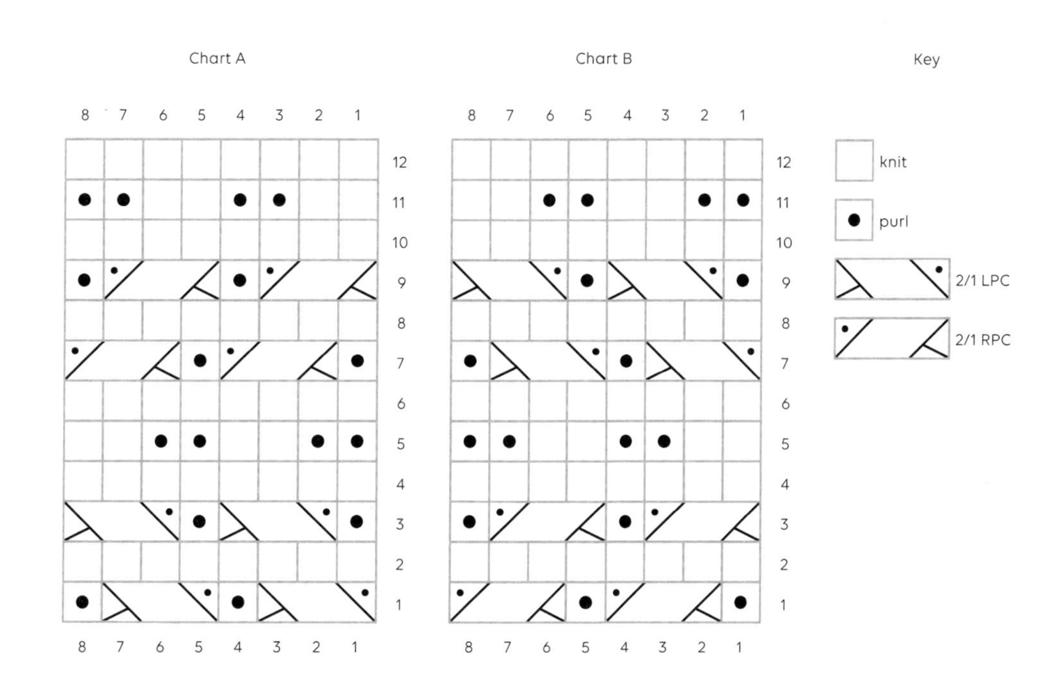

Pattern: Sheppard - Cable Wave Socks (DK)

Sizes: 1 (2, 3, 4)
To fit foot circumference: 20.5 (21.5, 23, 24.5)cm / 8 (8½, 9, 9¾)" – to be worn with approx. 2.5cm / 1" negative ease
Foot length is fully adjustable within the pattern. Finished sock measures 0.5cm / ¼" less than actual foot length to ensure a good fit.
Yarn: Approximately 195 (225, 250, 275)m / 212 (245, 272, 300)yds of DK-weight yarn; Short Row and Afterthought heels use slightly less yarn.
Sample 1 (Orange version, shown above)
Model wears a UK 7 / US 9 and is shown wearing a size 2.
Coop Knits Socks Yeah! DK (DK-weight; 75% superwash Merino wool, 25% nylon; 112m / 122yds per 50g skein).
Shade: Hecate; 2 (2, 3, 3) skeins
Gauge: 28 sts & 40 rounds = 10cm / 4" over St st on 3mm needles, after blocking.

Needles: 3mm / US 2.5 needles suitable for working small circumferences in the round
Always use a needle size that will result in the correct gauge after blocking.
Notions: 2 stitch markers, cable needle, tapestry needle
Notes: These socks are worked from the cuff down, with a ribbed cuff and a lace and rib pattern on the leg and foot. The sample shown is worked using the Heel Flap & Gusset method. Read all chart rounds from right to left.

Stitch Glossary
2/1 LPC: Slip 2 sts to cable needle and hold at front, p1, k2 from cable needle
2/1 RPC: Slip 2 sts to cable needle and hold at back, p1, k2 from cable needle

WRITTEN INSTRUCTIONS FOR CHARTS
Chart A
Worked over 8 sts
Round 1: [2/1 LPC, p1] twice.
Round 2 and all even-numbered rounds: Knit.
Round 3: [P1, 2/1 LPC] twice.
Round 5: [P2, k2] twice.
Round 7: [P1, 2/1 RPC] twice.
Round 9: [2/1 RPC, p1] twice.
Round 11: [K2, p2] twice.
Round 12: Knit.
Rep rounds 1-12 for patt.

Chart B
Worked over 8 sts
Round 1: [P1, 2/1 RPC] twice.
Round 2 and all even-numbered rounds: Knit.
Round 3: [2/1 RPC, p1] twice.
Round 5: [K2, p2] twice.
Round 7: [2/1 LPC, p1] twice.
Round 9: [P1, 2/1 LPC] twice.
Round 11: [P2, k2] twice.
Round 12: Knit.
Rep rounds 1-12 for patt.

Note: This design is also shown in fingering / 4-ply-weight yarn from page 72.

PATTERN BEGINS (both alike)

CUFF

Cast on 48 (52, 56, 60) sts. Join to work in the round, being careful not to twist sts. PM for beg of round.

Sizes 1 & 3 ONLY:

Rib round: *K1, p2, k1; rep from * to end.

Sizes 2 & 4 ONLY:

Rib round: *P2, k2; rep from * to end.

ALL sizes again:

Rep last round a further 11 times.

LEG

Sizes 1 & 3 ONLY:

Round 1: K1, p2, work round 1 of Chart A once, k2 (6), work round 1 of Chart B once, [p2, k2] 6 (7) times, p2, k1.

Sizes 2 & 4 ONLY:

Round 1: P2, work round 1 of Chart A once, k6 (10), work round 1 of Chart B once, [p2, k2] 7 (8) times.

ALL sizes again:

Last round sets patt. Working next round of Chart A and B each time, continue in patt as set until rounds 1-12 of charts have been completed 3 times in total.

HEEL

Work heel over 24 (26, 28, 30) sts using preferred method: Heel Flap & Gusset (below or page 128) OR Short Row (page 132) OR Afterthought (page 138). The sample shown is worked using the Heel Flap & Gusset method.

Heel Flap:

Turn work so WS is facing. Heel flap will be worked back and forth on the next 24 (26, 28, 30) sts, beg with a WS row. Keep rem 24 (26, 28, 30) sts on needles for instep.

Row 1 (WS): Sl1 wyif, p23 (25, 27, 29).

Row 2 (RS): *Sl1 wyib, k1; rep from * to end.

Rep rows 1-2 a further 10 times, then work row 1 only once more.

Heel Turn:

Row 1 (RS): Sl1 wyib, k14 (14, 16, 16), ssk, k1, turn, leaving rem 6 (8, 8, 10) sts unworked. *1 st dec*

Row 2 (WS): Sl1 wyif, p7 (5, 7, 5), p2tog, p1, turn, leaving rem 6 (8, 8, 10) sts unworked. *1 st dec*

Row 3: Sl1 wyib, k to 1 st before gap, ssk, k1, turn. *1 st dec*

Row 4: Sl1 wyif, p to 1 st before gap, p2tog, p1, turn. *1 st dec*

Rep rows 3-4 a further 2 (3, 3, 4) times. All heel sts have now been worked. *16 (16, 18, 18) heel sts rem*

Gusset:

Begin working in the round again as foll:

Sizes 1 & 3 ONLY:

Set-up round: Sl1 wyib, k15 (17), pick up and knit 12 sts along edge of heel flap (1 st in each slipped st along edge of flap); work across 24 (28) instep sts as foll: k1, p2, work round 1 of Chart A once, k2 (6), work round 1 of Chart B once, p2, k1; pick up and knit 12 sts along edge of heel flap, k28 (30), PM for beg of round at beg of instep sts.
64 (70) sts

Round 1 (dec): K1, p2, work next round of Chart A, k2 (6), work next round of Chart B, p2, k1, ssk, k to last 2 sts, k2tog.
2 sts dec

Round 2: K1, p2, work next round of Chart A, k2 (6), work next round of Chart B, p2, k1, k to end.

Sizes 2 & 4 ONLY:

Set-up round: Sl1 wyib, k15 (17), pick up and knit 12 sts along edge of heel flap (1 st in each slipped st along edge of the flap); work across 26 (30) instep sts as foll: p2, work round 1 of Chart A once, k6 (10), work round 1 of Chart B once, p2; pick up and knit 12 sts along edge of heel flap, k28 (30), PM for beg of round at beg of instep sts.
66 (72) sts

Round 1 (dec): P2, work next round of Chart A, k6 (10), work next round of chart, p2, ssk, k to last 2 sts, k2tog. *2 sts dec*

Round 2: P2, work next round of Chart A, k6 (10), work next round of Chart B, p2, k to end.

ALL sizes again:

Working next row of charts each time, rep rounds 1-2 a further 7 (6, 6, 5) times. *48 (52, 56, 60) sts: 24 (26, 28, 30) sts each for instep and sole*

FOOT

Work straight in pattern as set, working charts and St st on instep and St st on sole, until sock measures 4.5 (5, 5, 6) cm / 1¾ (2, 2, 2¼)" less than desired foot length.

TOE

Round 1: Knit.

Round 2 (dec): K1, ssk, k18 (20, 22, 24), k2tog, k1, PM, k1, ssk, k to last 3 sts, k2tog, k1. *44 (48, 52, 56) sts*

Round 3: Knit.

Round 4 (dec): *K1, ssk, k to 3 sts before marker, k2tog, k1, SM; rep from * once more. *4 sts dec*

Rep rounds 3-4 a further 6 (7, 7, 8) times. *16 (16, 20, 20) sts*

Break yarn, leaving a 30cm / 12" tail. Graft sts together (page 147).

FINISHING

Weave in ends and block to measurements.

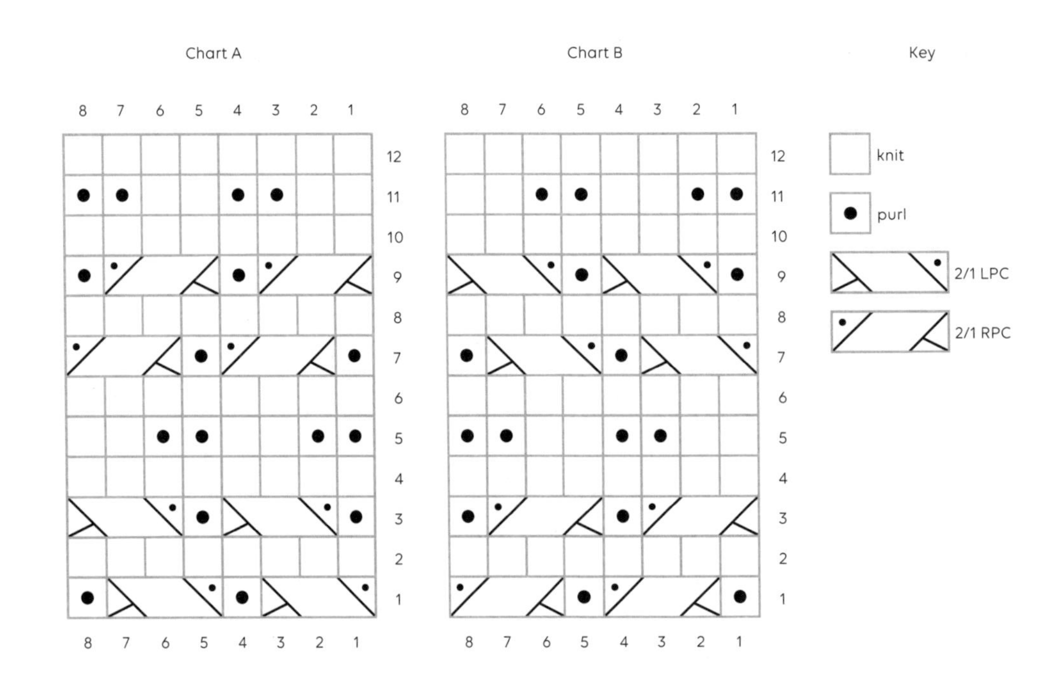

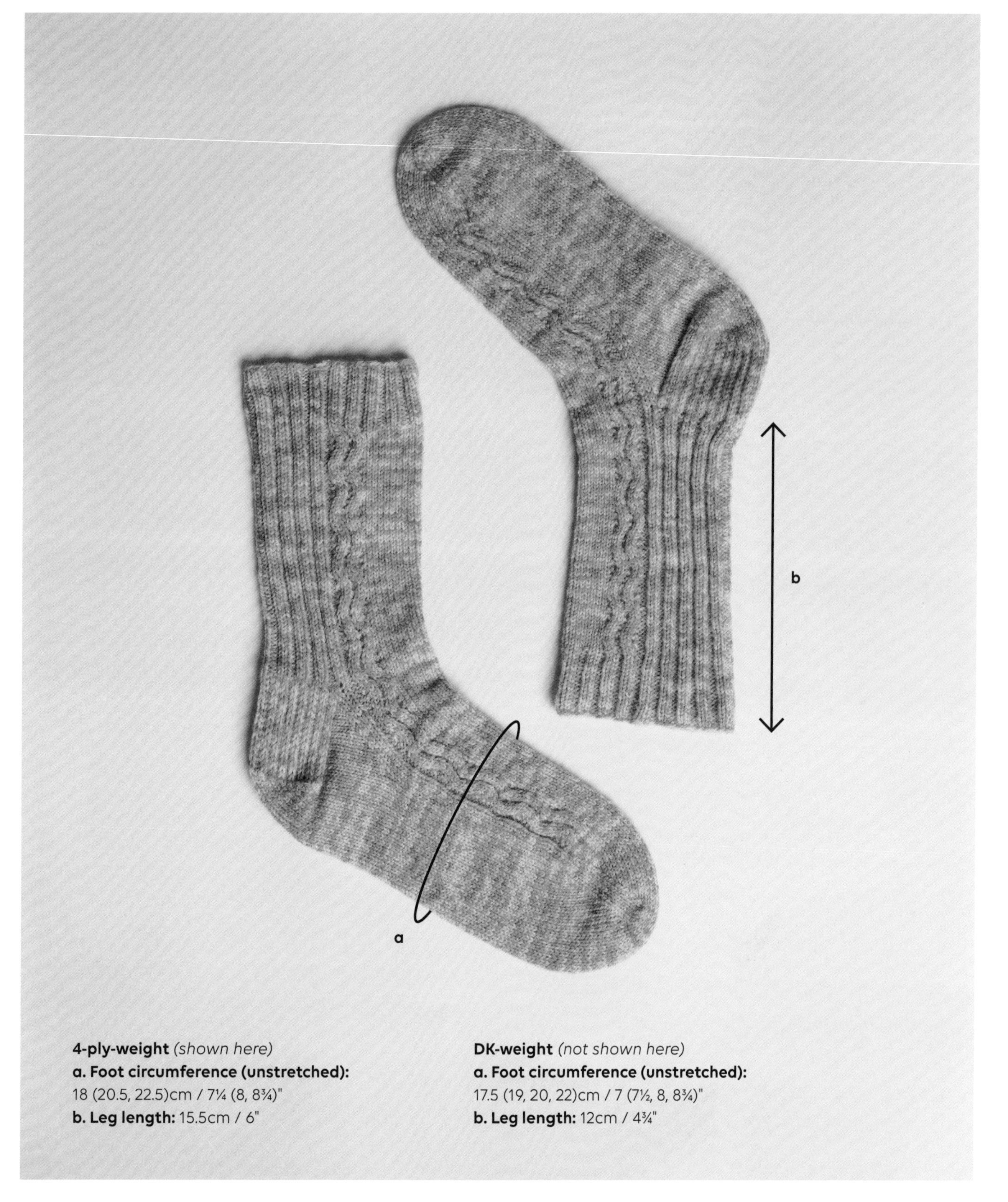

4-ply-weight *(shown here)*
a. Foot circumference (unstretched):
18 (20.5, 22.5)cm / 7¼ (8, 8¾)"
b. Leg length: 15.5cm / 6"

DK-weight *(not shown here)*
a. Foot circumference (unstretched):
17.5 (19, 20, 22)cm / 7 (7½, 8, 8¾)"
b. Leg length: 12cm / 4¾"

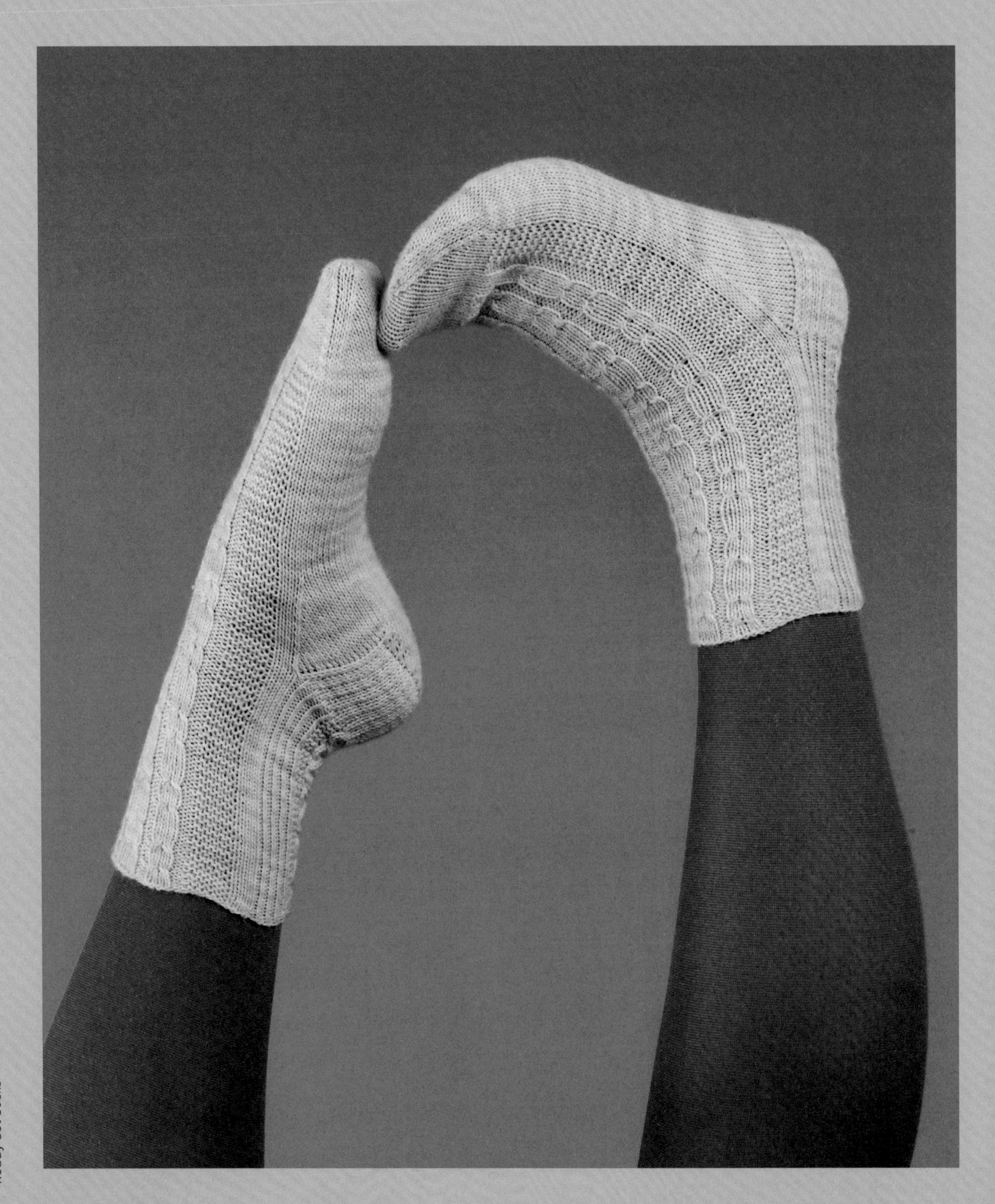

REYNOLDS

Gansey Style Socks

Twisted stitch, garter stitch, cables oh my! Inspired by the patterning on ganseys (traditional fisherman sweaters from coastal Britain), these socks can go practical or glam depending on your yarn choice. We love that this pair eschews the traditional cuff with the tops of the socks emulating the stand-up funnel collar of gansey sweaters. Knit your pair in a classic dark blue to really follow in the footsteps of fishermen's sweaters past.

#ReynoldsSocks

Pattern: Reynolds - Gansey Style Socks (4-ply)

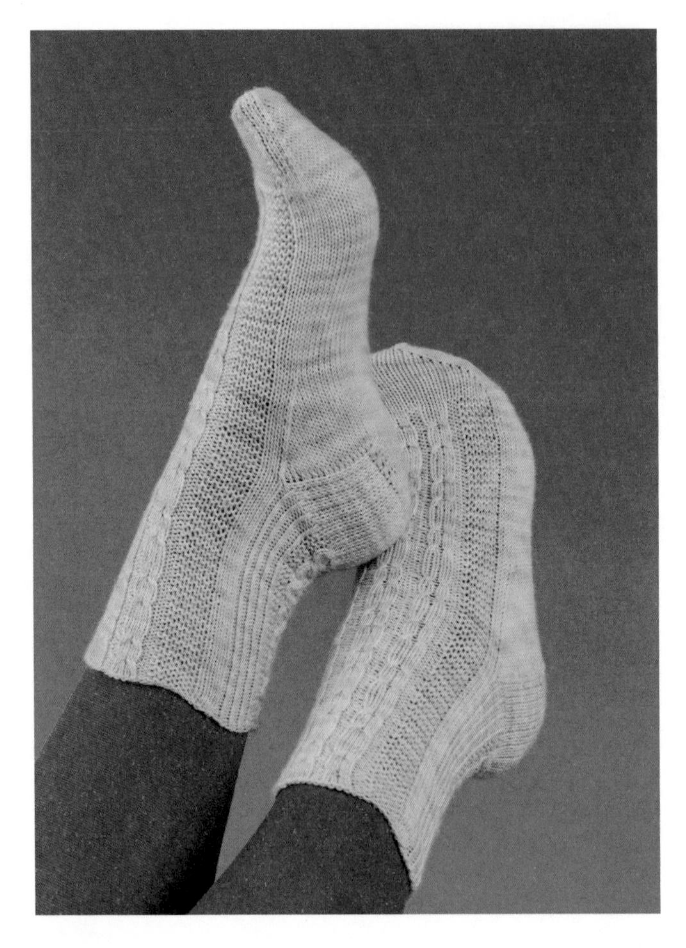

Sizes: 1 (2, 3)
To fit foot circumference: 20.5 (23, 25.5)cm / 8 (9, 10)" – to be worn with approx. 2.5cm / 1" negative ease
Foot length is fully adjustable within the pattern. Finished sock measures 0.5cm / ¼" less than actual foot length to ensure a good fit.
Yarn: Approximately 275 (325, 375)m / 300 (354, 409)yds of fingering / 4-ply-weight yarn for Heel Flap & Gusset version; Short Row and Afterthought heels use slightly less yarn.

Sample 1 (Pastel rainbow version, shown on this page)
Model wears a UK 7 / US 9 and is shown wearing a size 2.
The Wandering Flock Sock (fingering / 4-ply-weight; 75% Merino wool, 25% nylon; 380m / 415yds per 100g skein)
Shade: Cosmic Tye Dye; 1 skein
Gauge: 36 sts & 50 rounds = 10cm / 4" over St st on 2.5mm needles after blocking.
Needles: 2.5mm / US 1.5 needles suitable for working small circumferences in the round
Always use a needle size that will result in the correct gauge after blocking.
Notions: 2 stitch markers, cable needle, tapestry needle
Notes: These socks are worked from the cuff down, with cable patterns on the leg and foot. The samples shown are worked using the Heel Flap & Gusset method. Read all chart rounds from right to left. Ensure you are working from correct version of Chart B for 4-ply-weight sock.

Stitch Glossary
1/1 LC: Slip 1 st to cable needle and hold at front, k1, k1 from cable needle
1/1 RC: Slip 1 st to cable needle and hold at back, k1, k1 from cable needle
2/1 LC: Slip 2 sts to cable needle and hold at front, k1, k2 from cable needle
2/1 RC: Slip 2 sts to cable needle and hold at front, k1, k2 from cable needle
2/2 LC: Slip 2 sts to cable needle and hold at front, k2, k2 from cable needle
2/2 RC: Slip 2 sts to cable needle and hold at back, k2, k2 from cable
See pages 154-155 for how to work 1/1 LC and 1/1 RC without a cable needle.

WRITTEN INSTRUCTIONS FOR CHARTS

Chart A

Worked over 16 sts

Round 1: [K4, p2] twice, k4.

Rounds 2-5: Rep round 1 four times.

Round 6: 1/1 LC, 1/1 RC, p2, k4, p2, 1/1 LC, 1/1 RC.

Rounds 7-8: Rep round 1 twice.

Round 9: K4, p2, 1/1 LC, 1/1 RC, p2, k4.

Rounds 10-15: Rep rounds 4-9.

Round 16: Rep round 1.

Rep rounds 1-16 for patt.

Chart B – 4-ply Version ONLY

Worked over 18 sts

Round 1 and all odd-numbered rounds: [P2, k6] twice, p2.

Round 2: K11, 2/2 RC, k3.

Round 4: K2, 2/1 LC, 2/1 RC, k2, 2/1 RC, 2/1 LC, k2.

Round 6: K3, 2/2 LC, k11.

Round 8: K2, 2/1 RC, 2/1 LC, k2, 2/1 LC, 2/1 RC, k2.

Round 10: K11, 2/2 LC, k3.

Round 12: Rep round 4.

Round 14: K3, 2/2 RC, k11.

Round 16: Rep round 8.

Rep rounds 1-16 for patt.

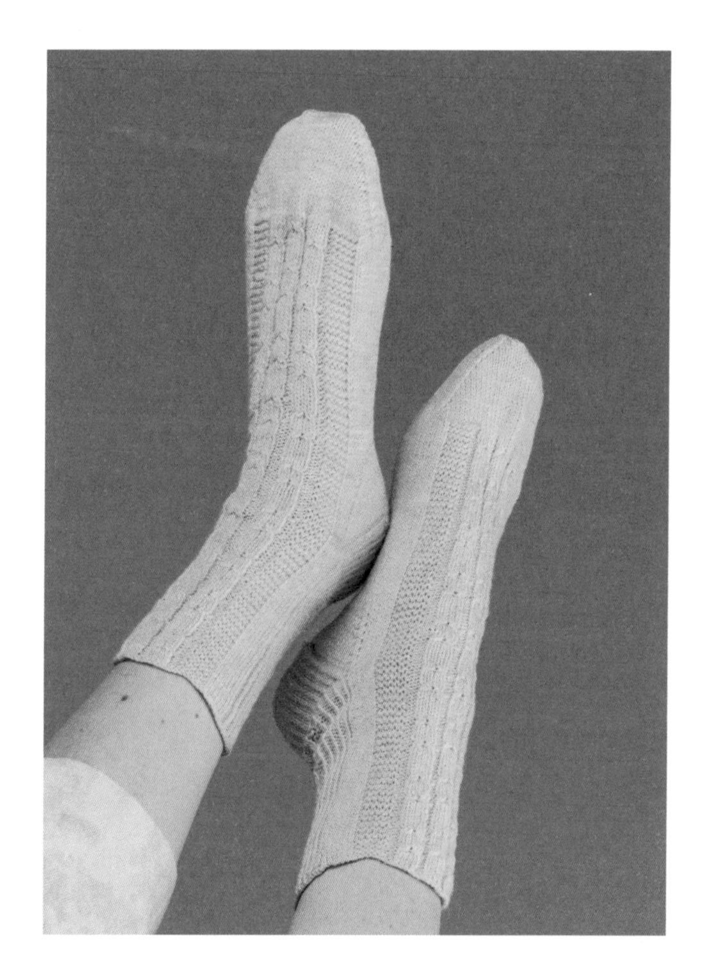

Sample 2 (Yellow version, shown above)
Model wears a UK 9 / US 10 and is shown wearing a size 3.
Neighborhood Fiber Co. Studio Sock (fingering / 4-ply-weight; 100% organic Merino wool; 365m / 400yds per 100g skein)
Shade: Penn North; 1 (1, 2) skeins

Note: This design is also shown in DK-weight yarn from page 86.

PATTERN BEGINS

SOCK ONE

LEG

Cast on 64 (72, 80) sts. Join to work in the round, being careful not to twist sts. PM for beg of round.

Round 1: K3 (3, 5), p3 (5, 5), p2, work round 1 of Chart A once, p2, p3 (5, 5), k4 (4, 6), [p1, k1tbl] 3 (4, 5) times, work round 1 of Chart B once, [k1tbl, p1] 3 (4, 5) times, k1.

Round 2: K3 (3, 5), k3 (5, 5), p2, work next round of Chart A, p2, k3 (5, 5), k4 (4, 6), [p1, k1tbl] 3 (4, 5) times, work next round of Chart B, [k1tbl, p1] 3 (4, 5) times, k1.

Last 2 rounds set Garter st, rib and chart pattern. Working next round of charts each time, work in patt as set until rounds 1-16 of charts have been completed 4 times in total.

HEEL

Work heel over 32 (36, 40) sts using preferred method: Heel Flap & Gusset (below page 128) OR Short Row (page 132) OR Afterthought (page 138). The samples shown are worked using the Heel Flap & Gusset method.

Heel Flap:

Turn work so WS is facing. Heel flap will be worked back and forth on the next 32 (36, 40) sts, beg with a WS row. Keep rem 32 (36, 40) sts on needles for instep.

Row 1 (WS): Sl1 wyif, p31 (35, 39).

Row 2 (RS): *Sl1 wyib, k1; rep from * to end.

Rep rows 1-2 a further 14 times, then work row 1 only once more.

Heel Turn:

Row 1 (RS): Sl1 wyib, k18 (20, 22), ssk, k1, turn, leaving rem 10 (12, 14) sts unworked. *1 st dec*

Row 2 (WS): Sl1 wyif, p7, p2tog, p1, turn, leaving rem 10 (12, 14) sts unworked. *1 st dec*

Row 3: Sl1 wyib, k to 1 st before gap, ssk, k1, turn. *1 st dec*

Row 4: Sl1 wyif, p to 1 st before gap, p2tog, p1, turn. *1 st dec*

Rep rows 3-4 a further 4 (5, 6) times. All heel sts have now been worked. *20 (22, 24) heel sts rem*

Gusset:

Begin working in the round again as foll:

Set-up round: Sl1 wyib, k19 (21, 23), pick up and knit 16 sts along edge of heel flap (1 st in each slipped st along edge of flap); work across 32 (36, 40) instep sts as foll:

k3 (3, 5), p3 (5, 5), p2, work round 1 of Chart A once, p2, p3 (5, 5), k3 (3, 5); pick up and knit 16 sts along edge of heel flap, k36 (38, 40), PM for beg of round at beg of instep sts.

84 (90, 96) sts

Round 1 (dec): K3 (3, 5), k3 (5, 5), p2, work next round of Chart A, p2, k3 (5, 5), k3 (3, 5), ssk, k to last 2 sts, k2tog.

2 sts dec

Round 2: K3 (3, 5), p3 (5, 5), p2, work next round of Chart A, p2, p3 (5, 5), k3 (3, 5), k to end.

Working next round of Chart A each time, rep rounds 1-2 a further 9 (8, 7) times. *64 (72, 80) sts: 32 (36, 40) sts each on instep and sole*

FOOT

Work straight in pattern as set, working Chart A and garter st on instep and St st on sole, until sock measures 4.5 (5, 6)cm / 1¾ (2, 2¼)" less than desired foot length.

TOE

Round 1: Knit.

Round 2 (dec): K1, ssk, k26 (30, 34), k2tog, k1, PM, k1, ssk, k to last 3 sts, k2tog, k1. *60 (68, 76) sts*

Round 3: Knit.

Round 4 (dec): *K1, ssk, k to 3 sts before marker, k2tog, k1, SM; rep from * once more. *4 sts dec*

Rep rounds 3-4 a further 9 (10, 12) times. *20 (24, 24) sts*

Break yarn, leaving a 30cm / 12" tail. Graft sts together (page 147).

SOCK TWO

LEG

Cast on 64 (72, 80) sts. Join to work in the round, being careful not to twist sts. PM for beg of round.

Note: For Sock Two, Chart A will begin with round 1, but Chart B will begin with round 5.

Round 1: K3 (3, 5), p3 (5, 5), p2, work round 1 of Chart A once, p2, p3 (5, 5), k4 (4, 6), [p1, k1tbl] 3 (4, 5) times, work round 5 of Chart B once, [k1tbl, p1] 3 (4, 5) times, k1.
Round 2: K3 (3, 5), k3 (5, 5), p2, work next round of Chart A, p2, k3 (5, 5), k4 (4, 6), [p1, k1tbl] 3 (4, 5) times, work next round of Chart B, [k1tbl, p1] 3 (4, 5) times, k1.

Last 2 rounds set Garter st, rib and chart pattern. Working next round of charts each time, work in patt as set until rounds 1-16 of Chart A have been completed 4 times in total (Chart B will end with round 4).

HEEL, FOOT & TOE
Work as for Sock One.

FINISHING
Weave in ends and block to measurements (page 89).

Key

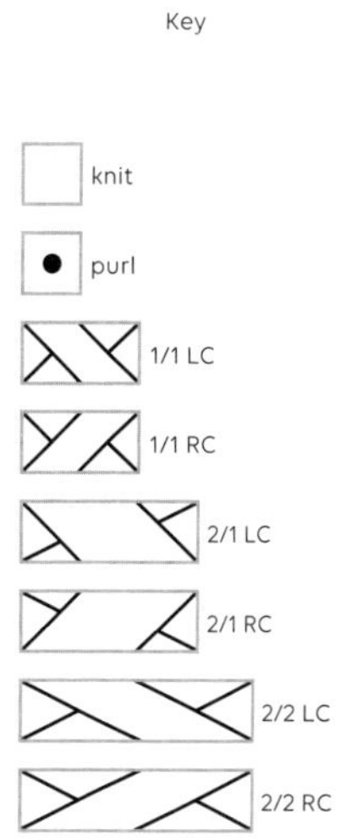

Chart A

Chart B - 4-ply Version ONLY

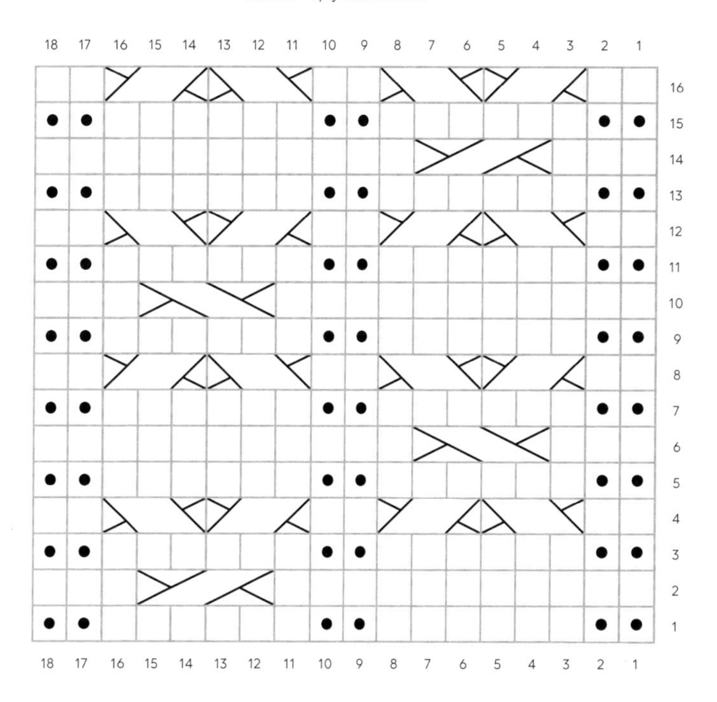

Pattern: Reynolds - Gansey Style Socks (DK)

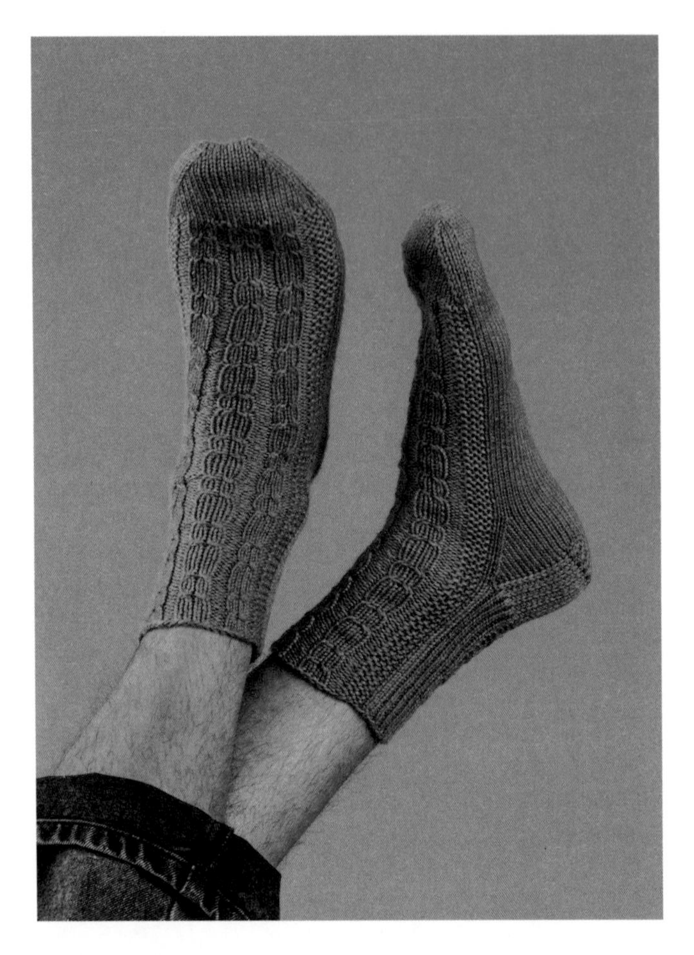

Sizes: 1 (2, 3, 4)
To fit foot circumference: 20.5 (21.5, 23, 24.5)cm / 8 (8½, 9, 9¾)" – to be worn with approx. 2.5cm / 1" negative ease
Foot length is fully adjustable within the pattern. Finished sock measures 0.5cm / ¼" less than actual foot length to ensure a good fit.
Yarn: Approximately 220 (256, 285, 310)m / 240 (279, 310, 338)yds of DK-weight yarn; Short Row and Afterthought heels use slightly less yarn.
Sample 1 (Blue version, shown above)
Model wears a UK 9 / US 10 and is shown wearing a size 3.
Opal Uni 6 ply (DK-weight; 75% virgin wool, 25% polyamide; 420m / 460yds per 150g ball)
Shade: Blue Jeans; 1 ball

Gauge: 28 sts & 40 rounds = 10cm / 4" over St st on 3mm needles, after blocking.
Needles: 3mm / US 2.5 needles suitable for working small circumferences in the round
Always use a needle size that will result in the correct gauge after blocking.
Notions: 2 stitch markers, cable needle, tapestry needle
Notes: These socks are worked from the cuff down, with cable patterns on the leg and foot. The sample shown is worked using the Heel Flap & Gusset method. Read all chart rounds from right to left. Ensure you are working from correct version of Chart B for DK-weight sock.

Stitch Glossary
1/1 LC: Slip 1 st to cable needle and hold at front, k1, k1 from cable needle
1/1 RC: Slip 1 st to cable needle and hold at back, k1, k1 from cable needle
2/1 LC: Slip 2 sts to cable needle and hold at front, k1, k2 from cable needle
2/1 RC: Slip 2 sts to cable needle and hold at front, k1, k2 from cable needle
2/2 LC: Slip 2 sts to cable needle and hold at front, k2, k2 from cable needle
2/2 RC: Slip 2 sts to cable needle and hold at back, k2, k2 from cable
See pages 154-155 for how to work 1/1 LC and 1/1 RC without a cable needle.

WRITTEN INSTRUCTIONS FOR CHARTS
Chart A
Worked over 16 sts
Round 1: [K4, p2] twice, k4.
Rounds 2-5: Rep round 1 four times.
Round 6: 1/1 LC, 1/1 RC, p2, k4, p2, 1/1 LC, 1/1 RC.
Rounds 7-8: Rep round 1 twice.
Round 9: K4, p2, 1/1 LC, 1/1 RC, p2, k4.
Rounds 10-15: Rep rounds 4-9.
Round 16: Rep round 1.
Rep rounds 1-16 for patt.

Chart B - DK Version ONLY
Worked over 10 sts
Round 1 and all odd-numbered rounds: P2, k6, p2.
Round 2: Knit.
Round 4: K2, 2/1 LC, 2/1 RC, k2.
Round 6: K3, 2/2 LC, k3.
Round 8: K2, 2/1 RC, 2/1 LC, k2.
Round 10: Knit.
Round 12: Rep round 4.
Round 14: K3, 2/2 RC, k3.
Round 16: Rep round 8.
Rep rounds 1-16 for patt.

Note: This design is also shown in fingering / 4-ply-weight yarn from page 82.

PATTERN BEGINS
SOCK ONE
LEG
Cast on 48 (52, 56, 60) sts. Join to work in the round, being careful not to twist sts. PM for beg of round.
Round 1: K1, p2 (2, 3, 4), p1 (2, 2, 2), work round 1 of Chart A once, p1 (2, 2, 2), p2 (2, 3, 4), k2 (3, 2, 3), [p1, k1tbl] 3 (3, 4, 4) times, work round 1 of Chart B once, [k1tbl, p1] 3 (3, 4, 4) times, k1 (2, 1, 2).
Round 2: K1, k2 (2, 3, 4), p1 (2, 2, 2), work next round of Chart A, p1 (2, 2, 2), k2 (2, 3, 4), k2 (3, 2, 3), [p1, k1tbl] 3 (3, 4, 4) times, work next round of Chart B, [k1tbl, p1] 3 (3, 4, 4) times, k1 (2, 1, 2).
Last 2 rounds set Garter st, rib and chart pattern. Working next round of charts each time, work in patt as set until rounds 1-16 of charts have been completed 3 times in total.

HEEL
Work heel over 24 (26, 28, 30) sts using preferred method: Heel Flap & Gusset (below or page 128) OR Short Row (page 132) OR Afterthought (page 138). The sample shown is worked using the Heel Flap & Gusset method.

Heel Flap:
Turn work so WS is facing. Heel flap will be worked back and forth on the next 24 (26, 28, 30) sts, beg with a WS row. Keep rem 24 (26, 28, 30) sts on needles for instep.
Row 1 (WS): Sl1 wyif, p23 (25, 27, 29).
Row 2 (RS): *Sl1 wyib, k1; rep from * to end.
Rep rows 1-2 a further 10 times, then work row 1 only once more.

Heel Turn:
Row 1 (RS): Sl1 wyib, k14 (14, 16, 16), ssk, k1, turn, leaving rem 6 (8, 8, 10) sts unworked. *1 st dec*
Row 2 (WS): Sl1 wyif, p7 (5, 7, 5), p2tog, p1, turn, leaving rem 6 (8, 8, 10) sts unworked. *1 st dec*
Row 3: Sl1 wyib, k to 1 st before gap, ssk, k1, turn. *1 st dec*
Row 4: Sl1 wyif, p to 1 st before gap, p2tog, p1, turn. *1 st dec*
Rep rows 3-4 a further 2 (3, 3, 4) times. All heel sts have now been worked. *16 (16, 18, 18) heel sts rem*

Gusset:
Begin working in the round again as foll:
Set-up round: Sl1 wyib, k15 (15, 17, 17), pick up and knit 12 sts along edge of heel flap (1 st in each slipped st along edge of the flap); work across 24 (26, 28, 30) instep sts as foll: k1, p2 (2, 3, 4), p1 (2, 2, 2), work round 1 of Chart A once, p1 (2, 2, 2), p2 (2, 3, 4), k1; pick up and knit 12 sts along edge of heel flap, k28 (28, 30, 30), PM for beg of round at beg of instep sts. *64 (66, 70, 72) sts*
Round 1 (dec): K1, k2 (2, 3, 4), p1 (2, 2, 2), work next round of Chart A, p1 (2, 2, 2), k2 (2, 3, 4), k1, ssk, k to last 2 sts, k2tog. *2 sts dec*
Round 2: K1, p2 (2, 3, 4), p1 (2, 2, 2), work next round of Chart A, p1 (2, 2, 2), p2 (2, 3, 4), k1, k to end.
Working next round of chart each time, rep rounds 1-2 a further 7 (6, 6, 5) times. *48 (52, 56, 60) sts: 24 (26, 28, 30) sts each for instep and sole*

FOOT
Work straight in pattern as set, working Chart A and Garter st on instep and St st on sole, until sock measures 4.5 (5, 5, 5.5)cm / 1¾ (2, 2, 2¼)" less than desired foot length.

TOE
Round 1: Knit.
Round 2 (dec): K1, ssk, k18 (20, 22, 24), k2tog, k1, PM, k1, ssk, k to last 3 sts, k2tog, k1. *44 (48, 52, 56) sts*
Round 3: Knit.
Round 4 (dec): *K1, ssk, k to 3 sts before marker, k2tog, k1, SM; rep from * once more. *4 sts dec*
Rep rounds 3-4 a further 6 (7, 7, 8) times. *16 (16, 20, 20) sts*
Break yarn, leaving a 30cm / 12" tail. Graft sts together (page 147).

SOCK TWO
LEG
Cast on 48 (52, 56, 60) sts. Join to work in the round, being careful not to twist sts. PM for beg of round.
Note: For Sock Two, Chart A will begin with round 1, but Chart B will begin with round 9.
Round 1: K1, p2 (2, 3, 4), p1 (2, 2, 2), work round 1 of Chart A once, p1 (2, 2, 2), p2 (2, 3, 4), k2 (3, 2, 3), [p1, k1tbl] 3 (3, 4, 4) times, work round 9 of Chart B once, [k1tbl, p1] 3 (3, 4, 4) times, k1 (2, 1, 2).
Round 2: K1, k2 (2, 3, 4), p1 (2, 2, 2), work next round of Chart A, p1 (2, 2, 2), k2 (2, 3, 4), k2 (3, 2, 3), [p1, k1tbl] 3 (3, 4, 4) times, work next round of Chart B, [k1tbl, p1] 3 (3, 4, 4) times, k1 (2, 1, 2).
Last 2 rounds set Garter st, rib and chart pattern.
Working next round of charts each time, work in patt as set until rounds 1-16 of Chart A have been completed 3 times (Chart B will end with round 8).

HEEL, FOOT & TOE
Work as for Sock One.

FINISHING
Weave in ends and block to measurements.

Chart A

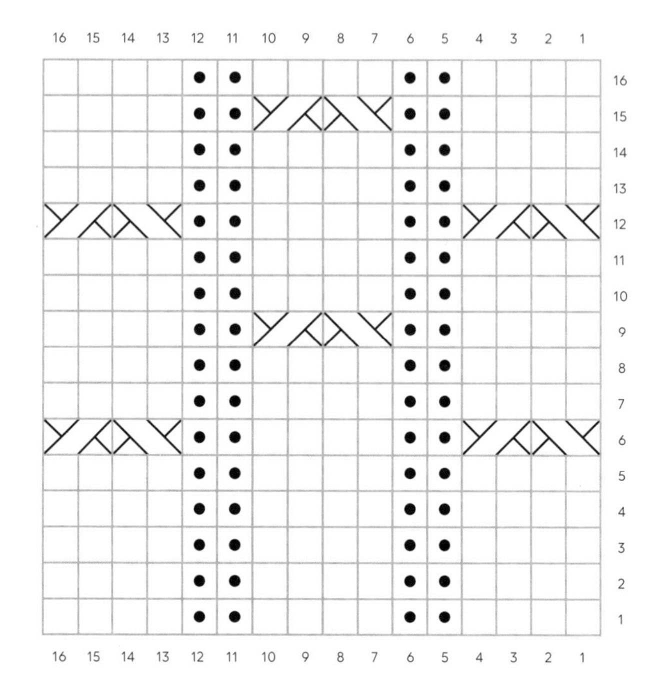

Chart B - DK Version ONLY

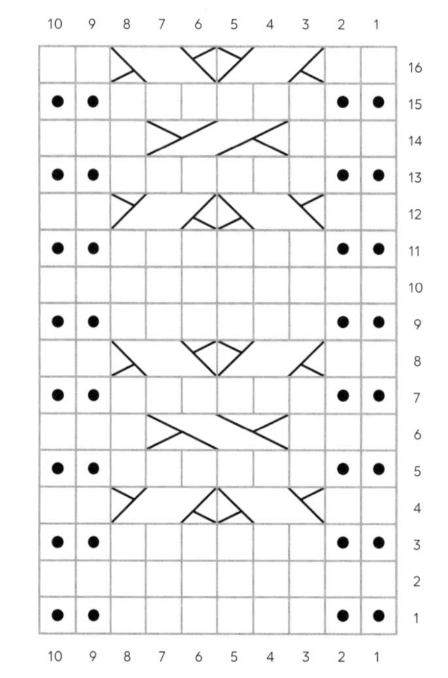

Key

- knit
- purl
- 1/1 LC
- 1/1 RC
- 2/1 LC
- 2/1 RC
- 2/2 LC
- 2/2 RC

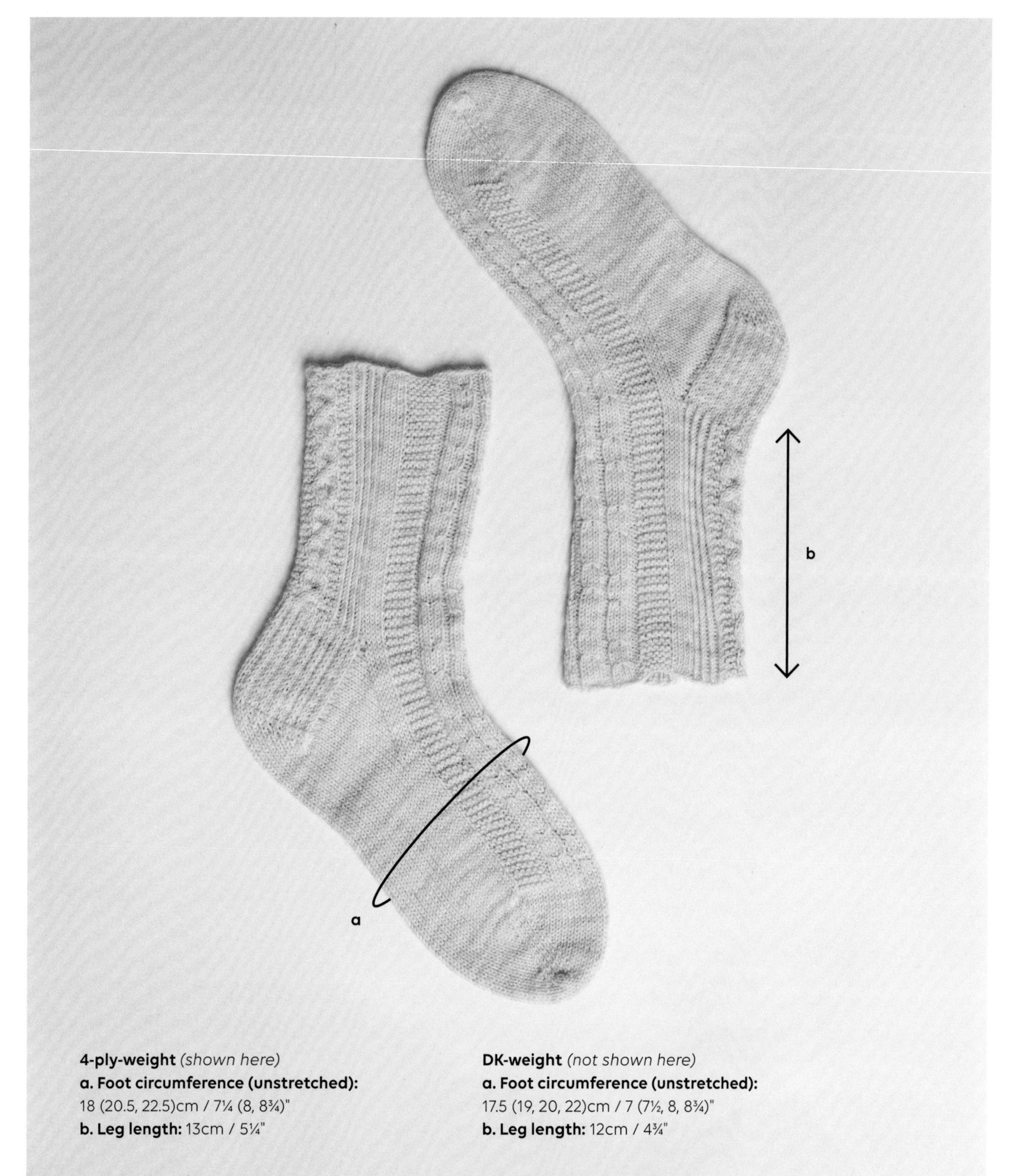

4-ply-weight *(shown here)*
a. Foot circumference (unstretched):
18 (20.5, 22.5)cm / 7¼ (8, 8¾)"
b. Leg length: 13cm / 5¼"

DK-weight *(not shown here)*
a. Foot circumference (unstretched):
17.5 (19, 20, 22)cm / 7 (7½, 8, 8¾)"
b. Leg length: 12cm / 4¾"

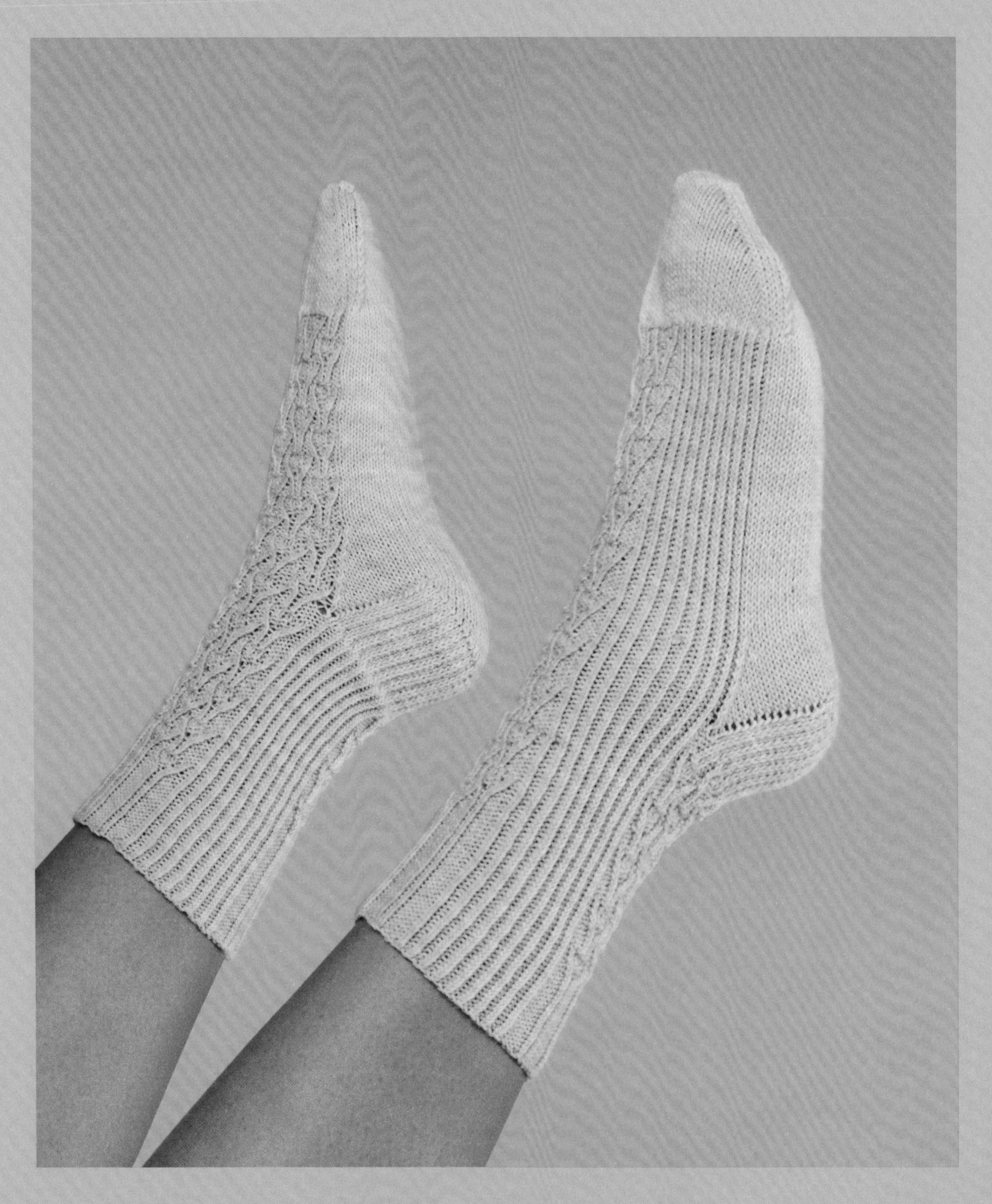

CHARISSE

Twisted Stitch Socks

These sophisticated socks blend swathes of elongated twisted stitches with fields of interlocking motifs that flow at an incline to the lower calf. Feet are often one of the most hard-wearing, utilitarian parts of our bodies, and yet they can't help but look elegant in the Charisse socks. Perhaps donning a pair will encourage you to put your feet up and enjoy some well-deserved rest.

#CharisseSocks

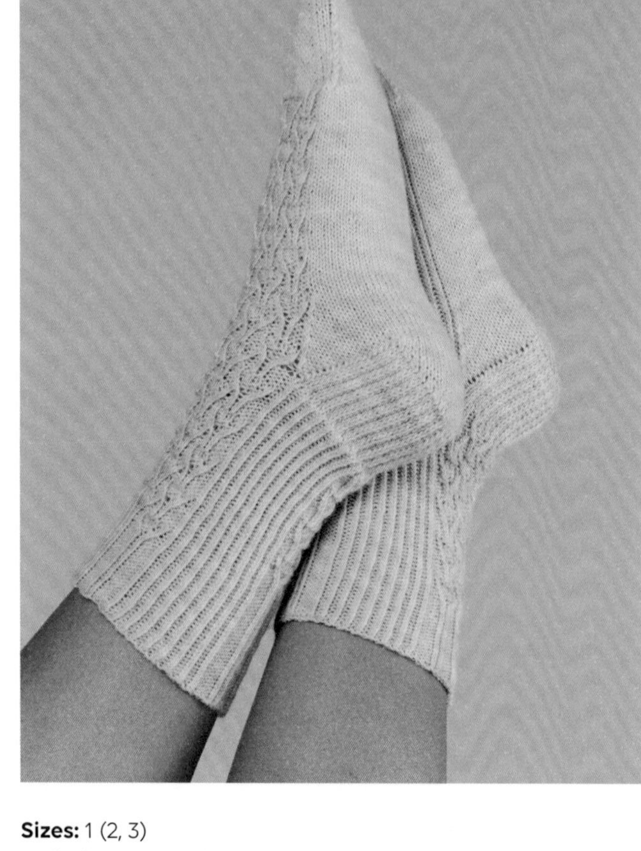

Sizes: 1 (2, 3)
To fit foot circumference: 20.5 (23, 25.5)cm / 8 (9, 10)" – to be worn with approx. 2.5cm / 1" negative ease
Foot length is fully adjustable within the pattern. Finished sock measures 0.5cm / ¼" less than actual foot length to ensure a good fit.
Yarn: Approximately 260 (300, 350)m / 283 (327, 381)yds of fingering / 4-ply-weight yarn for Heel Flap & Gusset version; Short Row and Afterthought heels use slightly less yarn.
Sample 1 (Neon version, shown above)
Model wears a UK 7 / US 9 and is shown wearing a size 3.
Qing Fibre Classic Sock (fingering / 4-ply-weight; 75% superwash Merino wool, 25% nylon; 400m / 437yds per 100g skein)
Shade: Neon Groove; 1 skein

Gauge: 36 sts & 50 rounds = 10cm / 4" over St st on 2.5mm needles after blocking.
Needles: 2.5mm / US 1.5 needles suitable for working small circumferences in the round
Always use a needle size that will result in the correct gauge after blocking.
Notions: 2 stitch markers, cable needle, tapestry needle
Notes: These socks are worked from the cuff down, with a ribbed cuff and a twisted rib and cable pattern on the leg and foot. The samples shown are worked using the Heel Flap & Gusset method (neon) and Afterthought method (camel). Read all chart rounds from right to left. Ensure you are working from correct charts for 4-ply or DK version as appropriate.

Stitch Glossary
1/1 LPT: Slip 1 st to cable needle and hold at front, p1, k1 tbl from cable needle
1/1 RPT: Slip 1 st to cable needle and hold at back, p1, k1 tbl from cable needle

WRITTEN INSTRUCTIONS FOR CHARTS
Chart A - 4-ply Version ONLY
Worked over 21 sts
Round 1: P2, [k2tbl, p3] 3 times, k2tbl, p2.
Round 2: P2, [k2tbl, p3] twice, k2tbl, p2, 1/1 RPT, 1/1 LPT, p1.
Round 3: P2, [k2tbl, p3] twice, k2tbl, [p2, k1tbl] twice, p1.
Round 4: P2, [k2tbl, p3] twice, k2tbl, p1, 1/1 RPT, p2, 1/1 LPT.
Rounds 5-6: P2, [k2tbl, p3] twice, k2tbl, p1, k1tbl, p1, k2, p1, k1tbl.
Round 7: P2, k2tbl, p3, k2tbl, p2, 1/1 RPT, 1/1 LPT, p6.
Round 8: P2, k2tbl, p3, k2tbl, [p2, k1tbl] twice, p2, k2tbl, p2.
Round 9: P2, k2tbl, p3, k2tbl, p1, 1/1 RPT, p2, 1/1 LPT, p1, k2tbl, p2.
Rounds 10-11: P2, k2tbl, p3, k2tbl, p1, k1tbl, p1, k2, p1, k1tbl, p1, k2tbl, p2.
Round 12: P2, k2tbl, p2, 1/1 RPT, 1/1 LPT, p6, 1/1 RPT, 1/1 LPT, p1.
Round 13: *P2, k2tbl, [p2, k1tbl] twice; rep from * once more, p1.
Round 14: P1, [p1, k2tbl, p1, 1/1 RPT, p2, 1/1 LPT] twice.
Rounds 15-16: P1, [p1, k2tbl, p1, k1tbl, p1, k2, p1, k1tbl] twice.
Round 17: P1, [1/1 RPT, 1/1 LPT, p6] twice.
Round 18: P1, *[k1tbl, p2] twice, k2tbl, p2; rep from * once more.
Round 19: [1/1 RPT, p2, 1/1 LPT, p1, k2tbl, p1] twice, p1.
Rounds 20-21: [K1tbl, p1, k2, p1, k1tbl, p1, k2tbl, p1] twice, p1.
Round 22: [P6, 1/1 RPT, 1/1 LPT] twice, p1.
Rep rounds 13-22 for patt.

Chart B - 4-ply Version ONLY
Worked over 21 sts
Round 1: P2, [k2tbl, p3] 3 times, k2tbl, p2.
Round 2: P1, 1/1 RPT, 1/1 LPT, p2, [k2tbl, p3] twice, k2tbl, p2.
Round 3: P1, [k1tbl, p2] twice, [k2tbl, p3] twice, k2tbl, p2.
Round 4: 1/1 RPT, p2, 1/1 LPT, p1, [k2tbl, p3] twice, k2tbl, p2.
Rounds 5-6: K1tbl, p1, k2, p1, k1tbl, p1, [k2tbl, p3] twice, k2tbl, p2.
Round 7: P6, 1/1 RPT, 1/1 LPT, p2, k2tbl, p3, k2tbl, p2.
Round 8: P2, k2tbl, [p2, k1tbl] twice, p2, k2tbl, p3, k2tbl, p2.
Round 9: P2, k2tbl, p1, 1/1 RPT, p2, 1/1 LPT, p1, k2tbl, p3, k2tbl, p2.
Rounds 10-11: P2, k2tbl, p1, k1tbl, p1, k2, p1, k1tbl, p1, k2tbl, p3, k2tbl, p2.
Round 12: P1, 1/1 RPT, 1/1 LPT, p6, 1/1 RPT, 1/1 LPT, p2, k2tbl, p2.
Round 13: P1, *[k1tbl, p2] twice, k2tbl, p2; rep from * once more.
Round 14: [1/1 RPT, p2, 1/1 LPT, p1, k2tbl, p1] twice, p1.
Rounds 15-16: [K1tbl, p1, k2, p1, k1tbl, p1, k2tbl, p1] twice, p1.
Round 17: [P6, 1/1 RPT, 1/1 LPT] twice, p1.
Round 18: *P2, k2tbl, [p2, k1tbl] twice; rep from * once more, p1.
Round 19: P1, [p1, k2tbl, p1, 1/1 RPT, p2, 1/1 LPT] twice.
Rounds 20-21: P1, [p1, k2tbl, p1, k1tbl, p1, k2, p1, k1tbl] twice.
Round 22: P1, [1/1 RPT, 1/1 LPT, p6] twice.
Rep rounds 13-22 for patt.

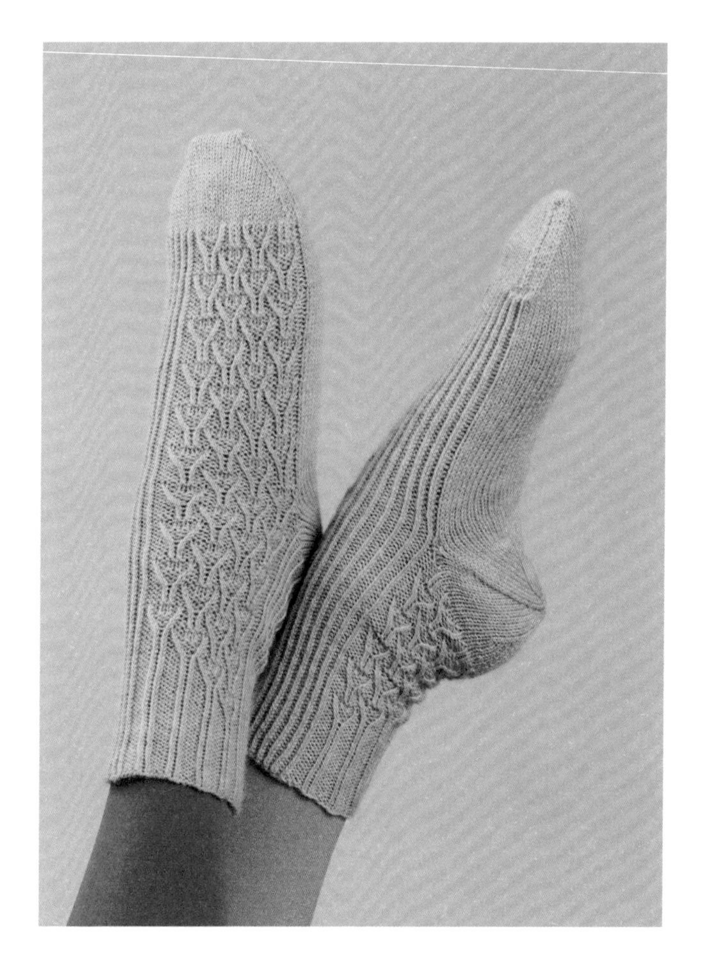

Sample 2 (Camel version, shown above and on page 95)
Model wears a UK 7 / US 9 and is shown wearing a size 2.
Opal Uni 4ply (fingering / 4-ply-weight; 75% virgin wool, 25% polyamide; 425m / 465yds per 100g skein)
Shade: 5189 Camel; 1 ball

Note: This design is also shown in DK-weight yarn from page 98.

PATTERN BEGINS

SOCK ONE

CUFF

Cast on 64 (72, 80) sts. Join to work in the round, being careful not to twist sts. PM for beg of round.

Rib round: *P1, [k1tbl, p1] 5 (7, 9) times, work round 1 of Chart A once; rep from * once more.

Repeating round 1 only of Chart A on each round, rep last round a further 19 times.

LEG

Round 1: *P1, [k1tbl, p1] 5 (7, 9) times, work round 2 of Chart A once; rep from * once more.

Last round sets patt. Working next round of Chart A each time, work in patt as set until round 22 of Chart A has been completed, then rep rounds 13-22 twice more, then rep rounds 13-21 only once more.

HEEL

Work heel over 32 (36, 40) sts using preferred method: Heel Flap & Gusset (below or page 128) OR Short Row (page 132) OR Afterthought (page 138). The samples shown are worked using the Heel Flap & Gusset method (neon) and Afterthought (camel).

Heel Flap:

Turn work so WS is facing. Heel flap will be worked back and forth on the next 32 (36, 40) sts, beg with a WS row. Keep rem 32 (36, 40) sts on needles for instep.

Row 1 (WS): Sl1 wyif, p31 (35, 39).

Row 2 (RS): *Sl1 wyib, k1; rep from * to end.

Rep rows 1-2 a further 14 times, then work row 1 only once more.

Heel Turn:

Row 1 (RS): Sl1 wyib, k18 (20, 22), ssk, k1, turn, leaving rem 10 (12, 14) sts unworked. *1 st dec*

Row 2 (WS): Sl1 wyif, p7, p2tog, p1, turn, leaving rem 10 (12, 14) sts unworked. *1 st dec*

Row 3: Sl1 wyib, k to 1 st before gap, ssk, k1, turn. *1 st dec*

Row 4: Sl1 wyif, p to 1 st before gap, p2tog, p1, turn. *1 st dec*

Rep rows 3-4 a further 4 (5, 6) times. All heel sts have now been worked. *20 (22, 24) heel sts rem*

Gusset:

Begin working in the round again as foll:

Set-up round: Sl1 wyib, k19 (21, 23), pick up and knit 16 sts along edge of heel flap (1 st in each slipped st along edge of flap); work across 32 (36, 40) instep sts as foll: p1, [k1tbl, p1] 5 (7, 9) times, work round 22 of Chart A once; pick up and knit 16 sts along edge of heel flap, k36 (38, 40), PM for beg of round at beg of instep sts. *84 (90, 96) sts*

Round 1 (dec): P1, [k1tbl, p1] 5 (7, 9) times, work round 13 of Chart A, ssk, k to last 2 sts, k2tog. *2 sts dec*

Round 2: P1, [k1tbl, p1] 5 (7, 9) times, work next round of Chart A, k to end.

Working next round of chart each time (repeating rounds 13-22 only), rep rounds 1-2 a further 9 (8, 7) times. *64 (72, 80) sts: 32 (36, 40) sts each on instep and sole*

FOOT

Work straight in patt as set, working Chart A and twisted rib on instep and St st on sole, until sock measures 4.5 (5, 6)cm / 1¾ (2, 2¼)" less than desired foot length.

TOE

Round 1: Knit.

Round 2 (dec): K1, ssk, k26 (30, 34), k2tog, k1, PM, k1, ssk, k to last 3 sts, k2tog, k1. *60 (68, 76) sts*

Round 3: Knit.

Round 4 (dec): *K1, ssk, k to 3 sts before marker, k2tog, k1, SM; rep from * once more. *4 sts dec*

Rep rounds 3-4 a further 9 (10, 12) times. *20 (24, 24) sts*

Break yarn, leaving a 30cm / 12" tail. Graft sts together (page 147).

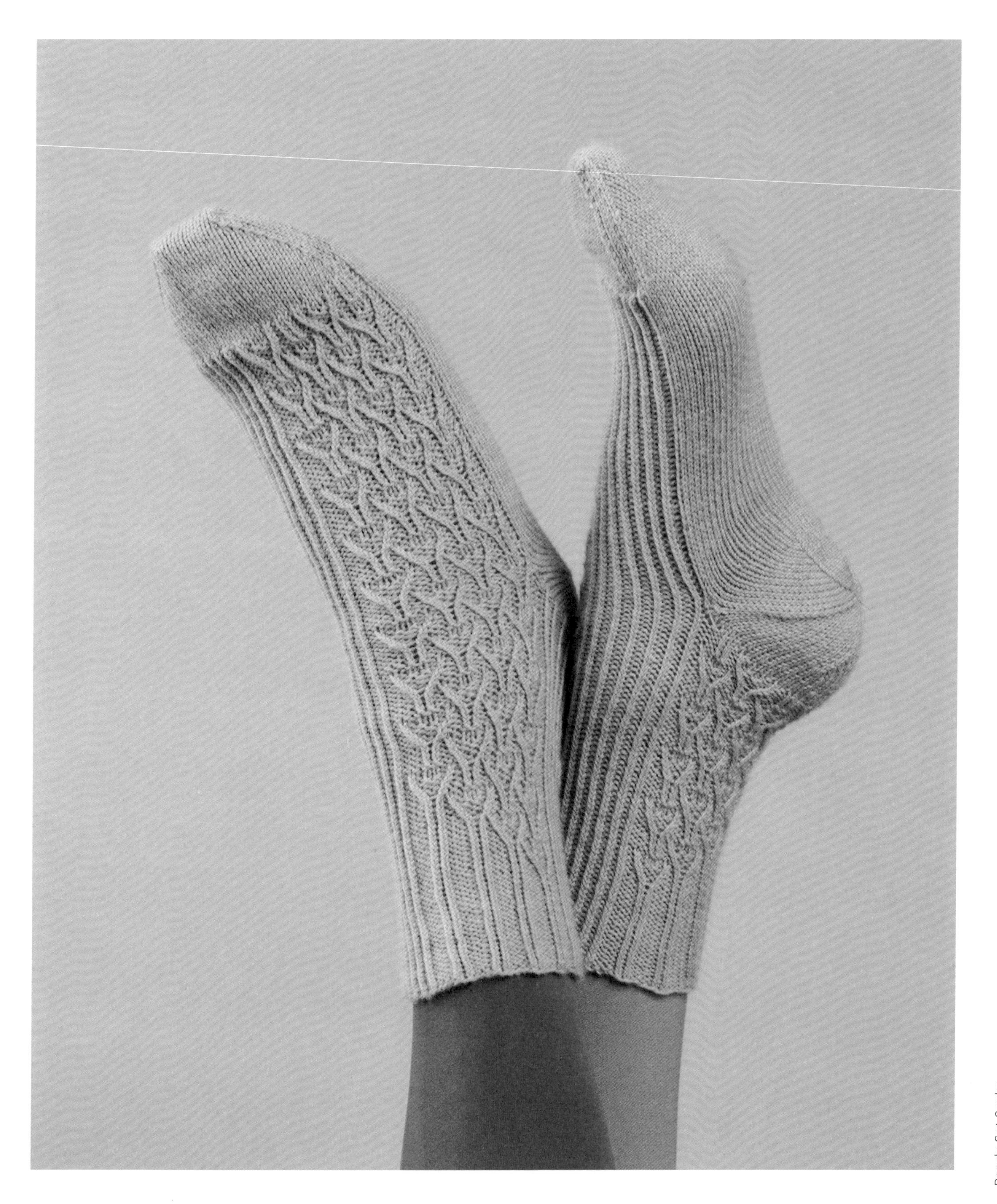

SOCK TWO

Cast on 64 (72, 80) sts. Join to work in the round, being careful not to twist sts. PM for beg of round.

Rib round: *Work round 1 of Chart B once, [p1, k1tbl] 5 (7, 9) times, p1; rep from * once more.

Repeating round 1 only of Chart B on each round, rep last round a further 19 times.

LEG

Round 1: *Work round 2 of Chart B, [p1, k1tbl] 5 (7, 9) times, p1; rep from * once more.

Last round sets patt. Working next round of Chart B each time, work in patt as set until round 22 of Chart B has been completed, then rep rounds 13-22 twice more, then rep rounds 13-21 only once more.

HEEL

Work Heel Flap and Heel Turn as for Sock One.

Chart A - 4-ply Version ONLY

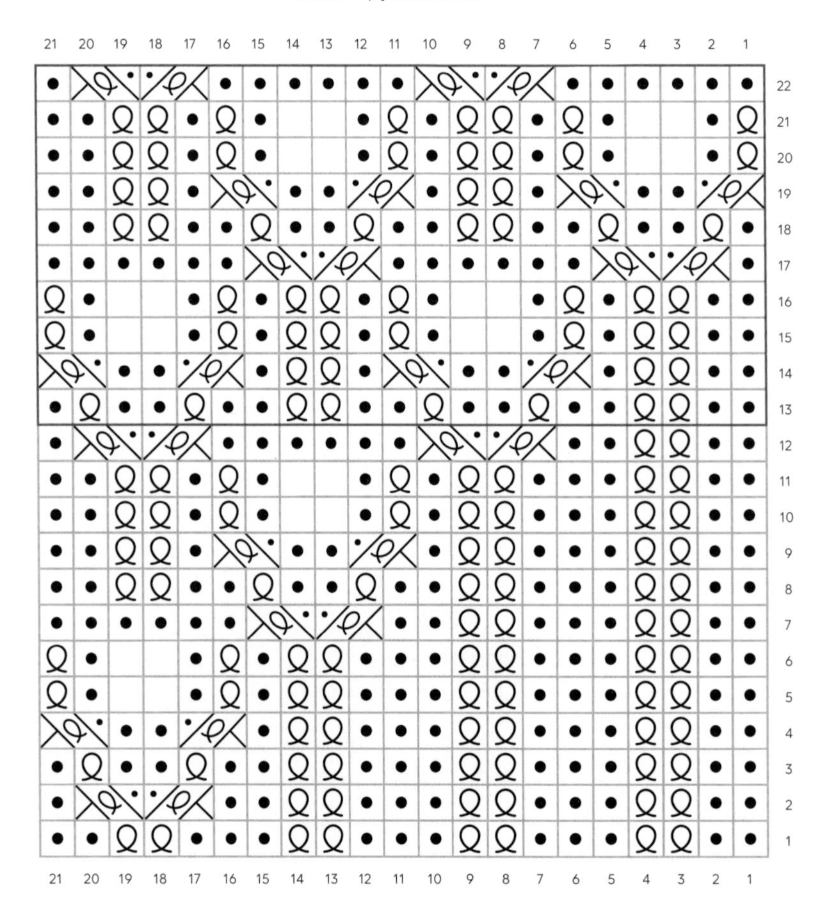

Gusset:
Begin working in the round again as foll:
Set-up round: Sl1 wyib, k19 (21, 23), pick up and knit 16 sts along edge of heel flap (1 st in each slipped st along edge of flap); work across 32 (36, 40) instep sts as foll: work round 22 of Chart B once, [p1, k1tbl] 5 (7, 9) times, p1; pick up and knit 16 sts along edge of heel flap, k36 (38, 40), PM for beg of round at beg of instep sts. *84 (90, 96) sts*
Round 1 (dec): Work round 13 of Chart B, [p1, k1tbl] 5 (7, 9) times, p1, ssk, k to last 2 sts, k2tog. *2 sts dec*
Round 2: Work next round of Chart B, [p1, k1tbl] 5 (7, 9) times, p1, k to end.
Working next round of chart each time (repeating rounds 13-22 only), rep rounds 1-2 a further 9 (8, 7) times. *64 (72, 80) sts: 32 (36, 40) sts each on instep and sole*

FOOT
Work straight in patt as set, working Chart B and twisted rib on instep and St st on sole, until sock measures 4.5 (5, 6)cm / 1¾ (2, 2¼)" less than desired foot length.

TOE
Work as for Sock One.

FINISHING
Weave in ends and block to measurements (page 103).

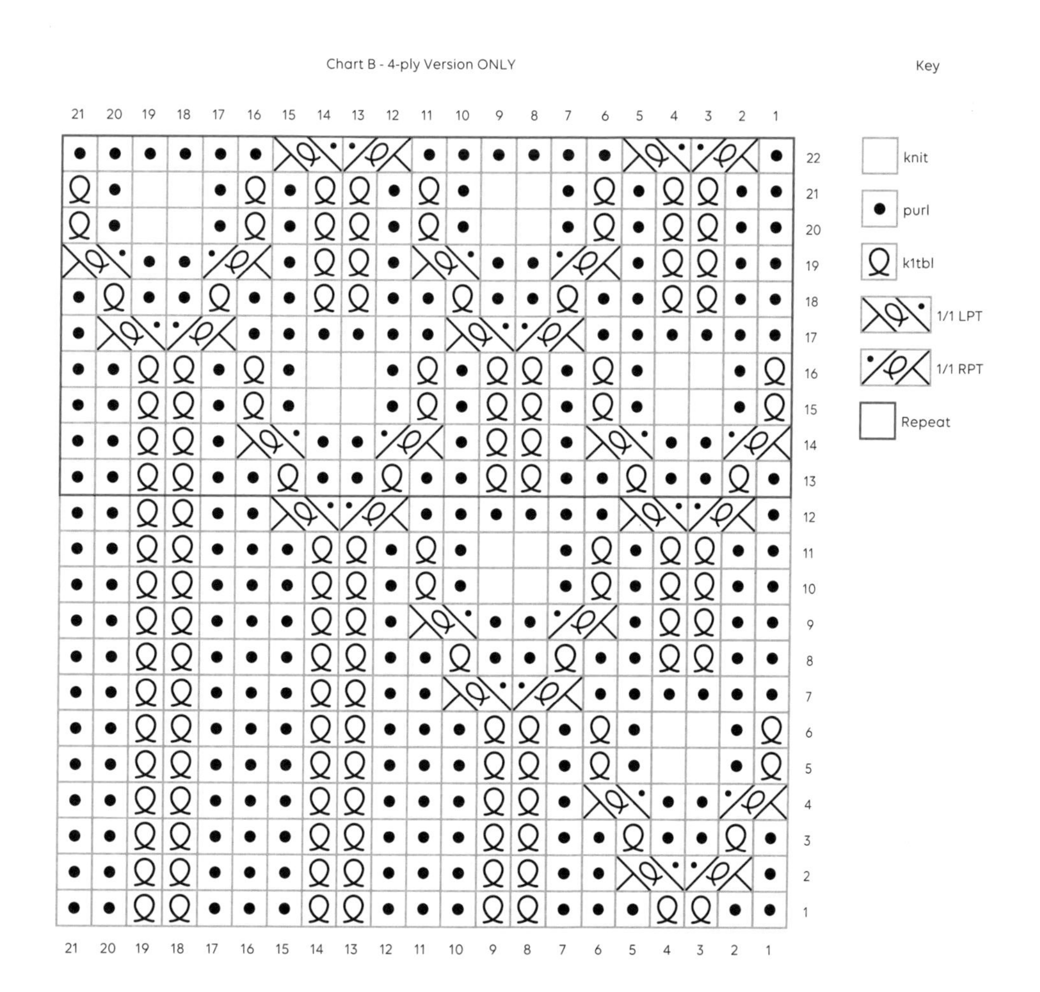

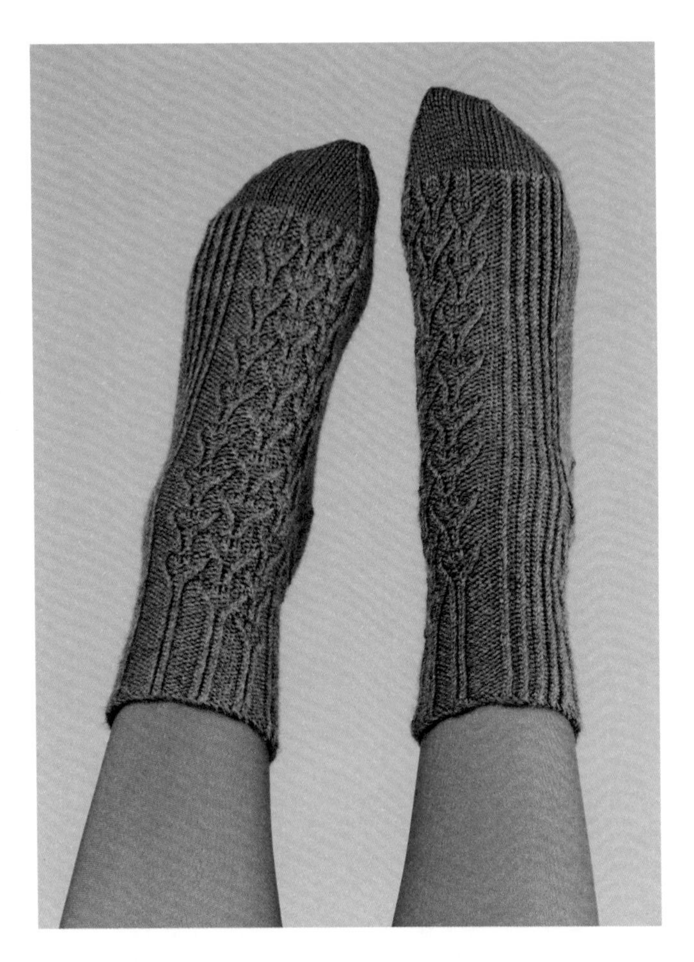

Sizes: 1 (2, 3, 4)
To fit foot circumference: 20.5 (21.5, 23, 24.5)cm / 8 (8½, 9, 9¾)" – to be worn with approx. 2.5cm / 1" negative ease
Foot length is fully adjustable within the pattern. Finished sock measures 0.5cm / ¼" less than actual foot length to ensure a good fit.
Yarn: Approximately 200 (230, 255, 280)m / 218 (250, 278, 305)yds of DK-weight yarn for Heel Flap & Gusset version; Short Row and Afterthought heels use slightly less yarn.

Sample 1 (Blue version, shown on this page)
Model wears a UK 7 / US 9 and is shown wearing a size 2.
Coop Knits Socks Yeah! DK (DK-weight; 75% superwash Merino wool, 25% nylon; 112m / 122yds per 50g skein)
Shades:
Main: Dollis (220); 2 (3, 3, 3) skeins
Toe: Demeter (209); 1 skein (or approx. 15g, 34m / 37yds)
Gauge: 28 sts & 40 rounds = 10cm / 4" over St st on 3mm needles, after blocking.
Needles: 3mm / US 2.5 needles suitable for working small circumferences in the round
Always use a needle size that will result in the correct gauge after blocking.
Notions: 2 stitch markers, cable needle, tapestry needle
Notes: These socks are worked from the cuff down, with a ribbed cuff and a twisted rib and cable pattern on the leg and foot. The samples shown are worked using the Heel Flap & Gusset method. Read all chart rounds from right to left. Ensure you are working from correct charts for 4-ply or DK version as appropriate.

Stitch Glossary
1/1 LPT: Slip 1 st to cable needle and hold at front, p1, k1 tbl from cable needle
1/1 RPT: Slip 1 st to cable needle and hold at back, p1, k1 tbl from cable needle

WRITTEN INSTRUCTIONS FOR CHARTS

Chart A - DK Version ONLY

Worked over 16 sts

Round 1: P2, [k2tbl, p3] twice, k2tbl, p2.
Round 2: P2, k2tbl, p3, k2tbl, p2, 1/1 RPT, 1/1 LPT, p1.
Round 3: P2, k2tbl, p3, k2tbl, [p2, k1tbl] twice, p1.
Round 4: P2, k2tbl, p3, k2tbl, p1, 1/1 RPT, p2, 1/1 LPT.
Rounds 5-6: P2, k2tbl, p3, k2tbl, p1, k1tbl, p1, k2, p1, k1tbl.
Round 7: P2, k2tbl, p2, 1/1 RPT, 1/1 LPT, p6.
Round 8: P2, k2tbl, [p2, k1tbl] twice, p2, k2tbl, p2.
Round 9: P2, k2tbl, p1, 1/1 RPT, p2, 1/1 LPT, p1, k2tbl, p2.
Rounds 10-11: P2, k2tbl, p1, k1tbl, p1, k2, p1, k1tbl, p1, k2tbl, p2.
Round 12: P1, 1/1 RPT, 1/1 LPT, p6, 1/1 RPT, 1/1 LPT, p1.
Round 13: P1, [k1tbl, p2] twice, k2tbl, [p2, k1tbl] twice, p1.
Round 14: 1/1 RPT, p2, 1/1 LPT, p1, k2tbl, p1, 1/1 RPT, p2, 1/1 LPT.
Rounds 15-16: K1tbl, p1, k2, p1, k1tbl, p1, k2tbl, p1, k1tbl, p1, k2, p1, k1tbl.
Round 17: P6, 1/1 RPT, 1/1 LPT, p6.
Rep rounds 8-17 for patt.

Chart B - DK Version ONLY

Worked over 16 sts

Round 1: P2, [k2tbl, p3] twice, k2tbl, p2.
Round 2: P1, 1/1 RPT, 1/1 LPT, p2, k2tbl, p3, k2tbl, p2.
Round 3: P1, [k1tbl, p2] twice, k2tbl, p3, k2tbl, p2.
Round 4: 1/1 RPT, p2, 1/1 LPT, p1, k2tbl, p3, k2tbl, p2.
Rounds 5-6: K1tbl, p1, k2, p1, k1tbl, p1, k2tbl, p3, k2tbl, p2.
Round 7: P6, 1/1 RPT, 1/1 LPT, p2, k2tbl, p2.
Round 8: P2, k2tbl, [p2, k1tbl] twice, p2, k2tbl, p2.
Round 9: P2, k2tbl, p1, 1/1 RPT, p2, 1/1 LPT, p1, k2tbl, p2.
Rounds 10-11: P2, k2tbl, p1, k1tbl, p1, k2, p1, k1tbl, p1, k2tbl, p2.
Round 12: P1, 1/1 RPT, 1/1 LPT, p6, 1/1 RPT, 1/1 LPT, p1.
Round 13: P1, [k1tbl, p2] twice, k2tbl, [p2, k1tbl] twice, p1.
Round 14: 1/1 RPT, p2, 1/1 LPT, p1, k2tbl, p1, 1/1 RPT, p2, 1/1 LPT.
Rounds 15-16: K1tbl, p1, k2, p1, k1tbl, p1, k2tbl, p1, k1tbl, p1, k2, p1, k1tbl.
Round 17: P6, 1/1 RPT, 1/1 LPT, p6.
Rep rounds 8-17 for patt.

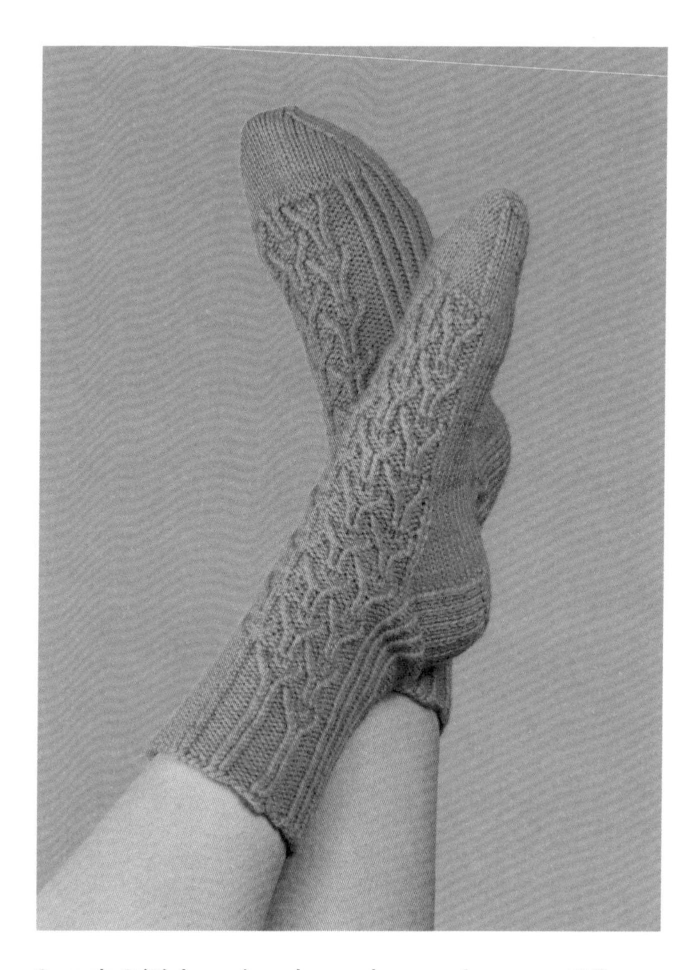

Sample 2 (Pink version, shown above and on page 101)
Model wears a UK 7 / US 9 and is shown wearing a size 2.
Purl Soho Posy (held double) (fingering / 4-ply-weight; 75% superwash Merino wool, 15% cashmere, 10% nylon; 145m / 159yds per 50g skein)
Shade: Pink Papaya; 3 (4, 4, 4) skeins

Note: This design is also shown in fingering / 4-ply-weight yarn from page 92.

PATTERN BEGINS

SOCK ONE

CUFF

Cast on 48 (52, 56, 60) sts. Join to work in the round, being careful not to twist sts. PM for beg of round.

Rib round: *[P1, k1tbl] 3 (4, 5, 6) times, p2, work round 1 of Chart A once; rep from * once more.

Repeating round 1 only of Chart A on each round, rep last round a further 15 times.

LEG

Round 1: *[P1, k1tbl] 3 (4, 5, 6) times, p2, work round 2 of Chart A; rep from * once more.

Working next round of Chart A each time, work in patt as set until round 17 of Chart A has been completed, then rep rounds 8-17 once more, then rep rounds 8-16 only once more.

HEEL

Work heel over 24 (26, 28, 30) sts using preferred method: Heel Flap & Gusset (below or page 128) OR Short Row (page 132) OR Afterthought (page 138). The sample shown is worked using the Heel Flap & Gusset method.

Heel Flap:

Turn work so WS is facing. Heel flap will be worked back and forth on the next 24 (26, 28, 30) sts, beg with a WS row. Keep rem 24 (26, 28, 30) sts on needles for instep.

Row 1 (WS): Sl1 wyif, p23 (25, 27, 29).

Row 2 (RS): *Sl1 wyib, k1; rep from * to end.

Rep rows 1-2 a further 10 times, then work row 1 only once more.

Heel Turn:

Row 1 (RS): Sl1 wyib, k14 (14, 16, 16), ssk, k1, turn, leaving rem 6 (8, 8, 10) sts unworked. *1 st dec*

Row 2 (WS): Sl1 wyif, p7 (5, 7, 5), p2tog, p1, turn, leaving rem 6 (8, 8, 10) sts unworked. *1 st dec*

Row 3: Sl1 wyib, k to 1 st before gap, ssk, k1, turn. *1 st dec*

Row 4: Sl1 wyif, p to 1 st before gap, p2tog, p1, turn. *1 st dec*

Rep rows 3-4 a further 2 (3, 3, 4) times. All heel sts have now been worked. *16 (16, 18, 18) heel sts rem*

Gusset:

Begin working in the round again as foll:

Set-up round: Sl1 wyib, k15 (15, 17, 17), pick up and knit 12 sts along edge of heel flap (1 st in each slipped st along edge of the flap); work across 24 (26, 28, 30) instep sts as foll: [p1, k1tbl] 3 (4, 5, 6) times, p2, work round 17 of Chart A once; pick up and knit 12 sts along edge of heel flap, k28 (28, 30, 30), PM for beg of round at beg of instep sts. *64 (66, 70, 72) sts*

Round 1 (dec): [P1, k1tbl] 3 (4, 5, 6) times, p2, work round 8 of Chart A, ssk, k to last 2 sts, k2tog. *2 sts dec*

Round 2: [P1, k1tbl] 3 (4, 5, 6) times, p2, work next round of Chart A, k to end.

Working next round of chart each time (repeating rounds 8-17 only), rep rounds 1-2 a further 7 (6, 6, 5) times. *48 (52, 56, 60) sts: 24 (26, 28, 30) sts each on instep and sole*

FOOT

Work straight in patt as set, working Chart A and twisted rib on instep and St st on sole, until sock measures 4.5 (5, 5, 5.5)cm / 1¾ (2, 2, 2¼)" less than desired foot length.

TOE

Round 1: Knit.

Round 2 (dec): K1, ssk, k18 (20, 22, 24), k2tog, k1, PM, k1, ssk, k to last 3 sts, k2tog, k1. *44 (48, 52, 56) sts*

Round 3: Knit.

Round 4 (dec): *K1, ssk, k to 3 sts before marker, k2tog, k1, SM; rep from * once more. *4 sts dec*

Rep rounds 3-4 a further 6 (7, 7, 8) times. *16 (16, 20, 20) sts*

Break yarn, leaving a 30cm / 12" tail. Graft sts together (page 147).

SOCK TWO

CUFF

Cast on 48 (52, 56, 60) sts. Join to work in the round, being careful not to twist sts. PM for beg of round.

Rib round: *Work round 1 of Chart B once, p2, [k1tbl, p1] 3 (4, 5, 6) times; rep from * once more.

Repeating round 1 only of Chart B on each round, rep last round a further 15 times.

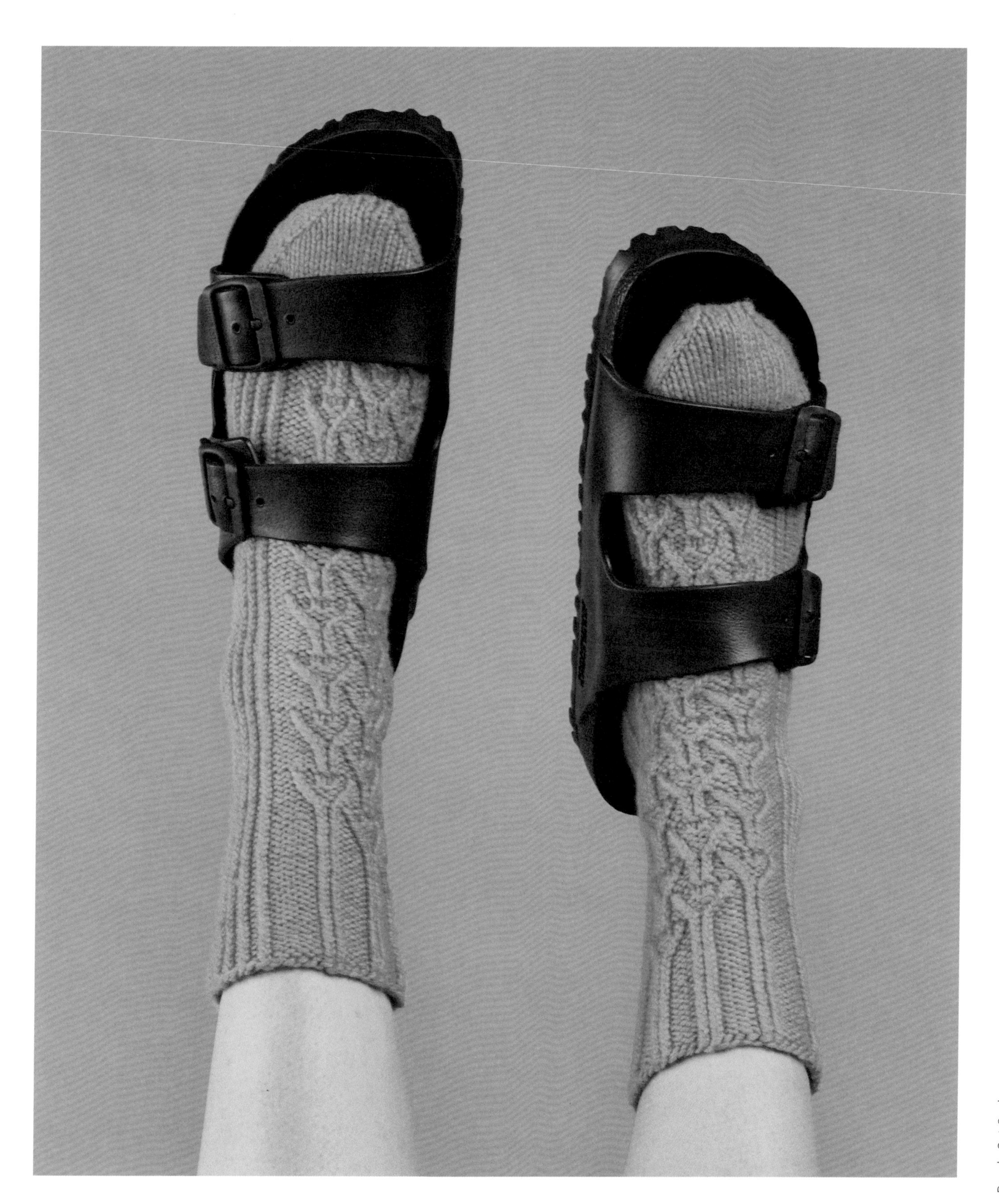

LEG

Round 1: *Work round 2 of Chart B, p2, [k1tbl, p1] 3 (4, 5, 6) times; rep from * once more.
Last round sets patt. Working next round of Chart B each time, work in patt as set until round 17 of Chart B has been completed, then rep rounds 8-17 once more, then rep rounds 8-16 only once more.

HEEL

Work Heel Flap and Heel Turn as for Sock One.

Gusset:
Begin working in the round again as foll:
Set-up round: Sl1 wyib, k15 (15, 17, 17), pick up and knit 12 sts along edge of heel flap (1 st in each slipped st along edge of the flap); work across 24 (26, 28, 30) instep sts as foll: work round 17 of Chart B once, p2, [k1tbl, p1] 3 (4, 5, 6) times; pick up and knit 12 sts along edge of heel flap, k28 (28, 30, 30), PM for beg of round at beg of instep sts. *64 (66, 70, 72) sts*

Round 1 (dec): Work round 8 of Chart B, p2, [k1tbl, p1] 3 (4, 5, 6) times, ssk, k to last 2 sts, k2tog. *2 sts dec*
Round 2: Work next round of Chart B, p2, [k1tbl, p1] 3 (4, 5, 6) times, k to end.
Working next round of chart each time (repeating rounds 8-17 only), rep rounds 1-2 a further 7 (6, 6, 5) times. *48 (52, 56, 60) sts: 24 (26, 28, 30) sts each on instep and sole*

FOOT

Work straight in patt as set, working Chart B and twisted rib on instep and St st on sole, until sock measures 4.5 (5, 5, 5.5) cm / 1¾ (2, 2, 2¼)" less than desired foot length.

TOE

Work as for Sock One.

FINISHING

Weave in ends and block to measurements.

Chart A - DK Version ONLY

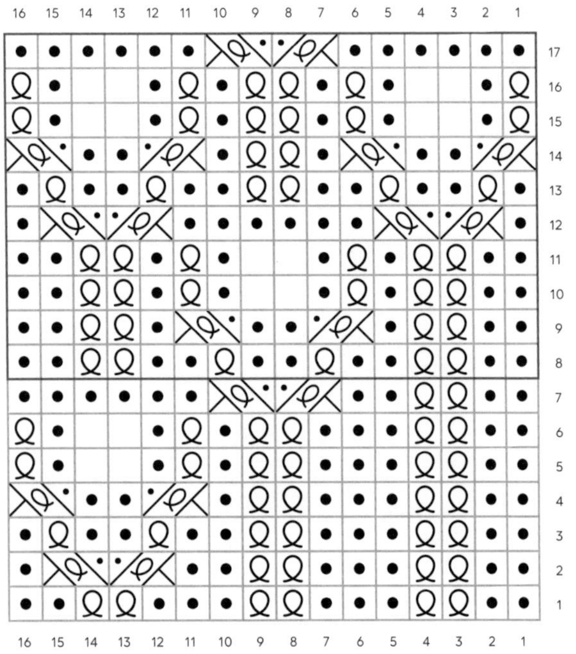

Chart B - DK Version ONLY

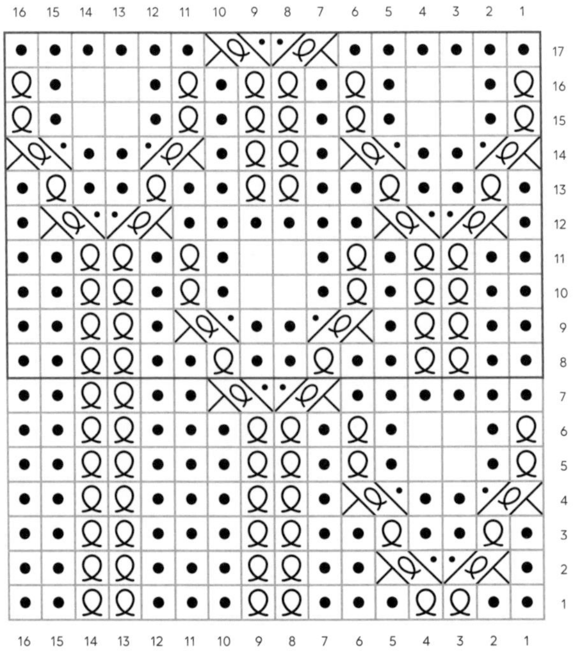

Key

- knit
- purl
- k1tbl
- 1/1 RPT
- 1/1 LPT
- Repeat

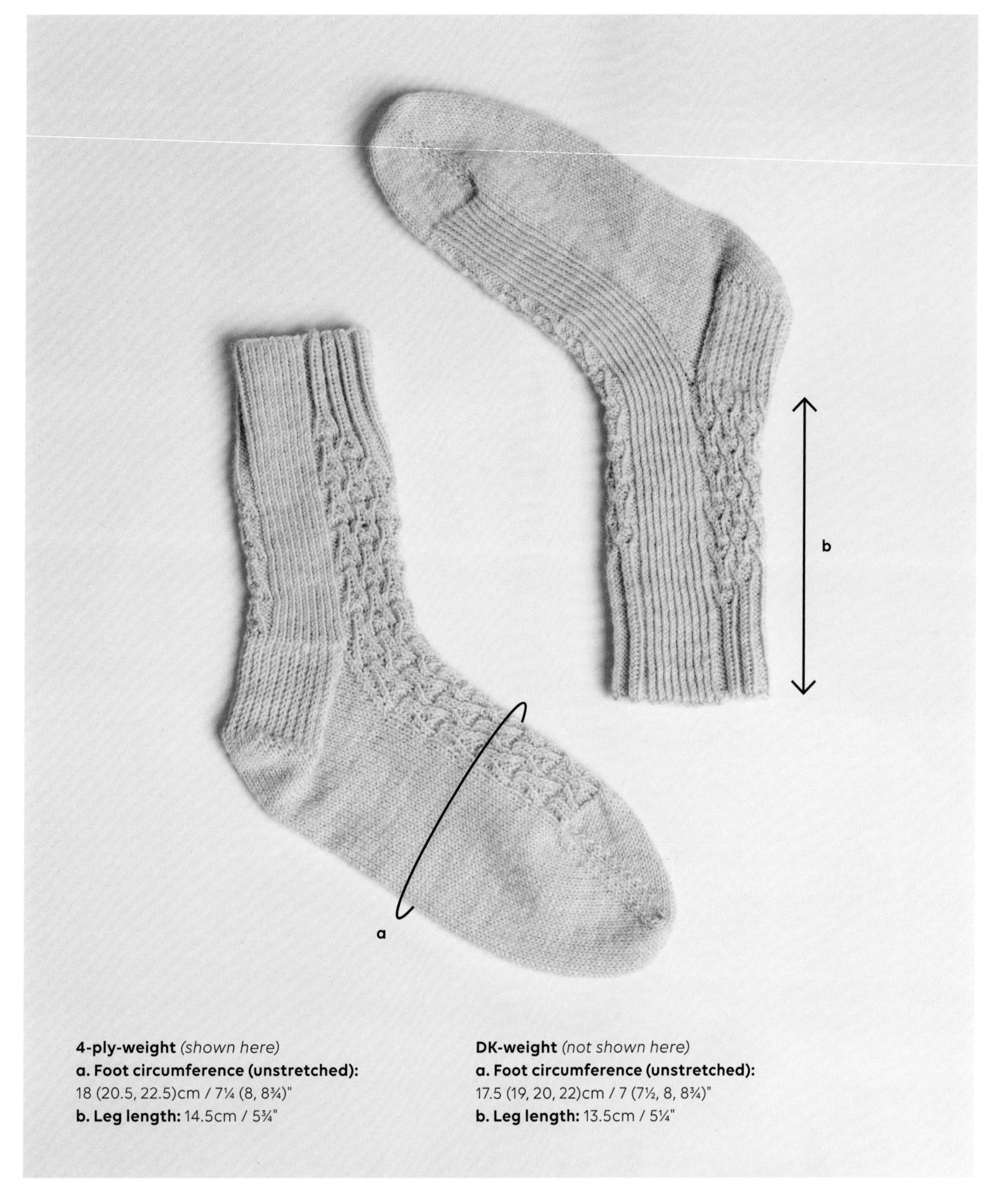

4-ply-weight *(shown here)*
a. Foot circumference (unstretched):
18 (20.5, 22.5)cm / 7¼ (8, 8¾)"
b. Leg length: 14.5cm / 5¾"

DK-weight *(not shown here)*
a. Foot circumference (unstretched):
17.5 (19, 20, 22)cm / 7 (7½, 8, 8¾)"
b. Leg length: 13.5cm / 5¼"

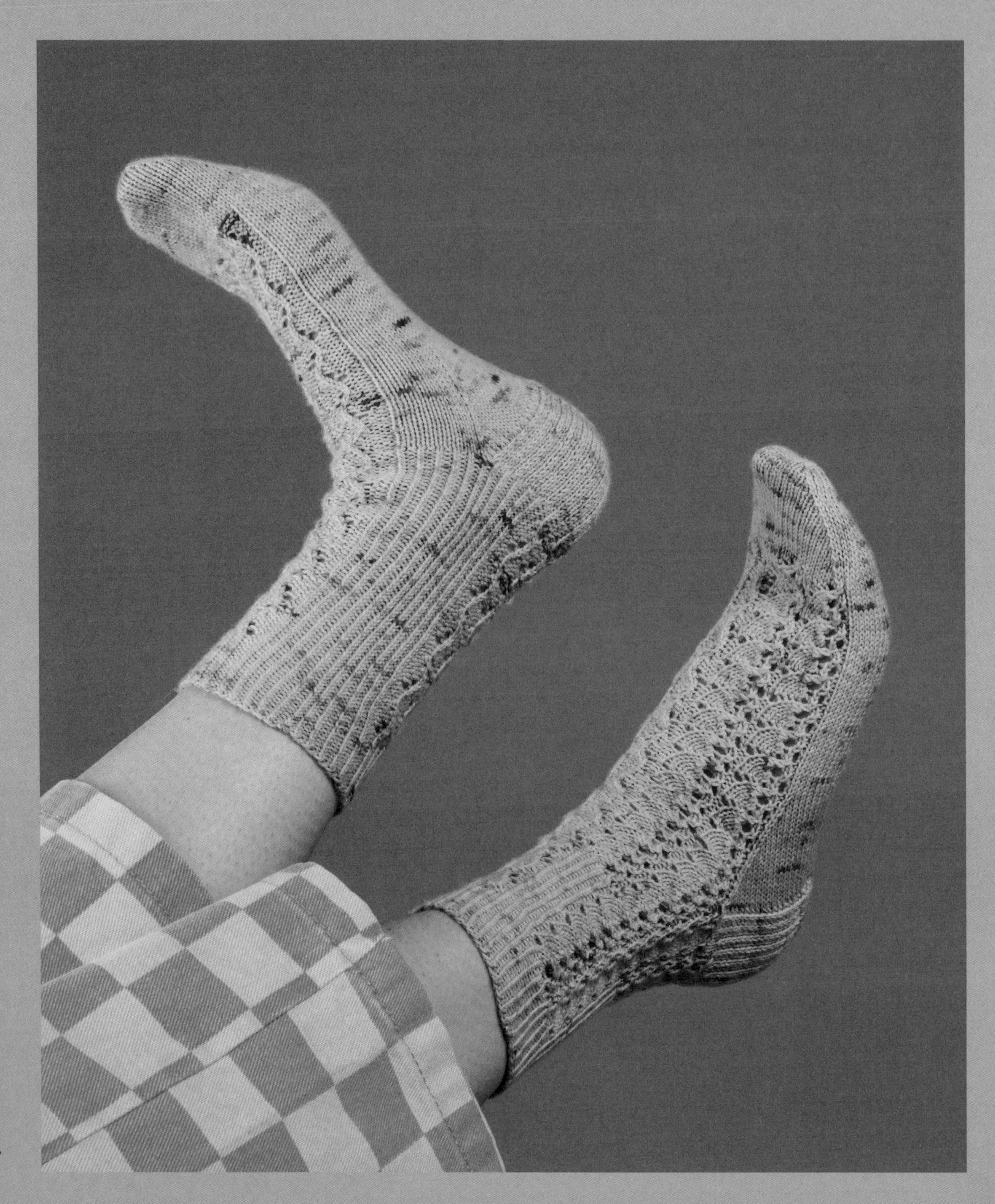

JACKSON

Twisted Rib + Lace Socks

Basically a party for your feet, the Jackson socks are a celebration of your mastery of sock knitting. Scalloped lace and zigzag twisted stitches interspersed with eyelets put us in mind of confetti thrown into the air and we know you'll be revelling in your incredible sock-knitting skills when you wear this pair. Try using a speckled, colourful yarn for an extra festive vibe.

#JacksonSocks

Sizes: 1 (2, 3)
To fit foot circumference: 20.5 (23, 25.5)cm / 8 (9, 10)" – to be worn with approx. 2.5cm / 1" negative ease
Foot length is fully adjustable within the pattern. Finished sock measures 0.5cm / ¼" less than actual foot length to ensure a good fit.
Yarn: Approximately 270 (315, 365)m / 294 (343, 397)yds of fingering / 4-ply-weight yarn for Heel Flap & Gusset version; Short Row and Afterthought heels use slightly less yarn.

Sample 1 (Lilac version, shown on this page)
Model wears a UK 7 / US 9 and is shown wearing a size 2.
The Wool Kitchen Sock (fingering / 4-ply-weight; 75% Merino wool, 25% nylon; 425m / 465m per 100g skein)
Shade: Parma Violets; 1 skein
Gauge: 36 sts & 50 rounds = 10cm / 4" over St st on 2.5mm needles after blocking.
Needles: 2.5mm / US 1.5 needles suitable for working small circumferences in the round
Always use a needle size that will result in the correct gauge after blocking.
Notions: 2 stitch markers, tapestry needle
Notes: These socks are worked from the cuff down, with a twisted ribbed cuff and a twisted rib and lace pattern on the leg and foot. The sample shown is worked using the Heel Flap & Gusset method. Read all chart rounds from right to left.

WRITTEN INSTRUCTIONS FOR CHARTS

Chart A
Worked over 3 sts
Round 1: Yo, ssk, p1.
Round 2: P1, k1 tbl, p1.
Round 3: P1, yo, ssk.
Rounds 4-6: P2, k1 tbl.
Round 7: P1, k2tog, yo.
Round 8: Rep round 2.
Round 9: K2tog, yo, p1.
Rounds 10-12: K1 tbl, p2.
Rep rounds 1-12 for patt.

Chart B
Worked over 7 sts
Round 1: Yo, k3, ssk, k2tog, yo.
Round 2: K1, yo, k2, ssk, k2.
Round 3: K2, yo, k1, ssk, yo, ssk.
Round 4: K3, yo, ssk, k2.
Round 5: K4, yo, ssk, k1.
Round 6: K5, yo, ssk.
Rep rounds 1-6 for patt.

Chart C
Worked over 7 sts
Round 1: Yo, ssk, k2tog, k3, yo.
Round 2: K2, k2tog, k2, yo, k1.
Round 3: K2tog, yo, k2tog, k1, yo, k2.
Round 4: K2, k2tog, yo, k3.
Round 5: K1, k2tog, yo, k4.
Round 6: K2tog, yo, k5.
Rep rounds 1-6 for patt.

Chart D
Worked over 3 sts
Round 1: P1, k2tog, yo.
Round 2: P1, k1 tbl, p1.
Round 3: K2tog, yo, p1.
Rounds 4-6: K1 tbl, p2.
Round 7: Yo, ssk, p1.
Round 8: Rep round 2.
Round 9: P1, yo, ssk.
Rounds 10-12: P2, k1 tbl.
Rep rounds 1-12 for patt.

Note: This design is also shown in DK-weight yarn from page 110.

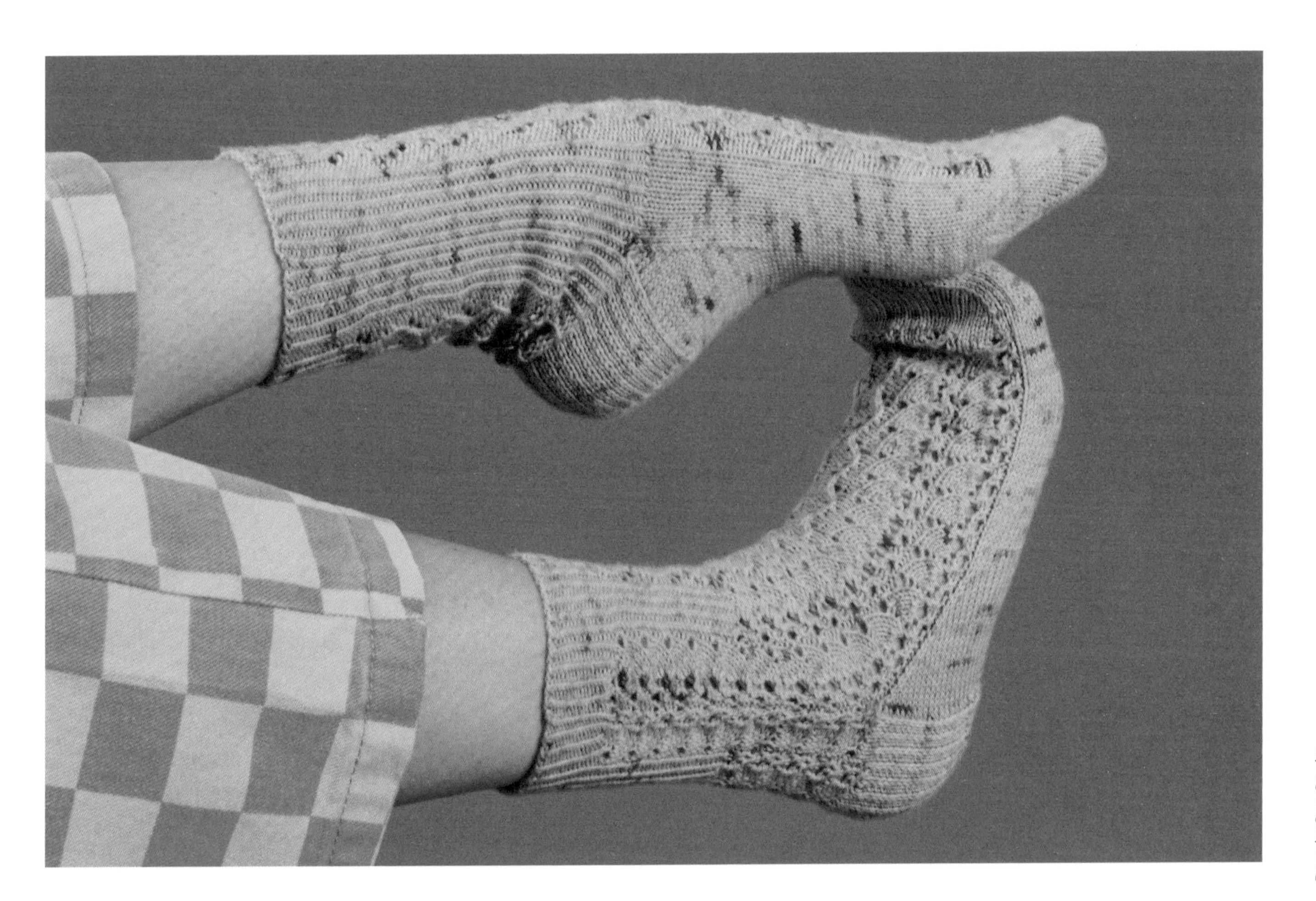

PATTERN BEGINS

SOCK ONE

CUFF

Cast on 64 (72, 80) sts. Join to work in the round, being careful not to twist. PM for beg of round.

Rib round: [P1, k1 tbl] 3 (5, 7) times, p2, [k1 tbl, p1] 24 times, [p1, k1 tbl] 4 (6, 8) times.

Rep last round a further 15 times.

LEG

Round 1: [P1, k1 tbl] 3 (5, 7) times, p2, [work round 1 of Chart A, p1] twice, [k1 tbl, p1] 4 times, work round 1 of Chart B, p1, work round 1 of Chart C, p1, [k1 tbl, p1] 4 times, [work round 1 of Chart D, p1] twice, [p1, k1 tbl] 4 (6, 8) times.

Working next round of charts each time, work in patt as set until rounds 1-6 of Charts B and C have been completed 5 times in total.

Round 31: [P1, k1 tbl] 3 (5, 7) times, p2, [work next round of Chart A, p1] twice, [work round 1 of Chart B, p1] twice, [work next round of Chart C, p1] twice, [work next round of Chart D, p1] twice, [p1, k1 tbl] 4 (6, 8) times.

Working next round of charts each time, work in patt as set until Charts B and C have been completed a further 5 times. *10 reps of Charts B & C in total*

HEEL

Work heel over 32 (36, 40) sts using preferred method: Heel Flap & Gusset (below or page 128) OR Short Row (page 132) OR Afterthought (page 138). The sample shown is worked using the Heel Flap & Gusset method.

Heel Flap:

Turn work so WS is facing. Heel flap will be worked back and forth on the next 32 (36, 40) sts, beginning with a WS row. Keep rem 32 (36, 40) sts on needles for instep.

Row 1 (WS): Sl1 wyif, p31 (35, 39).

Row 2 (RS): *Sl1 wyib, k1; rep from * to end.

Rep rows 1-2 a further 14 times, then work row 1 once more.

Heel Turn:

Row 1 (RS): Sl1 wyib, k18 (20, 22), ssk, k1, turn, leaving remaining 10 (12, 14) sts unworked. *1 st dec*

Row 2 (WS): Sl1 wyif, p7, p2tog, p1, turn, leaving remaining 10 (12, 14) sts unworked. *1 st dec*

Row 3: Sl1 wyib, k to 1 st before gap, ssk, k1, turn. *1 st dec*

Row 4: Sl1 wyif, p to 1 st before gap, p2tog, p1, turn. *1 st dec*

Rep rows 3-4 a further 4 (5, 6) times. All heel sts have been worked. *20 (22, 24) heel sts rem*

GUSSET

Begin working in the round again as foll:

Set-up round: Sl1 wyib, k19 (21, 23), pick up and knit 16 sts along edge of heel flap (1 stitch in each slipped stitch along edge of flap); work across 32 (36, 40) instep sts as foll: k6 (10, 14), p2, [work round 1 of Chart A, p1] twice, [work round 1 of Chart B, p1] twice; pick up and knit 16 sts along edge of heel flap, k36 (38, 40), PM for beg of round at beg of instep sts. *84 (90, 96) sts*

Round 1 (dec): K6 (10, 14), p2, [work next round of Chart A, p1] twice, [work next round of Chart B, p1] twice, ssk, k to last 2 sts, k2tog. *2 sts dec*

Round 2: K6 (10, 14), p2, [work next round of Chart A, p1] twice, [work next round of Chart B, p1] twice, k to end.

Working next round of charts each time, rep rounds 1-2 a further 9 (8, 7) times. *64 (72, 80) sts: 32 (36, 40) sts each on instep and sole*

FOOT

Work straight in patt as set, working Charts A and B on instep and St st on sole, until sock measures 4.5 (5, 5, 5.5) cm / 1¾ (2, 2, 2¼)" less than the desired foot length.

TOE

Round 1: Knit.

Round 2 (dec): K1, ssk, k26 (30, 34), k2tog, k1, PM, k1, ssk, knit to last 3 sts, k2tog, k1. *60 (68, 76) sts*

Round 3: Knit.

Round 4 (dec): *K1, ssk, k to 3 sts before marker, k2tog, k1, SM; rep from * once more. *4 sts dec*

Rep rounds 3-4 a further 9 (10, 12) times. *20 (24, 24) sts*

Break yarn, leaving a 30cm / 12" tail. Graft sts together (page 147).

SOCK TWO

CUFF

Cast on 64 (72, 80) sts. Join to work in the round, being careful not to twist. PM for beg of round.

Rib round: [P1, k1 tbl] 12 times, p2, [k1 tbl, p1] 7 (11, 15) times, [p1, k1tbl] 12 times.

Rep last round a further 15 times.

LEG

Round 1: P1, work round 1 of Chart C, [p1, k1 tbl] 4 times, p1, [work round 1 of Chart D, p1] twice, [p1, k1 tbl] 7 (11, 15) times, p2, [work round 1 of Chart A, p1] twice, [k1 tbl, p1] 4 times, work round 1 of Chart B.

Working next round of charts each time, work in patt as set until rounds 1-6 of Charts B and C have been completed 5 times in total.

Round 31: [P1, work next round of Chart C] twice, [p1, work next round of Chart D] twice, p1, [p1, k1 tbl] 7 (11, 15) times, p1, [p1, work next round of Chart A] twice, [p1, work next round of Chart B] twice.

Working next round of charts each time, work in patt as set until Charts B and C have been completed a further 5 times. *10 reps of Charts B & C in total*

HEEL

Work Heel Flap and Heel Turn as for Sock One.

GUSSET

Begin working in the round again as foll:

Set-up round: Sl1 wyib, k19 (21, 23), pick up and knit 16 sts along edge of heel flap (1 stitch in each slipped stitch along edge of flap); work across 32 (36, 40) instep sts as foll: [p1, work round 1 of Chart C] twice, [p1, work round 1 of Chart D] twice, p2, k6 (10, 14); pick up and knit 16 sts along edge of heel flap, k36 (38, 40), PM for beg of round at beg of instep sts. *84 (90, 96) sts*

Round 1 (dec): [P1, work next round of Chart C] twice, [p1, work next round of Chart D] twice, p2, k6 (10, 14), ssk, k to last 2 sts, k2tog. *2 sts dec*

Round 2: [P1, work next round of Chart C] twice, [p1, work next round of Chart D] twice, p2, k6 (10, 14), k to end.

Working next round of charts each time, rep rounds 1-2 a further 9 (8, 7) times. *64 (72, 80) sts: 32 (36, 40) sts each on instep and sole*

FOOT

Work straight in patt as set, working Charts C and D on instep and St st on sole, until sock measures 4.5 (5, 5, 5.5) cm / 1¾ (2, 2, 2¼)" less than the desired foot length.

TOE

Work as for Sock One.

FINISHING

Weave in ends and block to measurements (page 113).

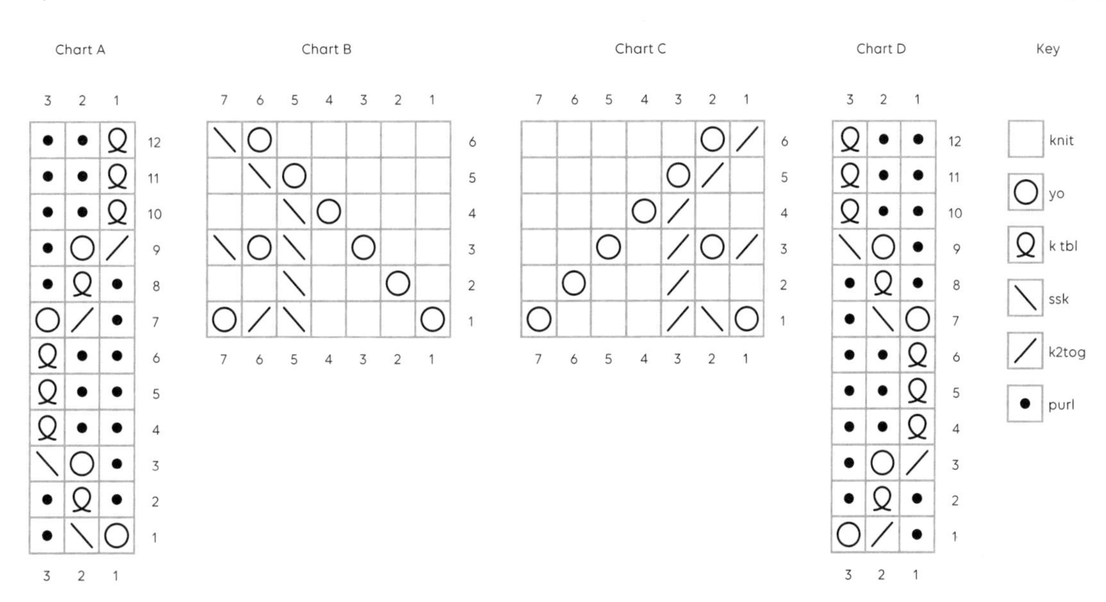

Pattern: Jackson - Twisted Rib + Lace Socks (DK)

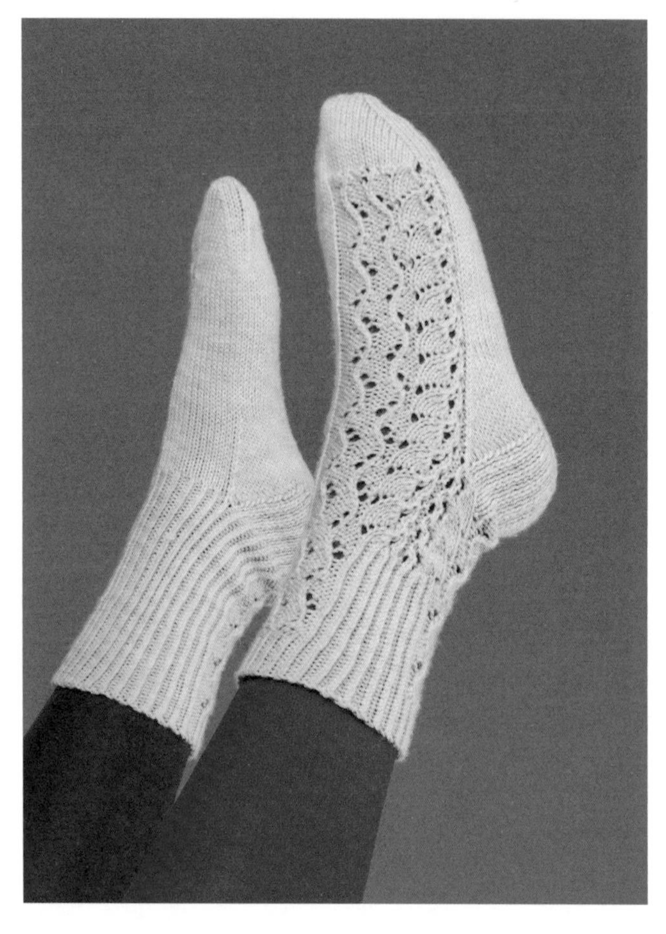

Sizes: 1 (2, 3, 4)
To fit foot circumference: 20.5 (21.5, 23, 24.5)cm / 8 (8½, 9, 9¾)" – to be worn with approx. 2.5cm / 1" negative ease
Foot length is fully adjustable within the pattern.
Finished sock measures 0.5cm / ¼" less than actual foot length to ensure a good fit.
Yarn: Approximately 215 (250, 275, 300)m / 234 (272, 300, 327)yds of DK-weight yarn for Heel Flap & Gusset version; Short Row and Afterthought heels use slightly less yarn.
Sample 1 (Cream version, shown above)
Model wears a UK 7 / US 9 and is shown wearing a size 2.
Coop Knits Socks Yeah! DK (DK-weight; 75% superwash Merino wool, 25% nylon; 112m / 122yds per 50g skein)
Shade: Quartz; 2 (3, 3, 3) skeins

Gauge: 28 sts & 40 rounds = 10cm / 4" over St st on 3mm needles, after blocking.
Needles: 3mm / US 2.5 needles suitable for working small circumferences in the round
Always use a needle size that will result in the correct gauge after blocking.
Notions: 2 stitch markers, tapestry needle
Notes: These socks are worked from the cuff down, with a twisted ribbed cuff and a twisted rib and lace pattern on the leg and foot. The sample shown is worked using the Heel Flap & Gusset method. Read all chart rounds from right to left.

WRITTEN INSTRUCTIONS FOR CHARTS
See page 106 for written instructions for charts - 4-ply-weight and DK versions both alike.

Note: This pattern is also shown in fingering / 4-ply-weight yarn on page 106.

PATTERN BEGINS
SOCK ONE
CUFF
Cast on 48 (52, 56, 60) sts. Join to work in the round, being careful not to twist. PM for beg of round.
Rib round: [P1, k1 tbl] 3 (4, 5, 6) times, p1, [p1, k1 tbl] 16 times, p1, [p1, k1 tbl] 4 (5, 6, 7) times.
Rep last round a further 9 times.

LEG
Round 1: [P1, k1 tbl] 3 (4, 5, 6) times, p2, [work round 1 of Chart A, p1] twice, [k1 tbl, p1] 8 times, [work round 1 of Chart D, p1] twice, [p1, k1 tbl] 4 (5, 6, 7) times.
Working next round of charts each time, continue as set until rounds 1-12 of Charts A and D have been worked twice.

Round 25: [P1, k1 tbl] 3 (4, 5, 6) times, p2, [work round 1 of Chart A, p1] twice, work round 1 of Chart B, p1, work round 1 of Chart C, p1, [work round 1 of Chart D, p1] twice, [p1, k1 tbl] 4 (5, 6, 7) times.
Working next round of charts each time, continue as set until rounds 1-6 of Charts B and C have been worked 4 times in total.

HEEL
Work heel over 24 (26, 28, 30) sts using preferred method: Heel Flap & Gusset (below or page 128) OR Short Row (page 132) OR Afterthought (page 138). The sample shown is worked using the Heel Flap & Gusset method.

Heel Flap:
Turn work so WS is facing. Heel flap will be worked back and forth on the next 24 (26, 28, 30) sts, beginning with a WS row. Keep rem 24 (26, 28, 30) sts on needles for instep.
Row 1 (WS): Sl1 wyif, p23 (25, 27, 29).
Row 2 (RS): *Sl1 wyib, k1; rep from * to end.
Rep rows 1-2 a further 10 times, then work row 1 once more.

Heel Turn:
Row 1 (RS): Sl1 wyib, k14 (14, 16, 16), ssk, k1, turn, leaving rem 6 (8, 8, 10) sts unworked. *1 st dec*
Row 2 (WS): Sl1 wyif, p7 (5, 7, 5), p2tog, p1, turn, leaving remaining 6 (8, 8, 10) sts unworked. *1 st dec*
Row 3: Sl1 wyib, knit to 1 st before gap, ssk, k1, turn. *1 st dec*
Row 4: Sl1 wyif, purl to 1 st before gap, p2tog, p1, turn. *1 st dec*
Rep rows 3-4 a further 2 (3, 3, 4) times. All heel sts have now been worked. *16 (16, 18, 18) heel sts rem*

Gusset:
Begin working in the round again as foll:
Set-up round: Sl1 wyib, k15 (15, 17, 17), pick up and knit 12 sts along edge of heel flap (1 st in each slipped st along edge of the flap); work across 24 (26, 28, 30) instep sts as foll: k6 (8, 10, 12), p2, [work round 1 of Chart A, p1] twice, work round 1 of Chart B once, p1; pick up and knit 12 sts along edge of heel flap, k28 (28, 30, 30), PM for beg of round at beg of instep sts. *64 (66, 70, 72) sts*

Round 1 (dec): K6 (8, 10, 12), p2, [work next round of Chart A, p1] twice, work next round of Chart B, p1, ssk, k to last 2 sts, k2tog. *2 sts dec*
Round 2: K6 (8, 10, 12), p2, [work next round of Chart A, p1] twice, work next round of Chart B, p1, k to end.
Working next round of charts each time, rep rounds 1-2 a further 7 (6, 6, 5) times. *48 (52, 56, 60) sts: 24 (26, 28, 30) sts each on instep and sole*

FOOT
Work straight in patt as set, working Charts A and B on instep and St st on sole, until sock measures 4.5 (5, 5, 5.5)cm / 1¾ (2, 2, 2¼)" less than the desired foot length.

TOE
Round 1: Knit.
Round 2 (dec): K1, ssk, k18 (20, 22, 24), k2tog, k1, PM, k1, ssk, knit to last 3 sts, k2tog, k1. *44 (48, 52, 56) sts*
Round 3: Knit.
Round 4 (dec): *K1, ssk, k to 3 sts before marker, k2tog, k1, SM; rep from * once more. *4 sts dec*
Rep rounds 3-4 a further 6 (7, 7, 8) times. *16 (16, 20, 20) sts*
Break yarn, leaving a 30cm / 12" tail. Graft sts together (page 147).

SOCK TWO
CUFF
Cast on 48 (52, 56, 60) sts. Join to work in the round, being careful not to twist. PM for beg of round.
Rib round: [P1, k1 tbl] 8 times, p1, [p1, k1 tbl] 7 (9, 11, 13) times, p1, [p1, k1 tbl] 8 times.
Rep last round a further 9 times.

LEG
Round 1: [P1, k1 tbl] 4 times, p1, [work round 1 of Chart D, p1] twice, [p1, k1 tbl] 7 (9, 11, 13) times, p1, [p1, work round 1 of Chart A] twice, [p1, k1 tbl] 4 times.
Working next round of charts each time, work in patt as set until rounds 1-12 of Charts A and D have been worked twice.

Round 25: P1, work round 1 of Chart C, p1, [work round 1 of Chart D, p1] twice, [p1, k1 tbl] 7 (9, 11, 13) times, p1, [p1, work round 1 of Chart A] twice, p1, work round 1 of Chart B.
Working next round of charts each time, work in patt as set until rounds 1-6 of Charts B and C have been worked 4 times in total.

HEEL
Work Heel Flap and Heel Turn as for Sock One.

GUSSET
Begin working in the round again as foll:
Set-up round: Sl1 wyib, k15 (15, 17, 17), pick up and knit 12 sts along edge of heel flap (1 st in each slipped st along edge of the flap); work across 24 (26, 28, 30) instep sts as foll: p1, work next round of Chart C, [p1, work next round of Chart D] twice, p2, k6 (8, 10, 12); pick up and knit 12 sts along edge of heel flap, k28 (28, 30, 30), PM for beg of round at beg of instep sts. *64 (66, 70, 72) sts*

Round 1 (dec): P1, work next round of Chart C, [p1, work next round of Chart D] twice, p2, k6 (8, 10, 12), ssk, k to last 2 sts, k2tog. *2 sts dec*
Round 2: P1, work next round of Chart C, [p1, work next round of Chart D] twice, p2, k6 (8, 10, 12), k to end.

Working next round of charts each time, rep rounds 1-2 a further 7 (6, 6, 5) times. *48 (52, 56, 60) sts: 24 (26, 28, 30) sts each on instep and sole*

FOOT
Work straight in patt as set, working Charts C and D on instep and St st on sole, until sock measures 4.5 (5, 5, 5.5)cm / 1¾ (2, 2, 2¼)" less than the desired foot length.

TOE
Work as for Sock One.

FINISHING
Weave in ends and block to measurements.

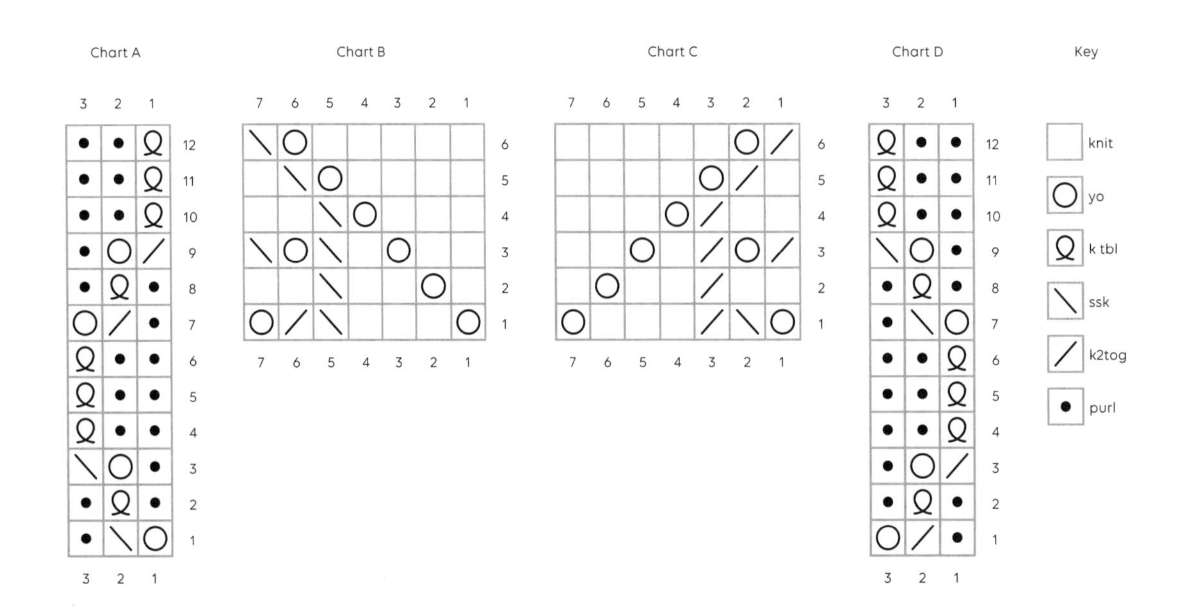

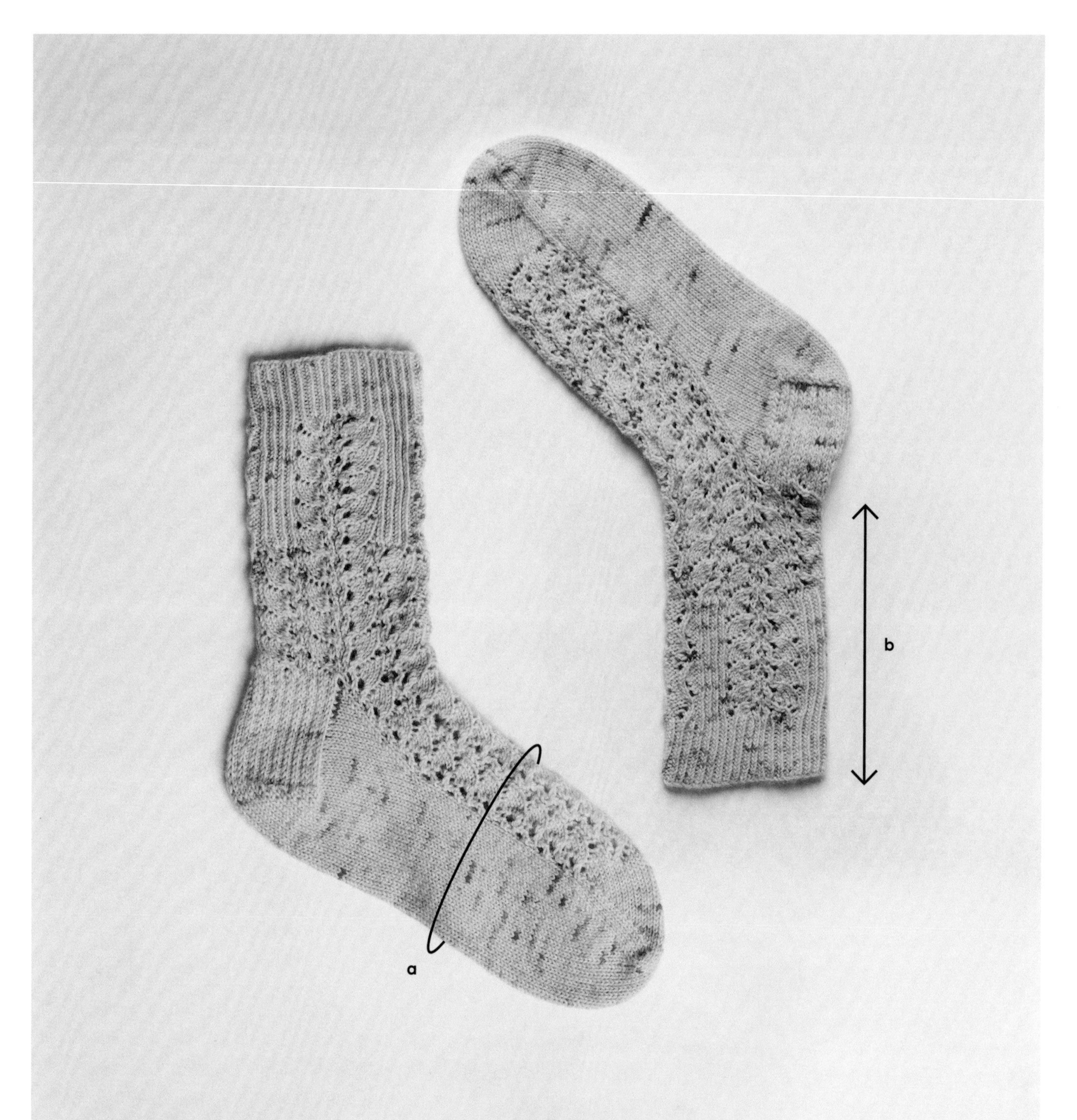

4-ply-weight *(shown here)*
a. Foot circumference (unstretched):
18 (20.5, 22.5)cm / 7¼ (8, 8¾)"
b. Leg length: 15cm / 6"

DK-weight *(not shown here)*
a. Foot circumference (unstretched):
17.5 (19, 20, 22)cm / 7 (7½, 8, 8¾)"
b. Leg length: 14.5cm / 5¾"

SHIRLEY

Mosaic Stitch Socks

The ultimate in fancy footwear, the Shirley socks are the showiest pair in these pages. Mosaic knitting offers maximum impact when mixed with stripes and we are agog over the possibilities that a variety of yarn combinations offers. For a simple but still very jazzy look, stick to two colours, or if you're feeling adventurous, put together a grab bag of scraps for yarn roulette. You may be surprised at which unexpected blends of colours really sing together!

#ShirleySocks

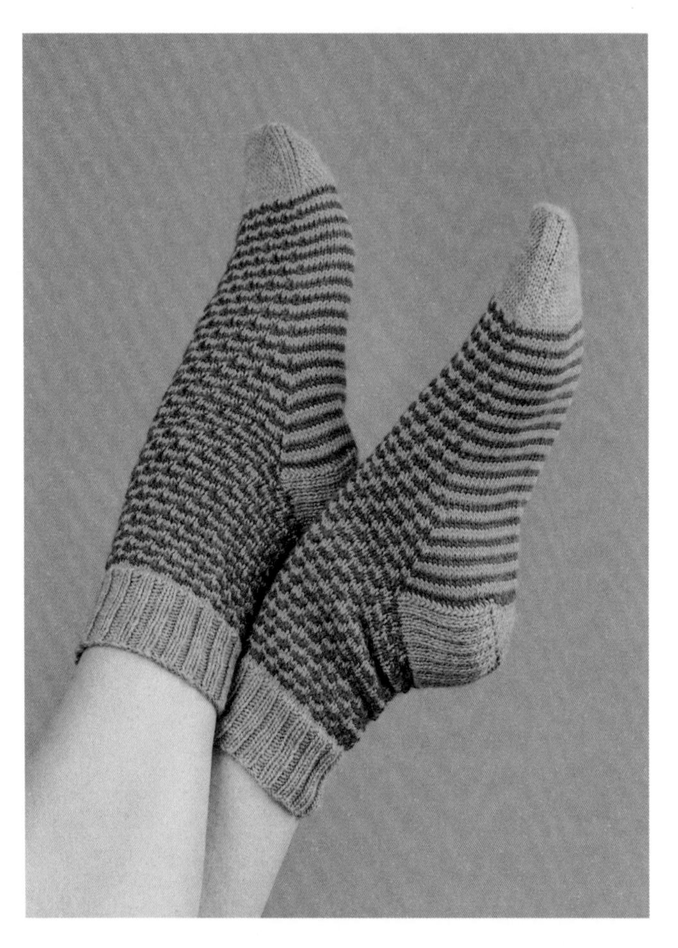

Sizes: 1 (2, 3)
To fit foot circumference: 20.5 (23, 25.5)cm / 8 (9, 10)" – to be worn with approx. 2.5cm / 1" negative ease
Foot length is fully adjustable within the pattern. Finished sock measures 0.5cm / ¼" less than actual foot length to ensure a good fit.
Yarn: Approximately 260 (300, 350)m / 283 (327, 381)yds of fingering / 4-ply-weight yarn for Heel Flap & Gusset version; Short Row and Afterthought heels use slightly less yarn.

Sample 1 (3 colour version, shown on this page)
Model wears a UK 7 / US 9 and is shown wearing a size 2.
Coop Knits Socks Yeah! (fingering / 4-ply-weight; 75% superwash Merino wool, 25% nylon; 212m / 231yds per 50g skein)
Yarn A: Chryso (108); 1 skein
Yarn B: Argon (1003); 1 skein
Yarn C: Topaz (113); 1 skein
Gauge: 36 sts & 50 rounds = 10cm / 4" over St st on 2.5mm needles after blocking.
Needles: 2.5mm / US 1.5 needles suitable for working small circumferences in the round
Always use a needle size that will result in the correct gauge after blocking.
Notions: 2 stitch markers, tapestry needle
Notes: These socks are worked from the cuff down, with a ribbed cuff and a lace striped pattern on the leg and foot. The samples shown are worked using the Heel Flap & Gusset method (blue & orange) and Short Row method (neon pastels). When changing yarns, ensure you twist the new colour with the previous colour between stripes to avoid holes. Take care not to pull yarns too tight between stripes to prevent the fabric from pulling.

Note: This design is also shown in DK-weight yarn from page 120.

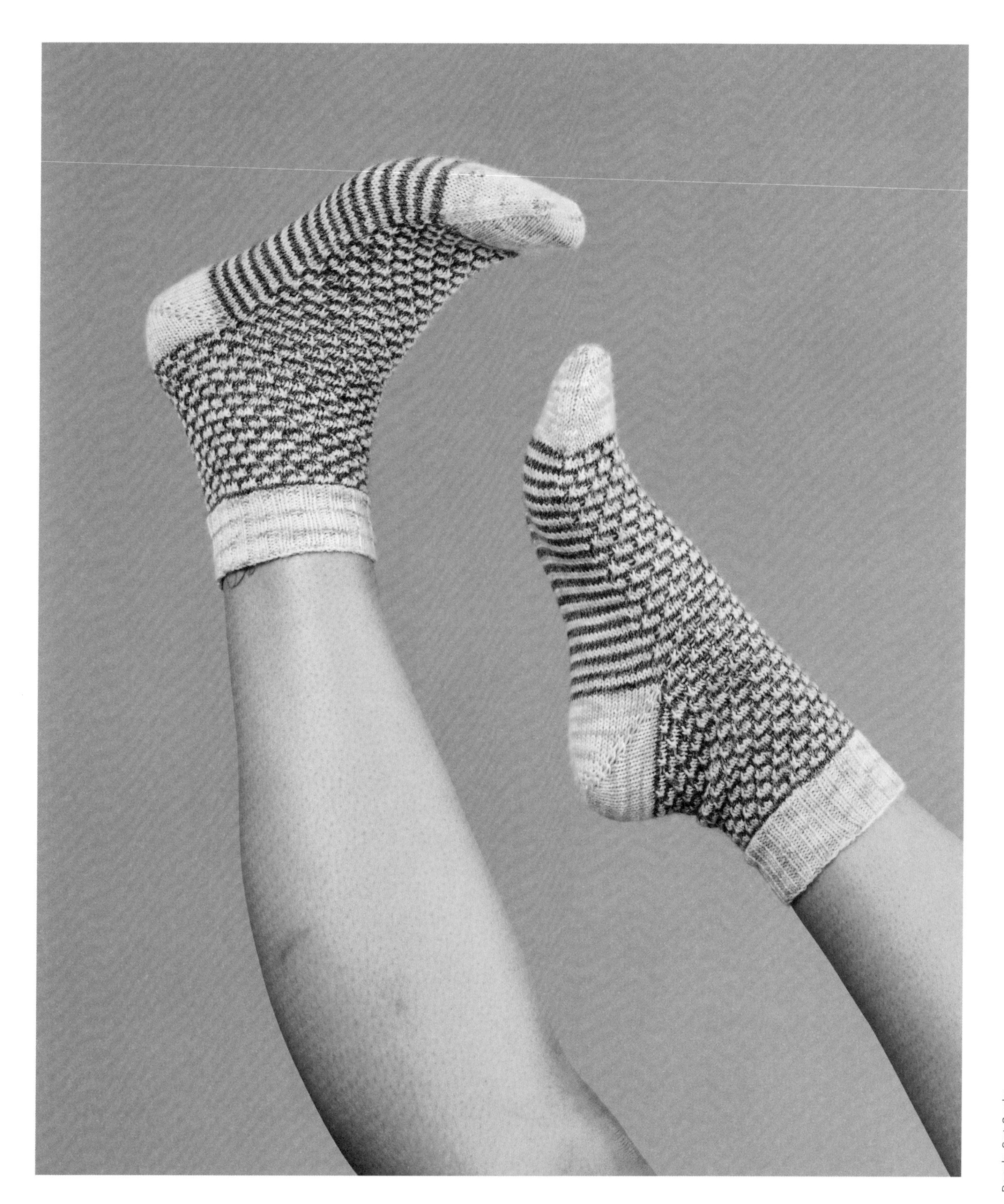

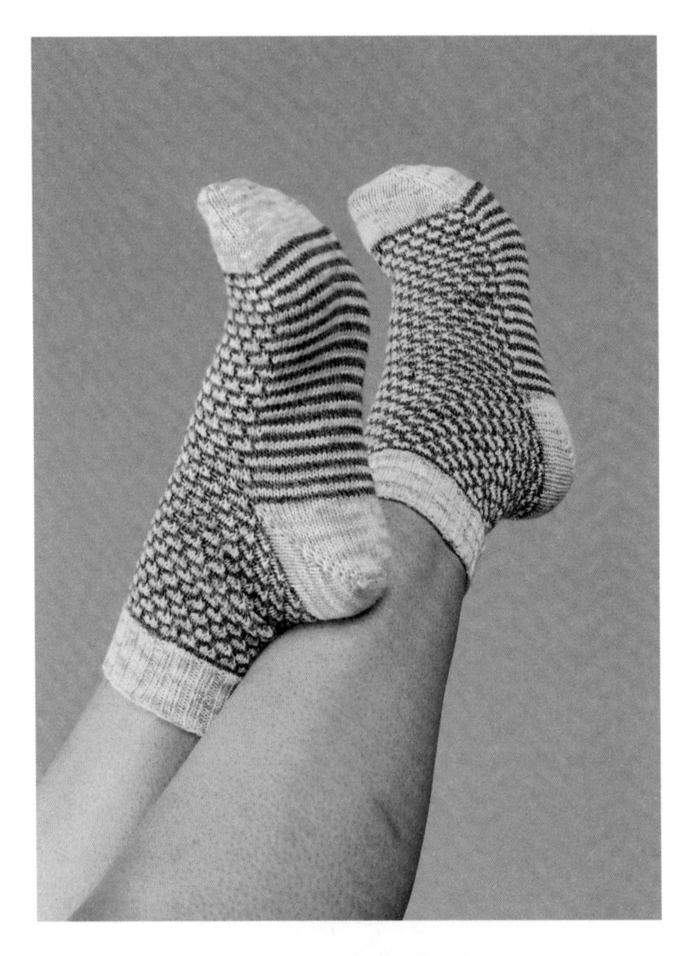

Sample 2 (4 colour version, shown above)
Model wears a UK 7 / US 9 and is shown wearing a size 2.
Vicki Brown Designs Sock Minis (fingering / 4-ply-weight; 75% superwash Merino wool, 25% nylon; 84m / 92yds per 20g skein)
Shades:
Pink: Hunchen; 1 skein
Yellow: Amarilo; 1 skein
Green: Spearmint; 1 skein
Lang Jawoll Sock Yarn (fingering / 4-ply-weight; 75% wool, 25% nylon; 202m / 221yds per 50g ball)
Grey: River (124); 1 ball

Note: Pattern instructions are written for the 3 colour version. Change colours as desired to use 4 or more shades.

PATTERN BEGINS
SOCK ONE
CUFF
With yarn A, cast on 64 (72, 80) sts. Join to work in the round, being careful not to twist sts. PM for beg of round.
Rib round: *P2, k2; rep from * to end.
Rep last round a further 19 times. Break yarn A.

LEG
Change to yarn B. Knit 2 rounds.
Join yarn C and begin working in lace stripe pattern as foll:
Round 1: With yarn C, knit.
Round 2: With yarn C, *k2, yo, ssk; rep from * to end.
Round 3: With yarn B, *k3, sl1 wyib; rep from * to end.
Round 4: With yarn B, knit.
Round 5: With yarn C, knit.
Round 6: With yarn C, *yo, ssk, k2; rep from * to end.
Round 7: With yarn B, *k1, sl1 wyib, k2; rep from * to end.
Round 8: With yarn B, knit.
Last 8 rounds set lace stripe patt. Rep rounds 1-8 a further 5 times, then work rounds 1-4 only once more.

HEEL
Work heel over 32 (36, 40) sts using preferred method: Heel Flap & Gusset (below or page 128) OR Short Row (page 132) OR Afterthought (page 138). The samples shown are worked using the Heel Flap & Gusset method (neon) and Afterthought (camel).

Heel Flap:
Turn work so WS is facing. Heel flap will be worked back and forth on the next 32 (36, 40) sts with yarn A, beg with a WS row. Keep rem 32 (36, 40) sts on needles for instep.
Change to yarn A.
Row 1 (WS): Sl1 wyif, p31 (35, 39).
Row 2 (RS): *Sl1 wyib, k1; rep from * to end.
Rep rows 1-2 a further 14 times, then work row 1 only once more.

Heel Turn:
Row 1 (RS): Sl1 wyib, k18 (20, 22), ssk, k1, turn, leaving rem 10 (12, 14) sts unworked. *1 st dec*
Row 2 (WS): Sl1 wyif, p7, p2tog, p1, turn, leaving rem 10 (12, 14) sts unworked. *1 st dec*
Row 3: Sl1 wyib, k to 1 st before gap, ssk, k1, turn. *1 st dec*
Row 4: Sl1 wyif, p to 1 st before gap, p2tog, p1, turn. *1 st dec*
Rep rows 3-4 a further 4 (5, 6) times. All heel sts have now been worked. *20 (22, 24) heel sts rem*

Gusset:
Begin working in the round again as foll:
Set-up round: With yarn C, sl1 wyib, k19 (21, 23), pick up and knit 16 sts along edge of heel flap (1 st in each slipped st along edge of flap), knit across 32 (36, 40) held instep sts, pick up and knit 16 sts along edge of heel flap, k36 (38, 40), PM for beg of round at beg of instep sts. *84 (90, 96) sts*
Round 1 (dec): Work round 6 of lace stripe pattern across 32 (36, 40) sts, ssk, k to last 2 sts, k2tog. *2 sts dec*
Round 2: With yarn B, work next round of lace stripe pattern across 32 (36, 40) sts, k to end.
Working next round of lace stripe pattern each time, changing colours as set by lace stripe pattern, rep rounds 1-2 a further 9 (8, 7) times. *64 (72, 80) sts: 32 (36, 40) sts each on instep and sole*

FOOT
Work straight in patt as set, working lace stripe pattern on instep and St st on sole, until sock measures 4.5 (5, 6)cm / 1¾ (2, 2¼)" less than desired foot length.

TOE
Break yarn B and C. Continue with yarn A only.
Round 1: Knit.
Round 2 (dec): K1, ssk, k26 (30, 34), k2tog, k1, PM, k1, ssk, k to last 3 sts, k2tog, k1. *60 (68, 76) sts*
Round 3: Knit.
Round 4 (dec): *K1, ssk, k to 3 sts before marker, k2tog, k1, SM; rep from * once more. *4 sts dec*
Rep rounds 3-4 a further 9 (10, 12) times. 20 (24, 24) sts
Break yarn, leaving a 30cm / 12" tail. Graft sts together (page 147).

SOCK TWO
CUFF
Work as for Sock One.

LEG
Change to yarn B. Knit 2 rounds.
Join yarn C and begin working in lace stripe pattern as foll:
Round 1: With yarn C, knit.
Round 2: With yarn C, *k2, k2tog, yo; rep from * to end.
Round 3: With yarn B, *k2, sl1 wyib, k1; rep from * to end.
Round 4: With yarn B, knit.
Round 5: With yarn C, knit.
Round 6: With yarn C, *k2tog, yo, k2; rep from * to end.
Round 7: With yarn B, *sl1 wyib, k3; rep from * to end.
Round 8: With yarn B, knit.
Last 8 rounds set lace stripe patt. Rep rounds 1-8 a further 5 times, then work rounds 1-4 only once more.

HEEL, FOOT & TOE
Work as for Sock One.

FINISHING
Weave in ends and block to measurements (page 123).

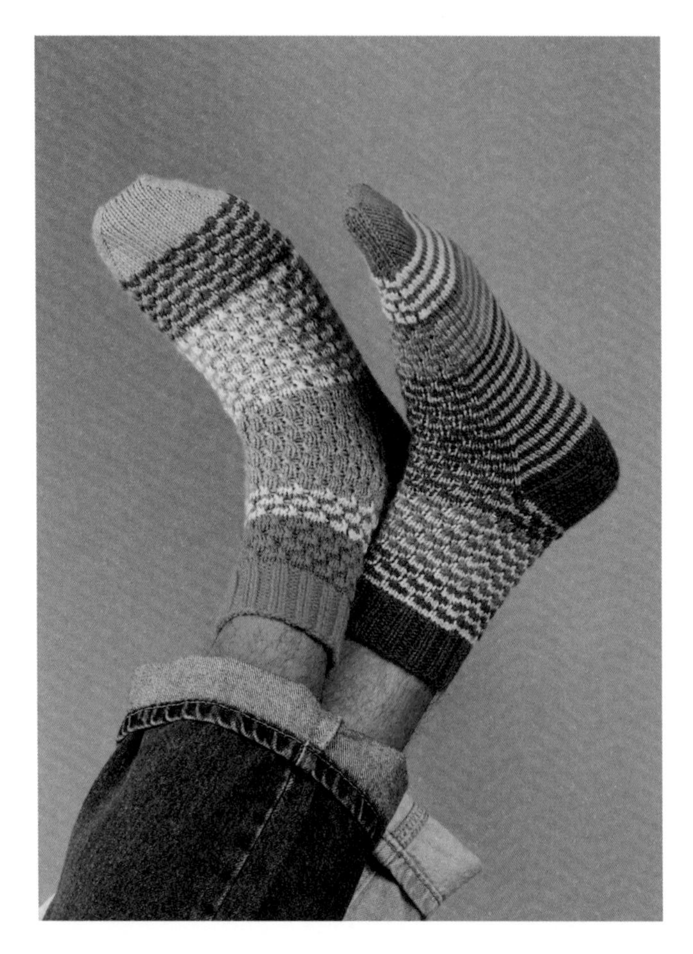

Sizes: 1 (2, 3, 4)
To fit foot circumference: 20.5 (21.5, 23, 24.5)cm / 8 (8½, 9, 9¾)" – to be worn with approx. 2.5cm / 1" negative ease
Foot length is fully adjustable within the pattern. Finished sock measures 0.5cm / ¼" less than actual foot length to ensure a good fit.
Yarn: Approximately 210 (240, 265, 290)m / 228 (261, 288, 316)yds of DK-weight yarn for Heel Flap & Gusset version; Short Row and Afterthought heels use slightly less yarn.
Sample 1 (Multicolour version, shown above)
Model wears a UK 9 / US 10 and is shown wearing a size 3.
Scrap DK-weight yarn
Shades: 10-15 assorted shades; scraps of approximately 10-15g

Gauge: 28 sts & 40 rounds = 10cm / 4" over St st on 3mm needles, after blocking.
Needles: 3mm / US 2.5 needles suitable for working small circumferences in the round
Always use a needle size that will result in the correct gauge after blocking.
Notions: 2 stitch markers, tapestry needle
Notes: These socks are worked from the cuff down, with a ribbed cuff and a lace striped pattern on the leg and foot. The sample shown is worked using the Heel Flap & Gusset method. When changing yarns, ensure you twist the new colour with the previous colour between stripes to avoid holes. Take care not to pull yarns too tight between stripes to prevent the fabric from pulling.

Note: This pattern is also shown in fingering / 4-ply-weight yarn from page 116.

PATTERN BEGINS
SOCK ONE
CUFF
With yarn A, cast on 48 (52, 56, 60) sts. Join to work in the round, being careful not to twist sts. PM for beg of round.
Rib round: *P2, k2; rep from * to end.
Rep last round a further 14 times. Break yarn A.

LEG
Change to yarn B. Knit 2 rounds.
Join yarn C and begin working in lace stripe pattern as foll:
Round 1: With yarn C, knit.
Round 2: With yarn C, *k2, yo, ssk; rep from * to end.
Round 3: With yarn B, *k3, sl1 wyib; rep from * to end.
Round 4: With yarn B, knit.
Round 5: With yarn C, knit.
Round 6: With yarn C, *yo, ssk, k2; rep from * to end.
Round 7: With yarn B, *k1, sl1 wyib, k2; rep from * to end.
Round 8: With yarn B, knit.
Last 8 rounds set lace stripe patt. Rep rounds 1-8 a further 4 times, then work rounds 1-4 only once more.

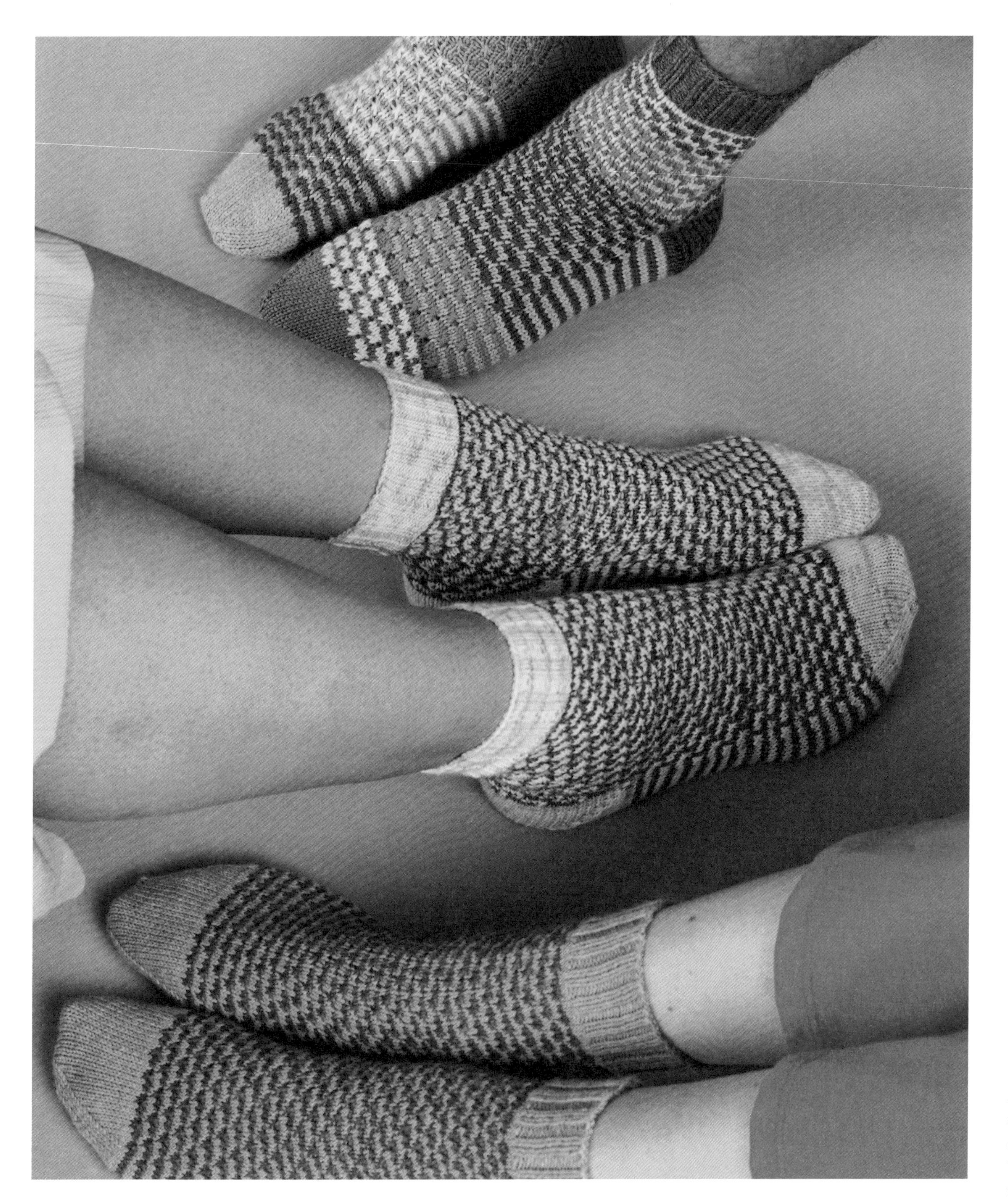

HEEL

Work heel over 24 (26, 28, 30) sts using preferred method: Heel Flap & Gusset (below or page 128) OR Short Row (page 132) OR Afterthought (page 138). The sample shown is worked using the Heel Flap & Gusset method.

Heel Flap:

Turn work so WS is facing. Heel flap will be worked back and forth on the next 24 (26, 28, 30) sts with yarn A, beg with a WS row. Keep rem 24 (26, 28, 30) sts on needles for instep. Change to yarn A.

Row 1 (WS): Sl1 wyif, p23 (25, 27, 29).

Row 2 (RS): *Sl1 wyib, k1; rep from * to end.

Rep rows 1-2 a further 10 times, then work row 1 only once more.

Heel Turn:

Row 1 (RS): Sl1 wyib, k14 (14, 16, 16), ssk, k1, turn, leaving rem 6 (8, 8, 10) sts unworked. *1 st dec*

Row 2 (WS): Sl1 wyif, p7 (5, 7, 5), p2tog, p1, turn, leaving rem 6 (8, 8, 10) sts unworked. *1 st dec*

Row 3: Sl1 wyib, k to 1 st before gap, ssk, k1, turn. *1 st dec*

Row 4: Sl1 wyif, p to 1 st before gap, p2tog, p1, turn. *1 st dec*

Rep rows 3-4 a further 2 (3, 3, 4) times. All heel sts have now been worked. *16 (16, 18, 18) heel sts rem*

Gusset:

Begin working in the round again as foll:

Set-up round: With yarn C, sl1 wyib, k15 (15, 17, 17), pick up and knit 12 sts along edge of heel flap (1 st in each slipped st along edge of the flap), knit across 24 (26, 28, 30) held instep sts, pick up and knit 12 sts along edge of heel flap, k28 (28, 30, 30), PM for new beg of round at beg of instep sts. *64 (66, 70, 72) sts*

Round 1 (dec): Work round 6 of lace stripe pattern across 24 (26, 28, 30) sts, ssk, k to last 2 sts, k2tog. *2 sts dec*

Round 2: With yarn B, work next round of lace stripe pattern across 24 (26, 28, 30) sts, k to end.

Working next round of lace stripe pattern each time, changing colours as set by lace stripe pattern, rep rounds 1-2 a further 7 (6, 6, 5) times. *48 (52, 56, 60) sts: 24 (26, 28, 30) sts each on instep and sole*

FOOT

Work straight in patt as set, working lace stripe pattern on instep and St st on sole, until sock measures 4.5 (5, 6)cm / 1¾ (2, 2¼)" less than desired foot length.

TOE

Break yarn B and C. Continue with yarn A only.

Round 1: Knit.

Round 2 (dec): K1, ssk, k18 (20, 22, 24), k2tog, k1, PM, k1, ssk, k to last 3 sts, k2tog, k1. *44 (48, 52, 56) sts*

Round 3: Knit.

Round 4 (dec): *K1, ssk, k to 3 sts before marker, k2tog, k1, SM; rep from * once more. *4 sts dec*

Rep rounds 3-4 a further 6 (7, 7, 8) times. *16 (16, 20, 20) sts*

Break yarn, leaving a 30cm / 12" tail. Graft sts together (page 147).

SOCK TWO

CUFF

Work as for Sock One.

LEG

Change to yarn B. Knit 2 rounds.

Join yarn C and begin working in lace stripe pattern as foll:

Round 1: With yarn C, knit.

Round 2: With yarn C, *k2, k2tog, yo; rep from * to end.

Round 3: With yarn B, *k2, sl1 wyib, k1; rep from * to end.

Round 4: With yarn B, knit.

Round 5: With yarn C, knit.

Round 6: With yarn C, *k2tog, yo, k2; rep from * to end.

Round 7: With yarn B, *sl1 wyib, k3; rep from * to end.

Round 8: With yarn B, knit.

Rep rounds 1-8 a further 4 times, then work rounds 1-4 only once more.

HEEL, FOOT & TOE

Work as for Sock One.

FINISHING

Weave in ends and block to measurements.

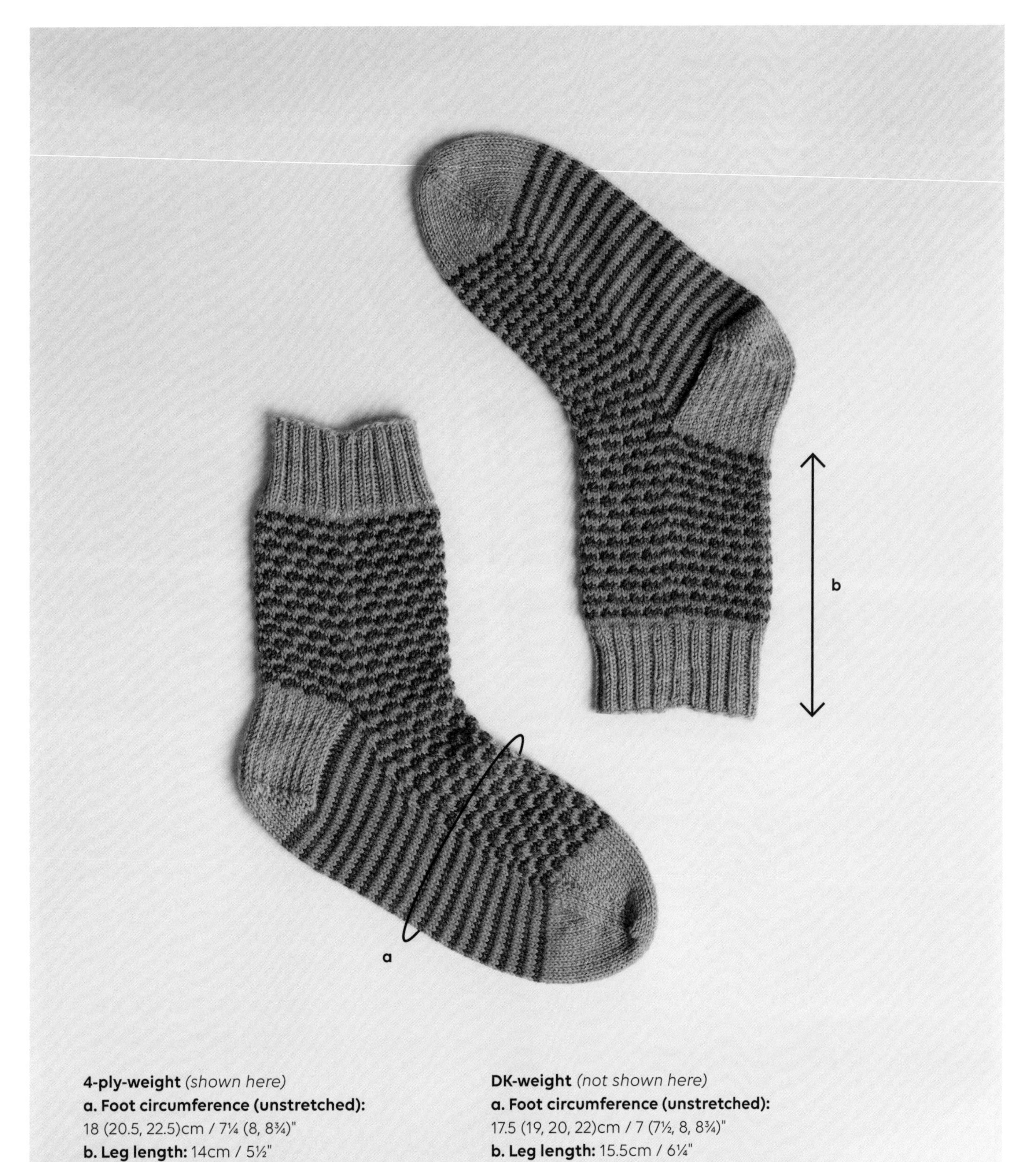

4-ply-weight *(shown here)*
a. Foot circumference (unstretched):
18 (20.5, 22.5)cm / 7¼ (8, 8¾)"
b. Leg length: 14cm / 5½"

DK-weight *(not shown here)*
a. Foot circumference (unstretched):
17.5 (19, 20, 22)cm / 7 (7½, 8, 8¾)"
b. Leg length: 15.5cm / 6¼"

VARIATIONS, TUTORIALS + ADJUSTMENTS

There is certainly more than one way to knit a sock and the patterns in this book are meant to work as stepping stones on your journey to sock-knitting confidence!

As you become more sure of yourself, and also figure out what feels best on your feet, you can make choices that will adapt your pairs to you!

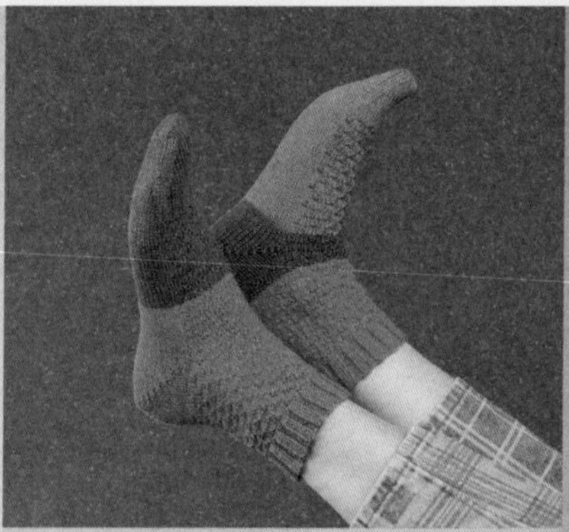

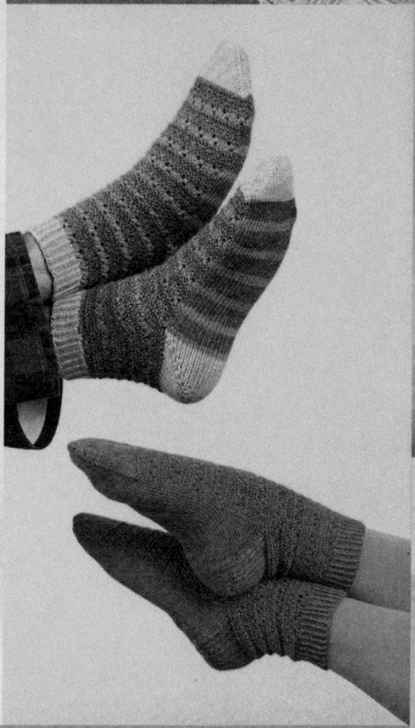

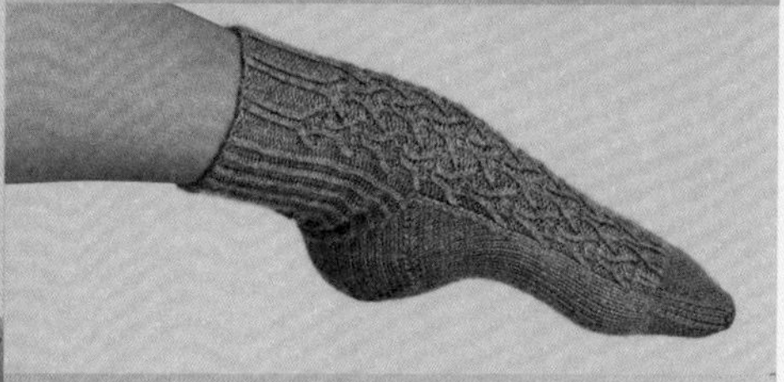

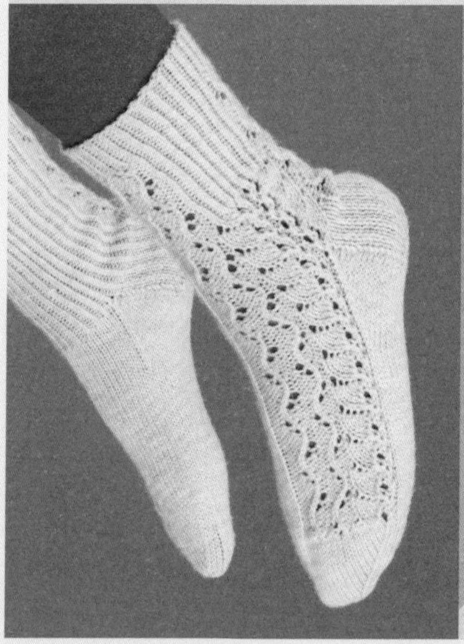

Types of Heel

Heels are arguably the best way to tailor your socks to your tastes. We've included three options for heels that are interchangeable in each pattern. Read on for a rundown of each style and some of their pros and cons.

One way to create heels is by making a heel flap (Fig.1). The flap (which becomes the back of the heel) is made by knitting the heel stitches back and forth until the correct length is reached. Stitches are then picked up along one side of the heel before knitting across the stitches for the top of the foot (the instep) and then picking up stitches for the other side of the heel so that you can continue to work in the round.

Alternatively, a short row heel (Fig.2) is created at the point where you've completed the ankle portion of your sock and you create a wedge of fabric by only knitting some of the stitches back and forth instead of in the round, and only working a portion of the total number of stitches at a time (so a short row instead of a full row). It sounds complicated, but if you follow the directions exactly as written, a magical heel will appear.

And as a third option, an afterthought heel (Fig.3) is made by using a piece of scrap yarn to work a row of stitches in the spot where the heel should go. You then come back to the heel once the rest of the sock is done and complete it (as an afterthought - kind of!). You unravel the scrap yarn and are left with live stitches that you pick up and then knit the heel onto the rest of the sock.

A heel flap style heel will fit most people best because the gusset created when the stitches are picked up around the heel increases the number of stitches. The extra fabric from this increase in stitches accommodates the widest part of the foot (the back of the heel to the top of the instep). A sock that fits this part of the foot well will be less likely to move around throughout the day. If you have a high instep or wide foot, extra room can be made in the sock by working more rows in the heel flap, picking up extra stitches for those rows and therefore increasing the size of the sock in that area. Similarly, if less room is needed, the heel flap (and so the number of stitches picked up) can be reduced.

If you are using a hand-dyed yarn that creates a repeated stripe or a colour pooling effect, changing the stitch count when the heel is worked will disturb the colour sequence. If that is something that you want to avoid, the other heel types, the short row heel or the afterthought heel, can be used. These two heels do not change the stitch count on the top of the foot and so the effect created by the yarn colours will continue without interruption.

The following pages contain step-by-step illustrations and instructions on how to work each one.

Fig.1

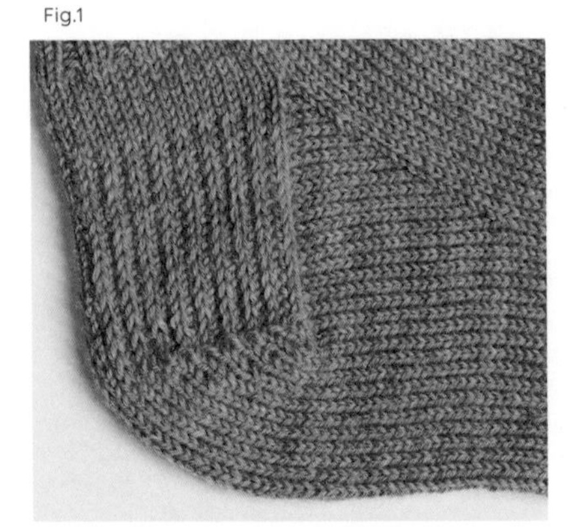

Fig.2

Fig.3

4-PLY WEIGHT

Heel Flap

Turn work so WS is facing. Heel flap will be worked back and forth on next 32 (36, 40) sts only, beg with a WS row. Keep rem 32 (36, 40) sts on needles for instep.

Row 1 (WS): Sl1 wyif, p31 (35, 39), turn.

Row 2 (RS): *Sl1 wyib, k1; rep from * to end.

Rep rows 1-2 a further 14 times, then work row 1 only once more.

Heel Turn

Row 1 (RS): Sl1 wyib, k18 (20, 22), ssk, k1, turn, leaving rem 10 (12, 14) sts unworked. *1 st dec*

Row 2 (WS): Sl1 wyif, p7, p2tog, p1, turn, leaving rem 10 (12, 14) sts unworked. *1 st dec*

Row 3: Sl1 wyib, k to 1 st before gap, ssk, k1, turn. *1 st dec*

Row 4: Sl1 wyif, p to 1 st before gap, p2tog, p1, turn. *1 st dec*

Rep rows 3-4 a further 4 (5, 6) times. All heel sts have now been worked. *20 (22, 24) heel sts rem*

Gusset

Begin working in the round again as foll:

Set-up round: Sl1 wyib, k19 (21, 23), pick up and knit 16 sts along edge of heel flap (1 st in each slipped st along edge of flap), work in patt across 32 (36, 40) instep sts, pick up and knit 16 sts along edge of heel flap, k36 (38, 40), PM for beg of round at beg of instep sts. *84 (90, 96) sts*

Round 1 (dec): Patt across 32 (36, 40) sts, ssk, k to last 2 sts, k2tog. *2 sts dec*

Round 2: Patt across 24 (26, 28, 30) sts, k to end.

Working next round of patt each time, rep rounds 1-2 a further 9 (8, 7) times. *64 (72, 80) sts: 32 (36, 40) sts each for instep and sole*

DK WEIGHT

Heel Flap

Turn work so WS is facing. Heel flap will be worked back and forth on the next 24 (26, 28, 30) sts, beg with a WS row. Keep rem 24 (26, 28, 30) sts on needles for instep.

Row 1 (WS): Sl1 wyif, p23 (25, 27, 29).

Row 2 (RS): *Sl1 wyib, k1; rep from * to end.

Rep rows 1-2 a further 10 times, then work row 1 only once more.

Heel Turn

Row 1 (RS): Sl1 wyib, k14 (14, 16, 16), ssk, k1, turn, leaving rem 6 (8, 8, 10) sts unworked. *1 st dec*

Row 2 (WS): Sl1 wyif, p7 (5, 7, 5), p2tog, p1, turn, leaving rem 6 (8, 8, 10) sts unworked. *1 st dec*

Row 3: Sl1 wyib, k to 1 st before gap, ssk, k1, turn. *1 st dec*

Row 4: Sl1 wyif, p to 1 st before gap, p2tog, p1, turn. *1 st dec*

Rep rows 3-4 a further 2 (3, 3, 4) times. All heel sts have now been worked. *16 (16, 18, 18) heel sts rem*

Gusset

Begin working in the round again as follows:

Set-up round: Sl1 wyib, k15 (15, 17, 17), pick up and knit 12 sts along edge of heel flap (1 st in each slipped st along edge of flap); work across 24 (26, 28, 30) instep sts in patt, pick up and knit 12 sts along edge of heel flap, k28 (28, 30, 30), PM for beg of round at beg of instep sts. *64 (66, 70, 72) sts*

Round 1 (dec): Patt across 24 (26, 28, 30) sts, ssk, k to last 2 sts, k2tog. *2 sts dec*

Round 2: Patt across 24 (26, 28, 30) sts, k to end.

Working next round of patt each time, rep rounds 1-2 a further 7 (6, 6, 5) times. *48 (52, 56, 60) sts: 24 (26, 28, 30) sts each on instep and sole*

Flow Chart

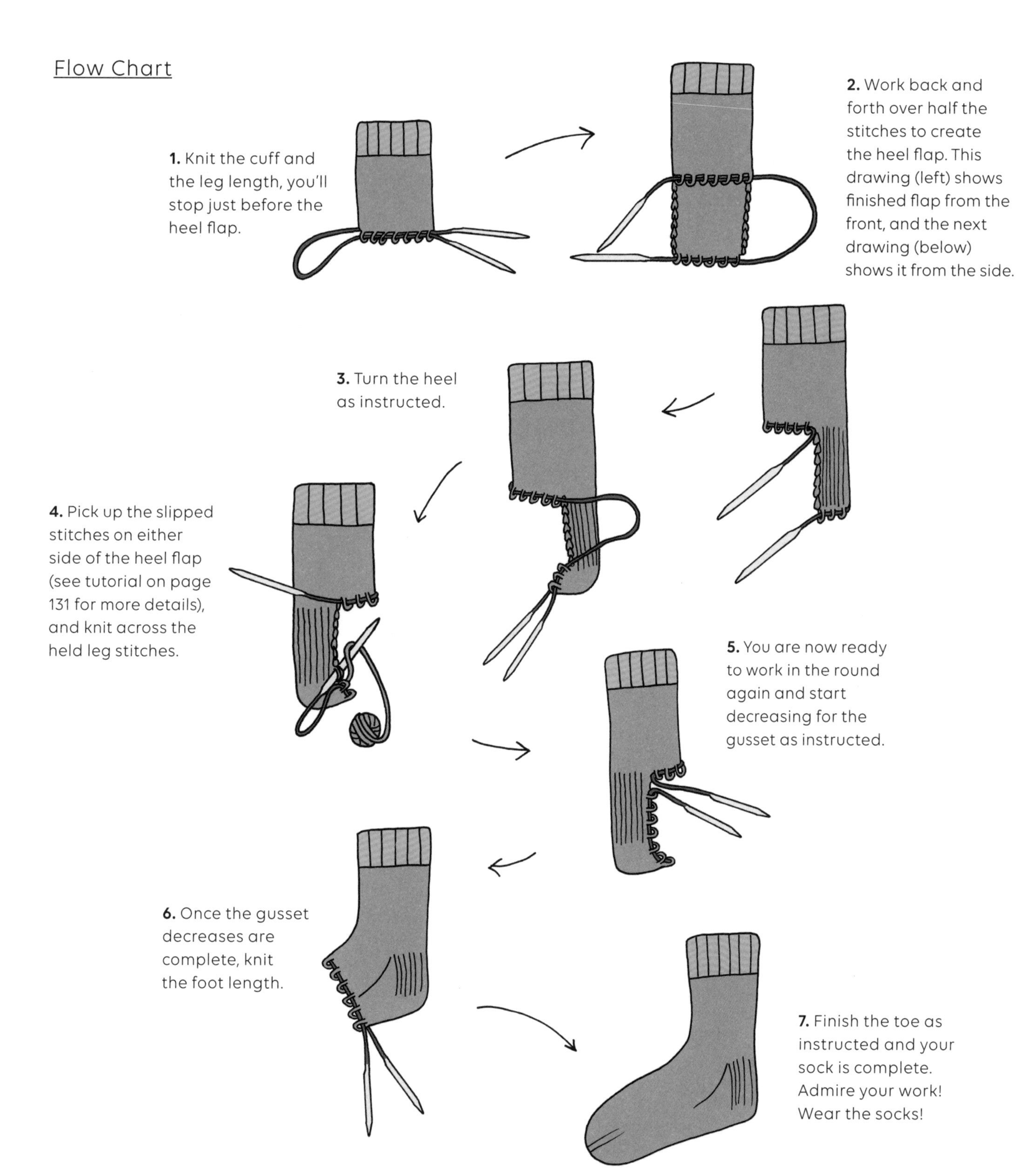
1. Knit the cuff and the leg length, you'll stop just before the heel flap.
2. Work back and forth over half the stitches to create the heel flap. This drawing (left) shows finished flap from the front, and the next drawing (below) shows it from the side.
3. Turn the heel as instructed.
4. Pick up the slipped stitches on either side of the heel flap (see tutorial on page 131 for more details), and knit across the held leg stitches.
5. You are now ready to work in the round again and start decreasing for the gusset as instructed.
6. Once the gusset decreases are complete, knit the foot length.
7. Finish the toe as instructed and your sock is complete. Admire your work! Wear the socks!

Picking Up Stitches in Heel Flap

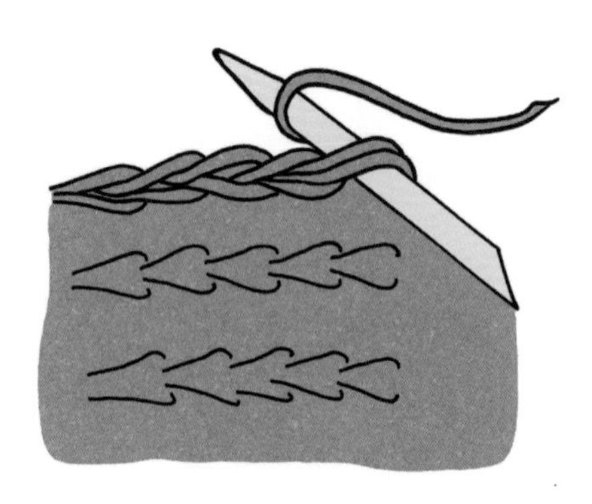

1. With right-side of the work facing, insert the right-hand needle tip under the first slipped stitch at the edge of the heel flap. Wrap the yarn around the needle as if to knit.

2. Pull the yarn through the stitch so the yarn sits on the right-hand needle.

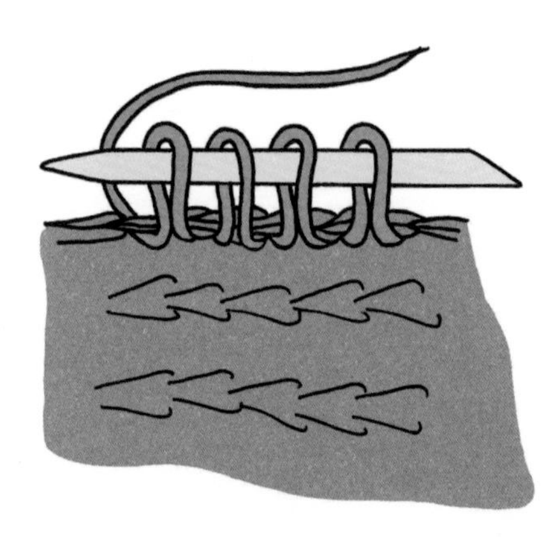

3. Repeat steps 1-2 across the heel flap slipped stitches, picking up as many stitches as required for the pattern.

SLIPPING STITCHES

Slip Stitches Pwise with Yarn in Back (Right Side)

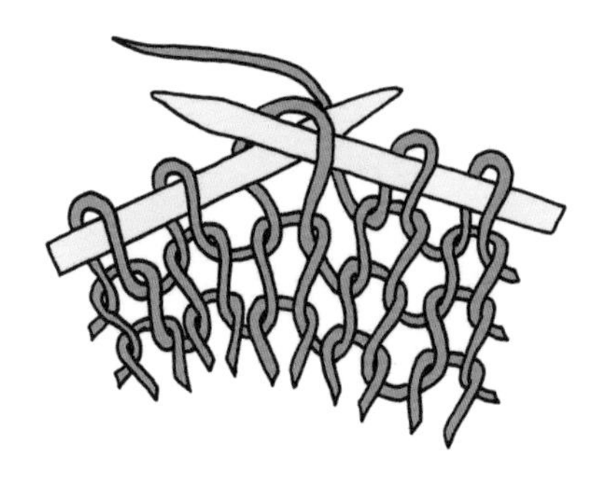

1. With yarn held in back, insert the right needle tip into the stitch you want to slip as if to purl.

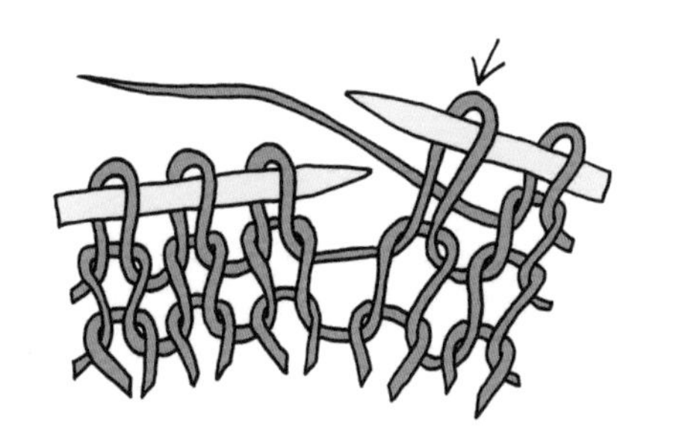

2. Pass stitch from left to right so that it's now sitting on the right needle as shown, but you haven't worked it by pulling the working yarn through.

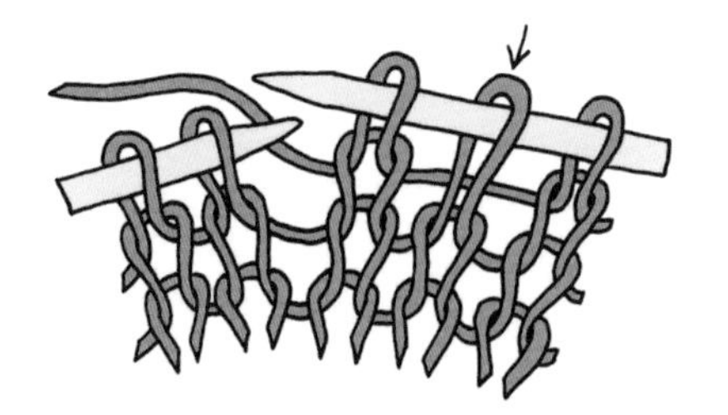

3. You can now continue working the next stitches as instructed. The working yarn will pass behind the slipped stitch before continuing to work with the subsequent stitches.

Slip Stitches Pwise with Yarn in Front (Wrong Side)

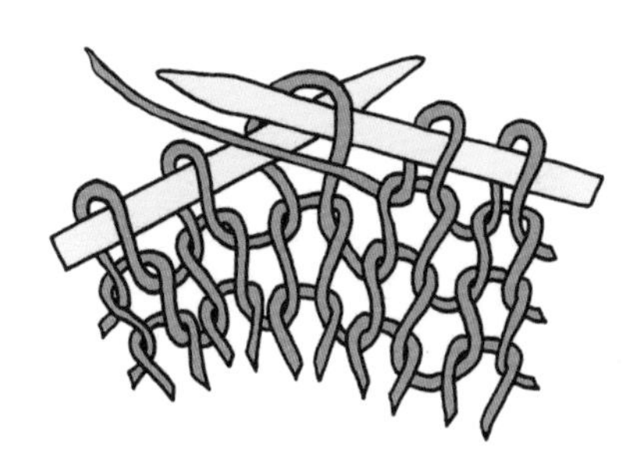

1. With yarn held in front, insert the right needle tip into the stitch you want to slip as if to purl.

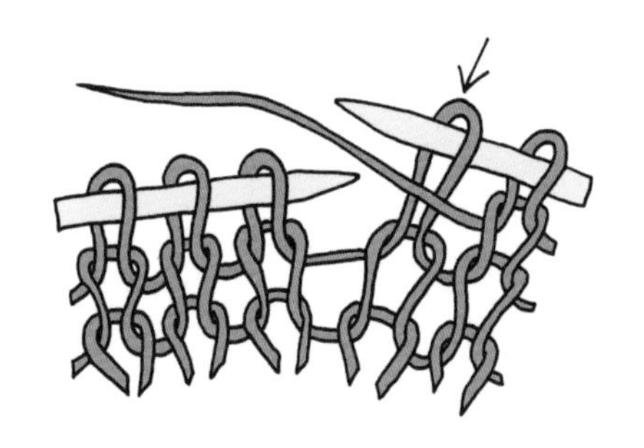

2. Pass stitch from left to right so that it's now sitting on the right needle as shown, but you haven't worked it by pulling the working yarn through.

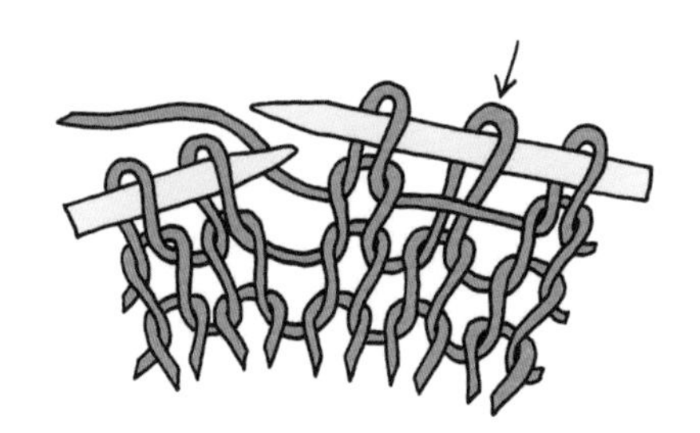

3. You can now continue working the next stitches as instructed. The working yarn will pass in front of the slipped stitch before continuing to work with the subsequent stitches.

4-PLY WEIGHT

The heel will be worked back and forth over the first 32 (36, 40) sts only.

Row 1 (RS): K31 (35, 39), w&t.
Row 2 (WS): P30 (34, 38), w&t.
Row 3: K to 1 st before next 'wrapped' st, w&t.
Row 4: P to 1 st before next 'wrapped' st, w&t.
Rep rows 3-4 until there are 12 (12, 14) unwrapped central sts with 10 (12, 13) wrapped sts on either side.

Row 1 (RS): K to first wrapped st, pick up the wrap and k the st tog with the wrap tbl, w&t the next st (this st is now wrapped twice).
Row 2 (WS): P to first wrapped st, pick up the wrap and p the st tog with the wrap, w&t the next st (this st is now wrapped twice).
Row 3: K to first wrapped st (which now has 2 wraps), pick up the wraps and k the st tog with the wraps tbl, w&t the next st (this st is now wrapped twice).
Row 4: P to first wrapped st (which now has 2 wraps), pick up the wraps and p the st tog with the wraps, w&t the next st (this st is now wrapped twice).
Rep rows 3-4 a further 7 (9, 10) times, then work row 3 only once more but do not w&t at end of row, PM for new beg of round, patt across 32 (36, 40) held instep sts, k the next st tog with its wraps, k to end.

DK WEIGHT

The heel will be worked back and forth over the first 24 (26, 28, 30) sts only.

Row 1 (RS): K23 (25, 27, 29), w&t.
Row 2 (WS): P22 (24, 26, 28), w&t.
Row 3: K to 1 st before next 'wrapped' st, w&t.
Row 4: P to 1 st before next 'wrapped' st, w&t.
Rep rows 3-4 until there are 8 (8, 10, 10) unwrapped central sts with 8 (9, 9, 10) wrapped sts on either side.

Row 1 (RS): K to first wrapped st, pick up the wrap and k the st tog with the wrap tbl, w&t the next st (this st is now wrapped twice).
Row 2 (WS): P to first wrapped st, pick up the wrap and p the st tog with the wrap, w&t the next st (this st is now wrapped twice).
Row 3: K to first wrapped st (which now has 2 wraps), pick up the wraps and k the st tog with the wraps tbl, w&t the next st (this st is now wrapped twice).
Row 4: P to first wrapped st (which now has 2 wraps), pick up the wraps and p the st tog with the wraps, w&t the next st (this st is now wrapped twice).
Rep rows 3-4 a further 5 (6, 6, 7) times, then work row 3 only once more but do not w&t at end of row, PM for new beg of round, patt across 24 (26, 28, 30) held instep sts, k the next st tog with its wraps, k to end.

Flow Chart

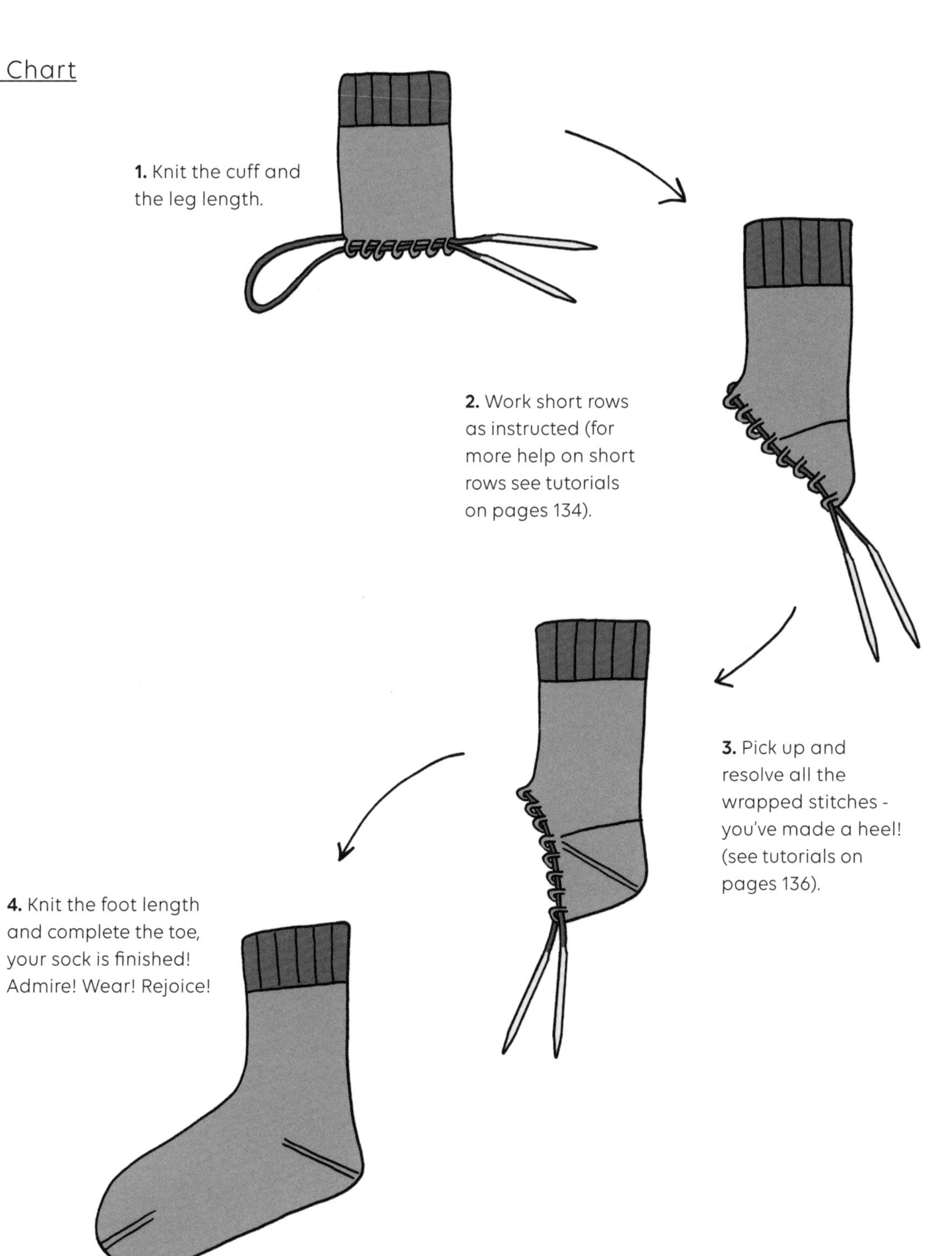

1. Knit the cuff and the leg length.
2. Work short rows as instructed (for more help on short rows see tutorials on pages 134).
3. Pick up and resolve all the wrapped stitches - you've made a heel! (see tutorials on pages 136).
4. Knit the foot length and complete the toe, your sock is finished! Admire! Wear! Rejoice!

W+T Knit Side Facing

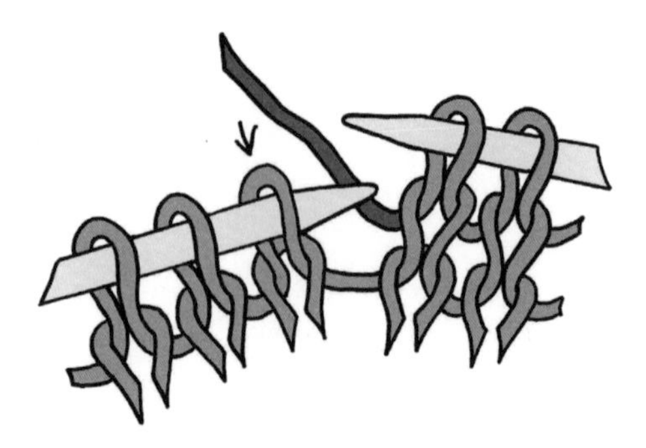

1. Knit to the stitch specified in the pattern. The arrow here shows where the turn will happen and the stitch that will be wrapped.

2. With yarn held in back, slip this stitch purlwise onto the right-hand needle.

3. Bring your yarn to the front of your work, between the two needle tips, as if to purl.

4. Slip the first stitch on the right-hand needle back to the left-hand needle, ensuring this stitch is not twisted. Bring your yarn to the back of your work between the two needle tips.

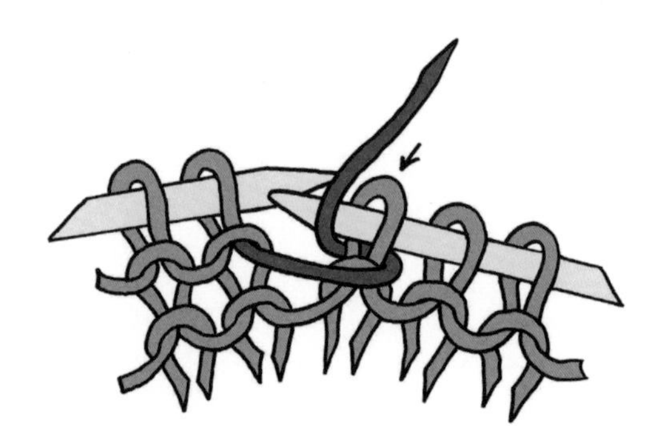

5. Turn your work 180 degrees. The arrow shows the stitch has now been wrapped and your yarn should be at the front of your work, ready to purl.

W+T Purl Side Facing

1. Purl to the stitch specified in the pattern. The arrow here shows where the turn will happen and the stitch is to be wrapped

2. With yarn held in front, slip this stitch purlwise onto the right-hand needle.

3. Bring your yarn to the back of your work, between the two needle tips, as if to knit.

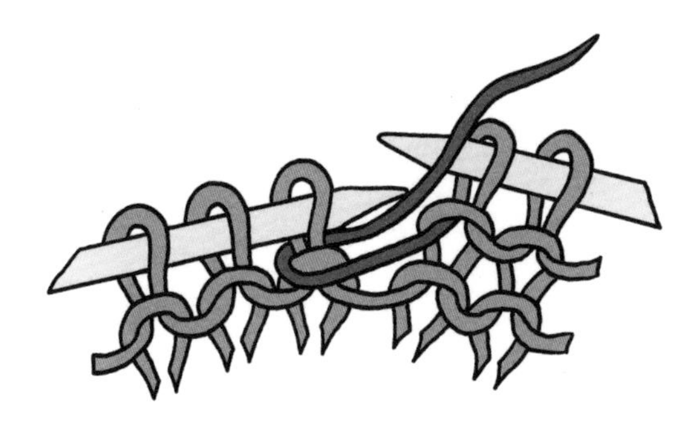

4. Slip the first stitch on the right-hand needle back to the left-hand needle, ensuring this stitch is not twisted. Bring your yarn to the front of your work between the two needle tips, as if to purl.

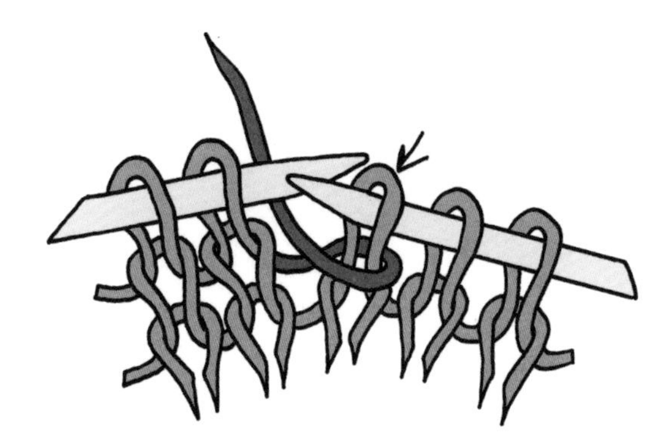

5. Turn your work 180 degrees. The stitch has been wrapped and your yarn should be at the back of your work, ready to knit.

Picking Up Wrap Knit Side

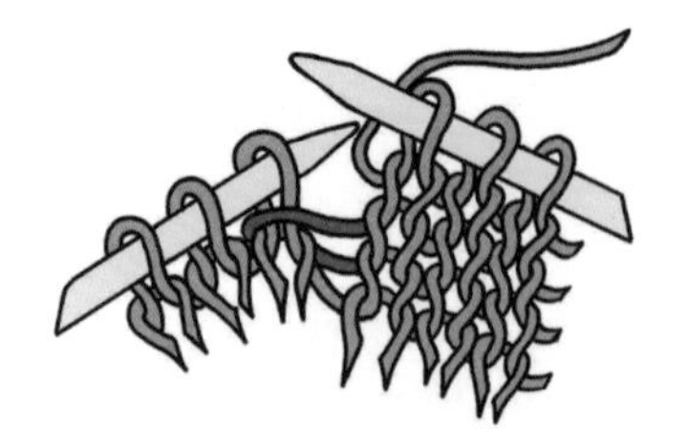

1. Work to the wrapped stitch. You will see a loop of yarn that sits around the neck of a stitch.

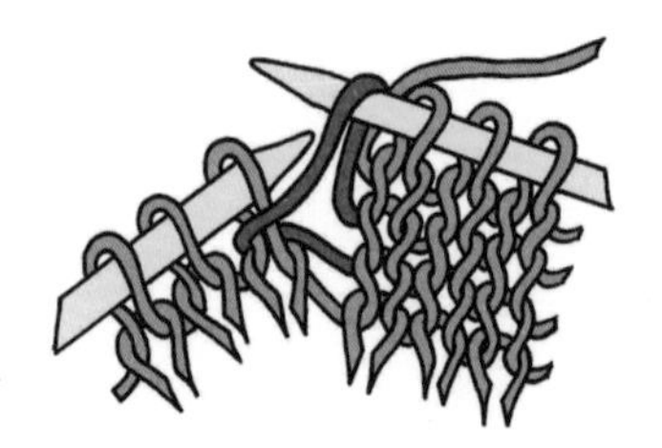

2. Bring the right-hand needle to the front of your work and pick up the wrap from front to back.

3. Insert the tip of the right-hand needle knitwise into the stitch the wrap is sat around. Slip the stitch, so now the wrap and this stitch sit on the right-hand needle.

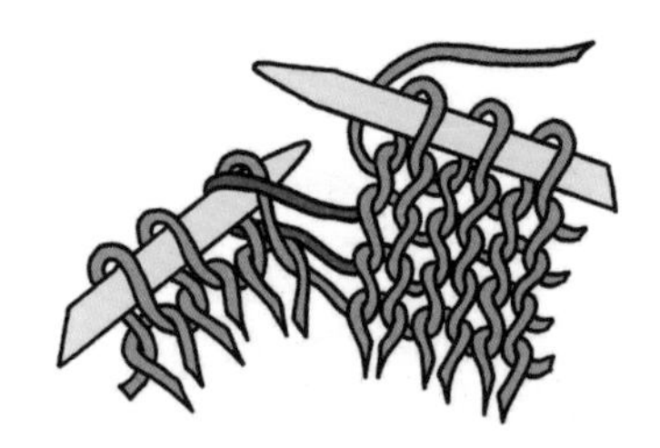

4. Slip the wrap, then the stitch, to the left-hand needle to sit as shown.

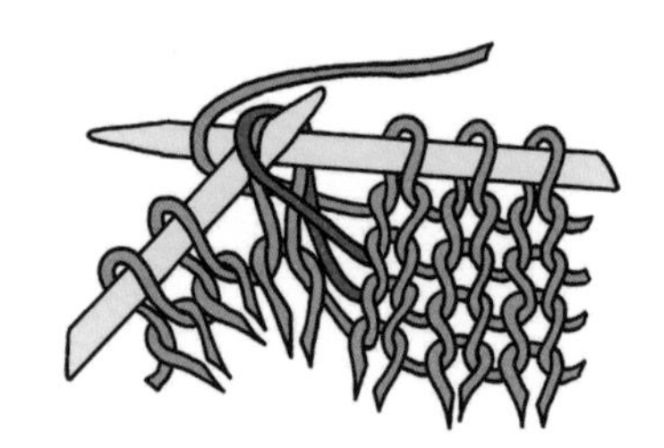

5. Knit the wrap and the stitch together through the back loop.

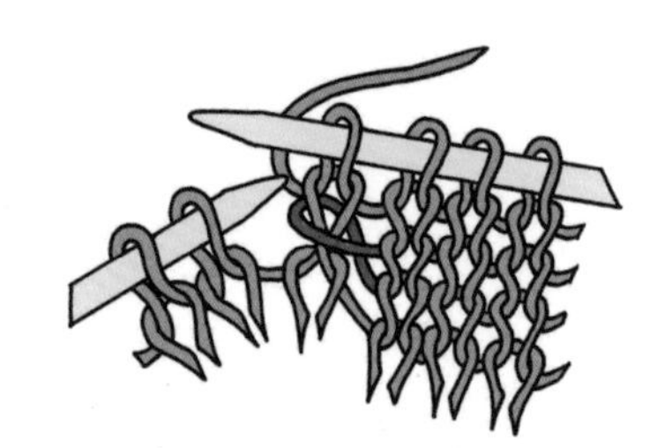

6. Ta-da!

Picking Up Double Wrap Knit Side

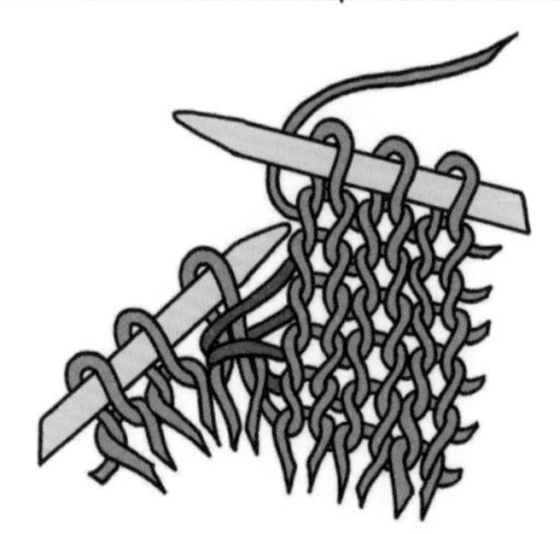

1. Knit to the double wrap, this is the two loops of yarn that sit around the neck of a stitch.

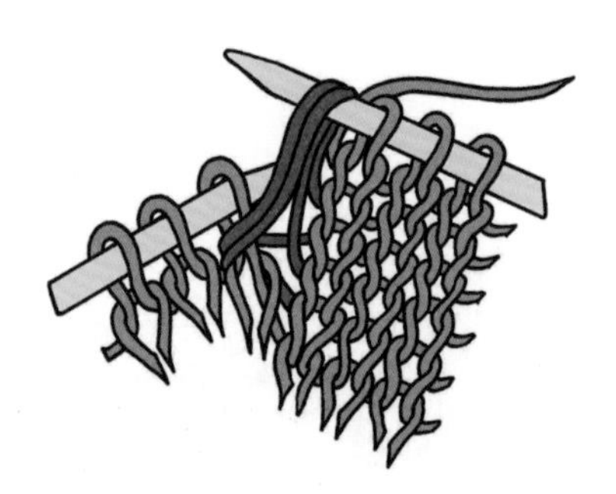

2. Move right-hand needle to front of work, pick up the two wraps from front to back. Follow steps 3-6 above for a single wrap, but ensuring you move and knit both picked-up wraps.

Picking Up Wrap Purl Side

1. Purl to wrapped stitch. You will see a loop of yarn that sits around the neck of a stitch.

2. Move your right-hand needle to the back of your work and pick up the wrap from back to front.

3. Place the picked-up wrap onto the left-hand needle.

4. Purl together the wrap and the wrapped stitch.

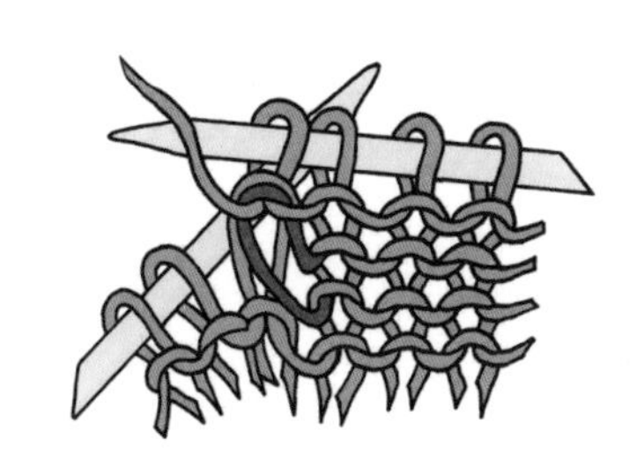

5. Ta-da!

Picking Up Double Wrap Purl Side

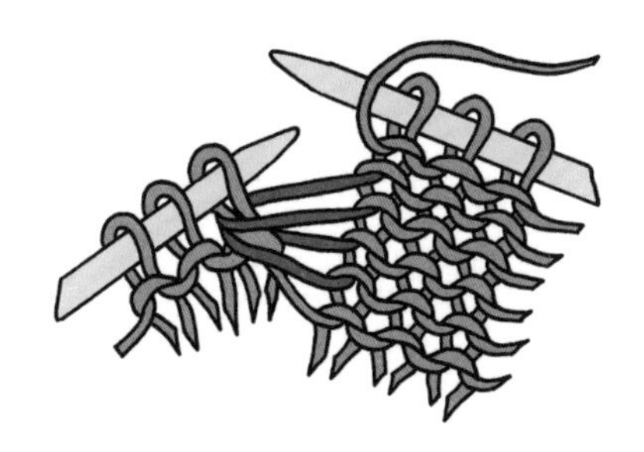

1. Purl to the double wrap, this is the two loops of yarn that sit around the neck of a stitch.

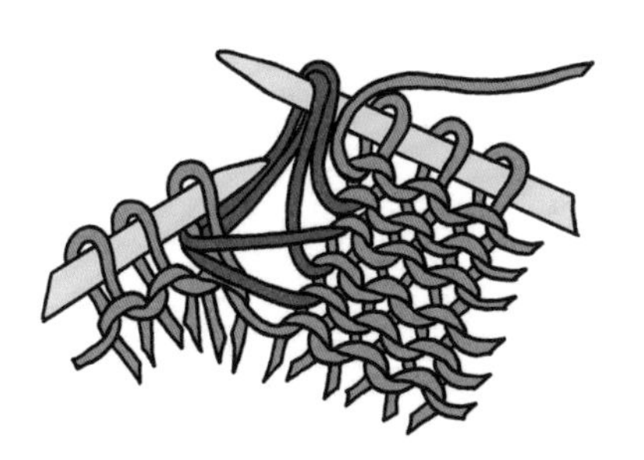

2. Move right-hand needle to back of work, pick up the two wraps from back to front. Place on left needle as shown in step 3 above, then purl together the wraps and wrapped stitch.

4-PLY WEIGHT
Set-up round: Work 32 (36, 40) sts in patt, use a piece of waste yarn to knit 32 (36, 40) sts to end of round, slip these 32 (36, 40) sts back to LH needle and knit them again with working yarn.
You now have 32 (36, 40) sts of waste yarn in your fabric. After completion of the toe, you will return to these sts, unpick the waste yarn and work an 'afterthought' heel.

Work Afterthought Heel
Pick up the RH leg of each of the 32 (36, 40) main yarn sts under the row of waste yarn sts. Turn the sock and rep the process again, picking up 32 (36, 40) sts from the other side of the waste yarn. You should now have 64 (72, 80) sts on your needles. Carefully remove the waste yarn, ensuring all sts are safely on your needles.
With working yarn, beg to work in the round as foll:
Next round: K32 (36, 40), pick up and knit 2 sts in gap between sole and instep, k32 (36, 40), pick up and knit 2 sts in gap between sole and instep. *68 (76, 84) sts*

Sizes 1 & 2 ONLY:
Next round (dec): *K32 (17), k2tog; rep from * to end.
66 (72) sts

ALL sizes again:
Knit 8 (8, 9) rounds.

Shape Heel
Sizes 2 & 3 ONLY:
Next round (dec): *K10 (12), k2tog; rep from * to end.
66 (78) sts
Next round: Knit.
Size 2 ONLY: Go to "ALL sizes again."
Size 3 ONLY: Continue as foll:
Next round (dec): *K11, k2tog; rep from * to end. *72 sts*
Next round: Knit.
Next round (dec): *K10, k2tog; rep from * to end. *66 sts*
Next round: Knit.

ALL sizes again:
Round 1 (dec): *K9, k2tog; rep from * to end. *60 sts*
Round 2: Knit.
Round 3 (dec): *K8, k2tog; rep from * to end. *54 sts*
Round 4: Knit.
Round 5 (dec): *K7, k2tog; rep from * to end. *48 sts*
Round 6: Knit.
Round 7 (dec): *K6, k2tog; rep from * to end. *42 sts*
Round 8: Knit.
Round 9 (dec): *K5, k2tog; rep from * to end. *36 sts*
Round 10: Knit.
Round 11 (dec): *K4, k2tog; rep from * to end. *30 sts*
Round 12: Knit.
Round 13 (dec): *K3, k2tog; rep from * to end. *24 sts*
Round 14: Knit.
Round 15 (dec): *K2, k2tog; rep from * to end. *18 sts*
Round 16 (dec): *K1, k2tog; rep from * to end. *12 sts*
Round 17 (dec): *K2tog; rep from * to end. *6 sts*
Break yarn, leaving a 15cm / 6" tail, thread tail through rem sts and pull tightly to close the heel.

DK WEIGHT

Set-up round: Work 24 (26, 28, 30) sts in patt, use a piece of waste yarn to knit 24 (26, 28, 30) sts to end of round, slip these 24 (26, 28, 30) sts back to LH needle and then knit them again with working yarn.

You now have 24 (26, 28, 40) sts of waste yarn in your fabric. After completion of the toe, you will return to these sts, unpick the waste yarn and work an 'afterthought' heel.

Work Afterthought Heel

Pick up the RH leg of each of the 24 (26, 28, 30) main yarn sts under the row of waste yarn sts. Turn the sock and rep the process again, picking up 24 (26, 28, 30) sts from the other side of the waste yarn. You should now have 48 (52, 56, 60) sts on your needles. Carefully remove the waste yarn, ensuring all sts are safely on your needles.

With working yarn, beg to work in the round as foll:

Next round: K24 (26, 28, 30), pick up and knit 2 sts in gap between sole and instep, k24 (26, 28, 30), pick up and knit 2 sts in gap between sole and instep. *52 (56, 60, 64) sts*

Sizes 1, 2 & 4 ONLY:

Next round (dec): *K11 (26, 14), k2tog; rep from * to end. *48 (54, 60) sts*

ALL sizes again:

Knit 8 (8, 9, 8) rounds.

Shape Heel

Sizes 2, 3 & 4 ONLY:

Next round (dec): *K7 (8, 8), k2tog; rep from * to end. *48 (54, 54) sts*

Next round: Knit.

Size 2 ONLY: Go to "ALL sizes again".

Sizes 3 & 4 ONLY: Continue as foll:

Next round (dec): *K7, k2tog; rep from * to end. *48 sts*

Next round: Knit.

ALL sizes again:

Round 1 (dec): *K6, k2tog; rep from * to end. *42 sts*

Round 2: Knit.

Round 3 (dec): *K5, k2tog; rep from * to end. *36 sts*

Round 4: Knit.

Round 5 (dec): *K4, k2tog; rep from * to end. *30 sts*

Round 6: Knit.

Round 7 (dec): *K3, k2tog; rep from * to end. *24 sts*

Round 8: Knit.

Round 9 (dec): *K2, k2tog; rep from * to end. *18 sts*

Round 10 (dec): *K1, k2tog; rep from * to end. *12 sts*

Round 11 (dec): *K2tog; rep from * to end. *6 sts*

Break yarn, leaving a 15cm / 6" tail, thread tail through rem sts and pull tightly to close the heel.

Flow Chart

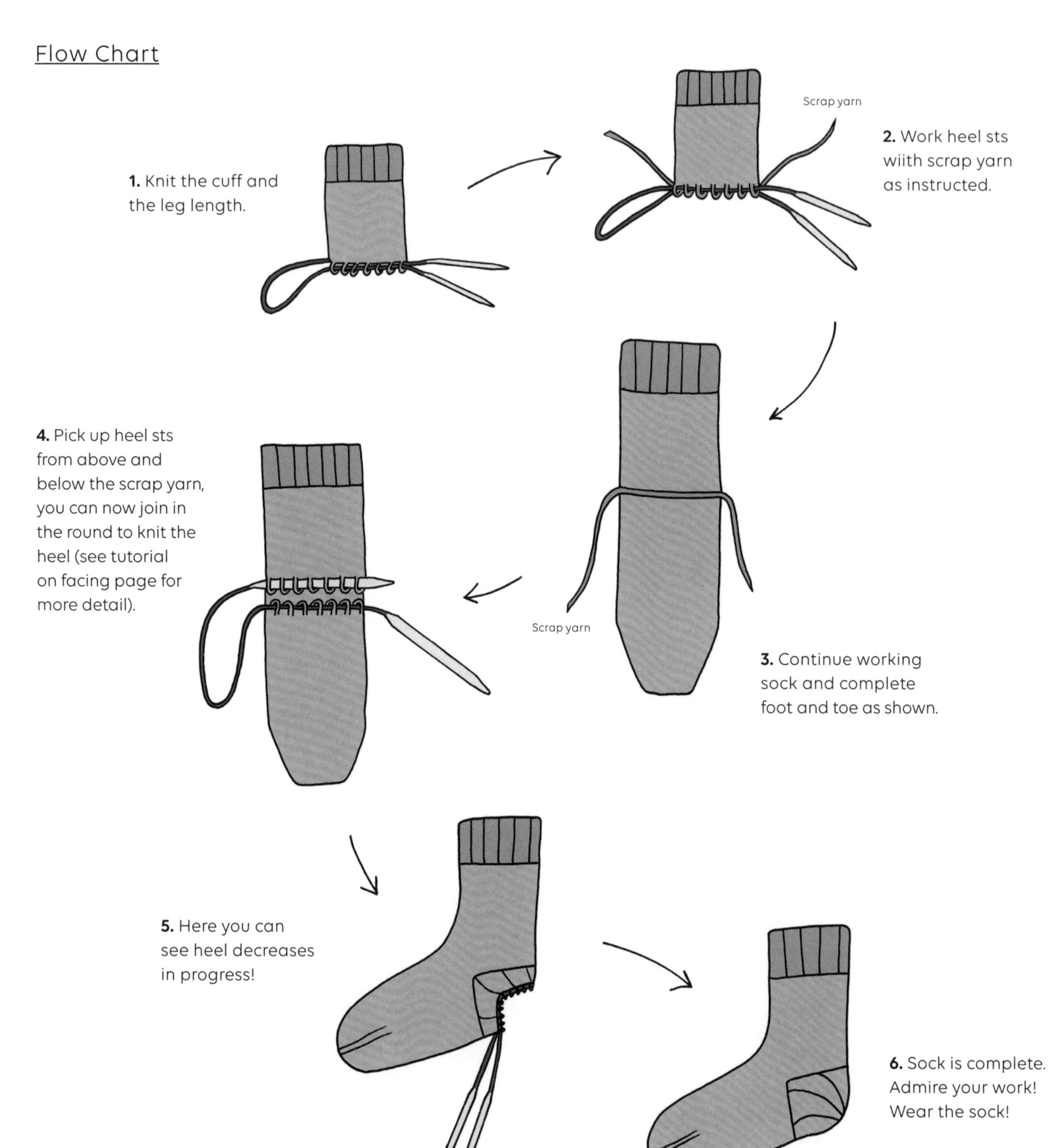

1. Knit the cuff and the leg length.
Scrap yarn
2. Work heel sts wiith scrap yarn as instructed.
3. Continue working sock and complete foot and toe as shown.
Scrap yarn
4. Pick up heel sts from above and below the scrap yarn, you can now join in the round to knit the heel (see tutorial on facing page for more detail).
5. Here you can see heel decreases in progress!
6. Sock is complete. Admire your work! Wear the sock!

Picking Up Stitches from Scrap Yarn

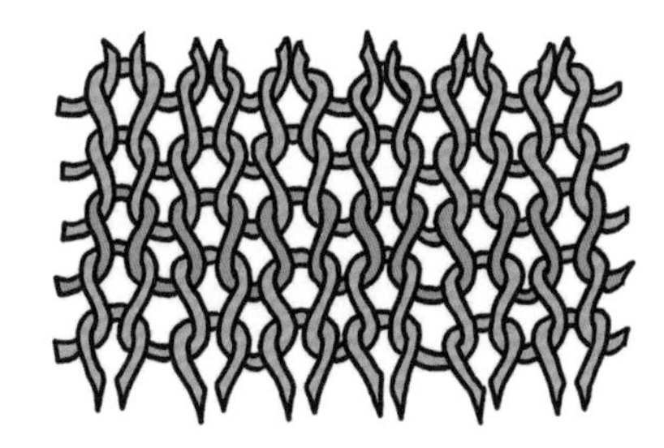

1. For an afterthought heel, you will be picking up stitches above and below the scrap yarn you knitted into the sock. You'll then remove the scrap yarn and work in the round to make the heel. Here the scrap yarn is shown in blue.

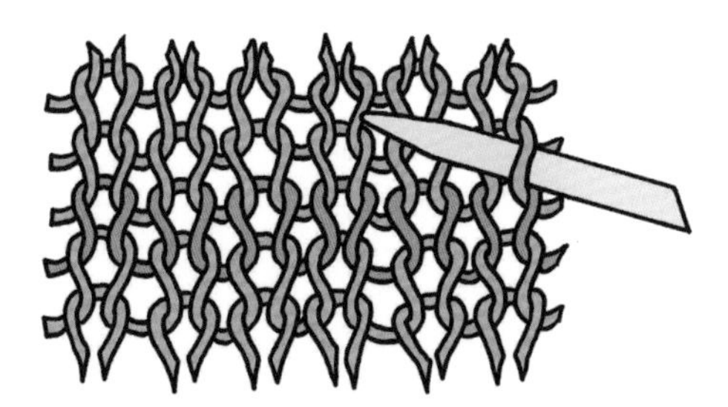

2. Locate the last scrap yarn stitch on the right-hand end of the row. Using your right-hand needle tip, pick up the stitch directly above it, making sure you only pick up the right-hand leg of the stitch as shown.

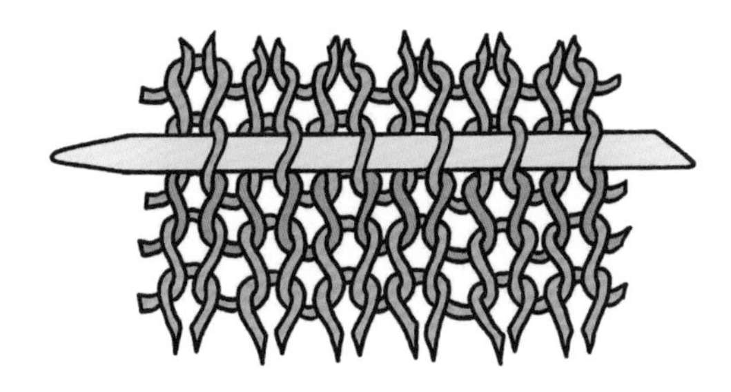

3. Continue picking up stitches in this manner from right to left, one for every stitch in the scrap yarn.

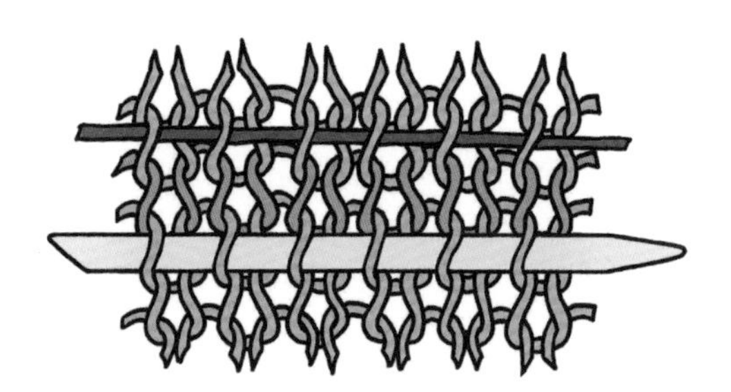

4. Manoeuvre your work so these stitches can slide onto the cable of your circular needle, and bring the needle round to pick up the stitches below the scrap yarn. As before you are only picking up the right leg of each stitch.

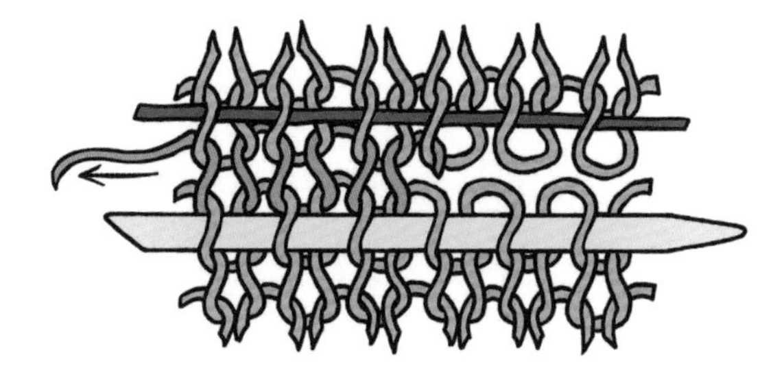

5. Now remove the waste yarn. You can use a spare needle to gently pull this out stitch by stitch, or very carefully snip the scrap yarn out with a pair of small, sharp scissors. Your picked up stitches will now be sat on the needles ready to work the heel.

Fibre + Colour

Socks probably endure the most challenging circumstances of any knitted clothing. They are exposed to friction between the foot and floor and also within footwear. To mitigate this, yarns designed to be made into socks are often spun with a high twist and include a strengthening fibre such as nylon, silk, or mohair. The majority of the fibre in a sock yarn is often wool. This is because wool has a natural memory that will allow the sock to stretch to fit and maintain its shape while it is being worn rather than become baggy and fall down or move around. Some of the fibres that are used to strengthen the sock yarn don't have the same elastic properties, so yarns with a high silk content, for example, may not be suitable for socks.

Socks that are worn in boots or shoes may felt while they are being worn. The properties for felting - heat, friction, and moisture - are all present in a shoe or boot. Superwash yarns (yarns that have been treated with a chemical process that makes them suitable for machine washing) will felt less easily. However, felting on the sole of a sock could actually slow wear and tear on the sock! Felting fuses fibres of the yarns together, creating an extra dense fabric and therefore making darning or fixing holes in socks a less frequent necessity.

If you are intending to wear your socks exclusively indoors around your home, and therefore decreasing the need for utility, you can cast your net wider in terms of yarn choice, perhaps by making some luxurious cashmere or Angora-infused bed socks.

When it comes to colour, keep in mind that solid colours will showcase stitch patterns clearly, especially more subtle designs such as gansey-inspired knit and purl patterns. If you choose hand-dyed or variegated yarns for these stitches, the detail may be obscured by the yarn. Multi-coloured yarns may be more suited to bolder stitches such as cables. Patterns with strong vertical elements like ribbing can work well with yarns that stripe or pool horizontally.

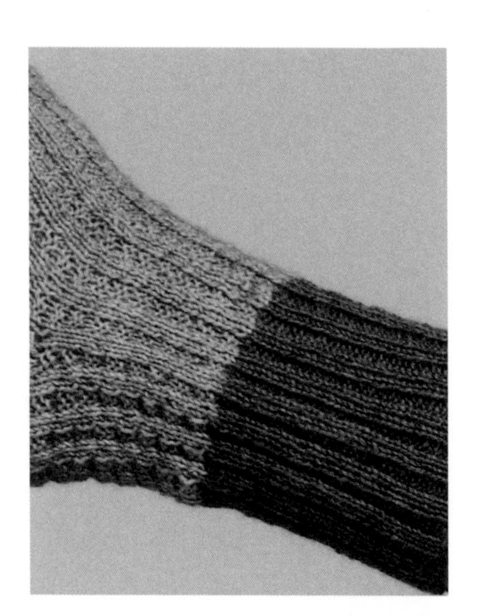

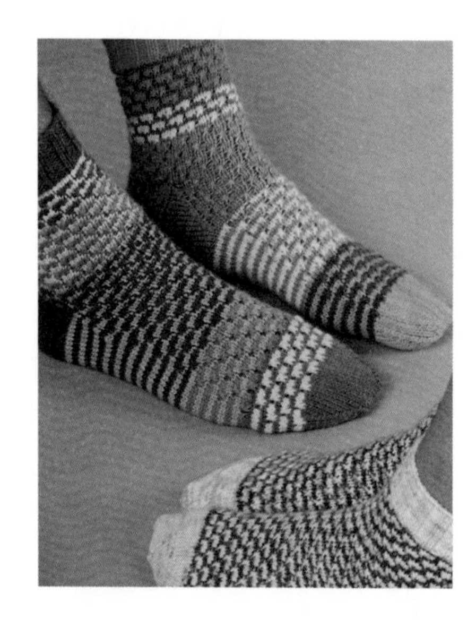

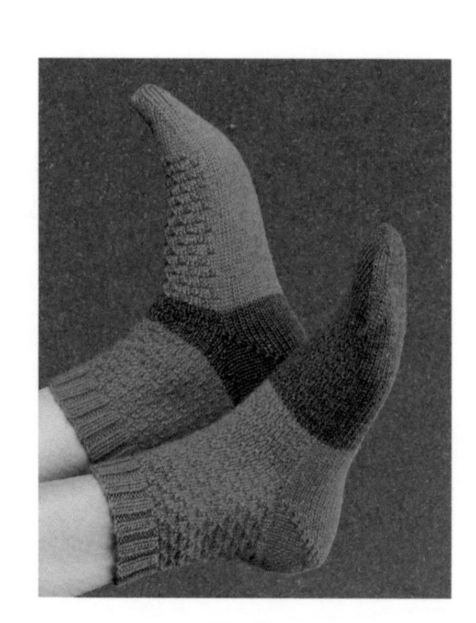

CHANGING COLOUR

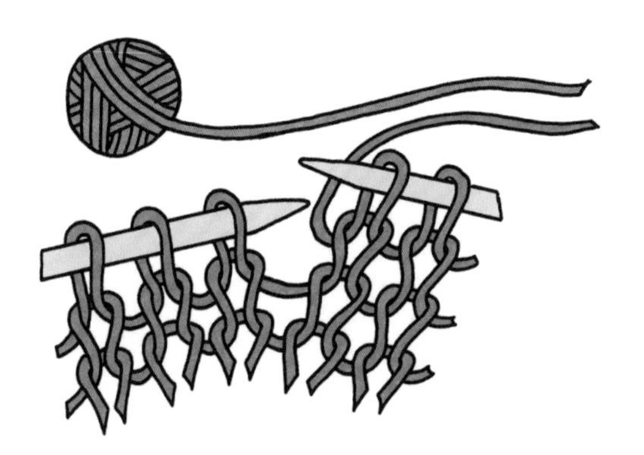

1. Leave a tail of at least 20cm / 8" of your 'old' yarn (shown in blue) and drop this yarn. Pick up the new yarn, ready to knit.

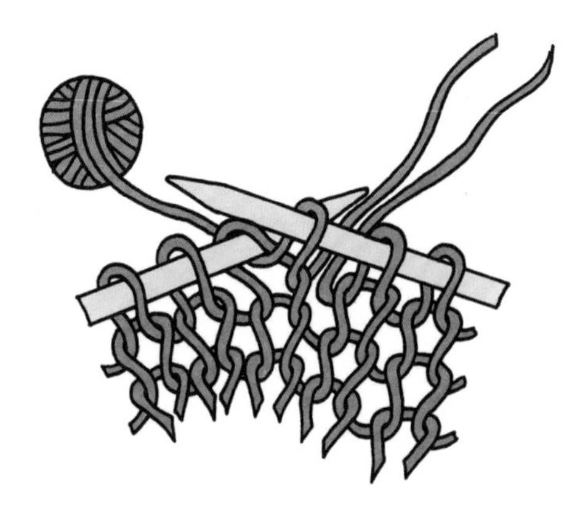

2. Insert right needle into next stitch to knit as normal but wrap with new yarn. Draw needle through to make stitch.

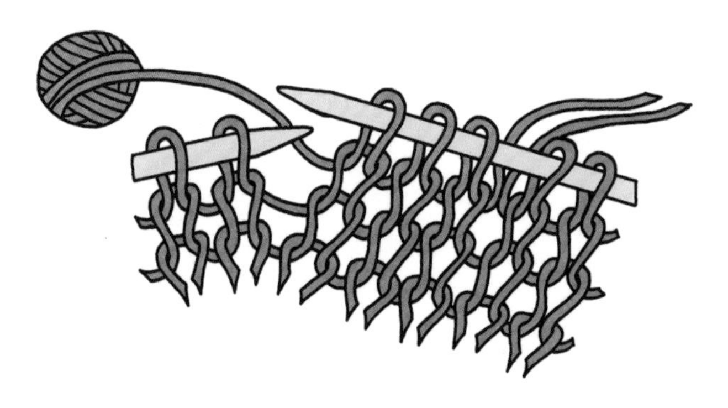

3. Continue knitting with new yarn, pulling tail ends to tighten the stitches if necessary. Weave in loose ends at the end of the project.

Types of Cuff

There's more than one way to knit a cuff! Typically, a knitted rib pattern is used to impart some elasticity to the top of the sock so that it stays up. Rib stitch patterns are made up of combinations of knit and purl stitches and are naturally stretchy, making them perfectly suited to cuffs. Here are some ways you can customise yours:

- Play with the length of your cuff - they can be quite short or very long. You can even make the cuff long enough to fold over.

- Change up the rib pattern - try [p2, k2] (Fig.1), [p4, k4] (Fig.2), or even [p3, k1tbl] (Fig.3)

- Experiment with different cast-ons to achieve various levels of elasticity or a particularly tailored look.

- Make sure you use a loose and/or stretchy cast-on! The top of your sock has to stretch over each part of your foot, heel, ankle, and calf. See page 146 for our long-tail cast-on tutorial.

Fig.1

Fig.2

Fig.3

KNIT THROUGH BACK LOOP (ktbl)

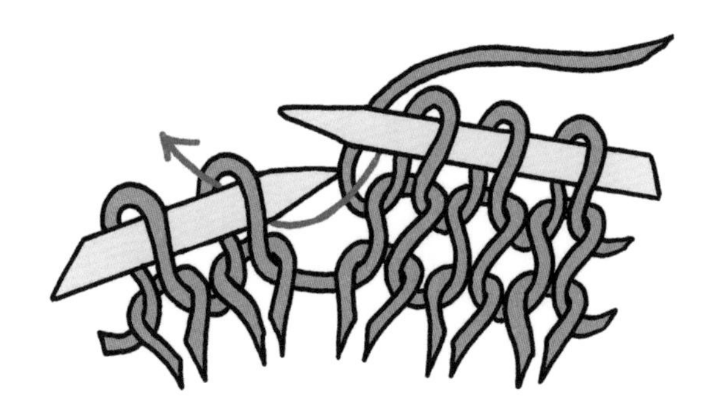

1. Bring the right-hand needle to the back of your work and insert the needle tip into the back of the first stitch.

2. Wrap the yarn around the tip of the right-hand needle and pull the yarn through the stitch - as if you were working a regular knit stitch.

3. Ta-da! ktbl is a twisted stitch which now sits on the right-hand needle

LONG-TAIL CAST-ON

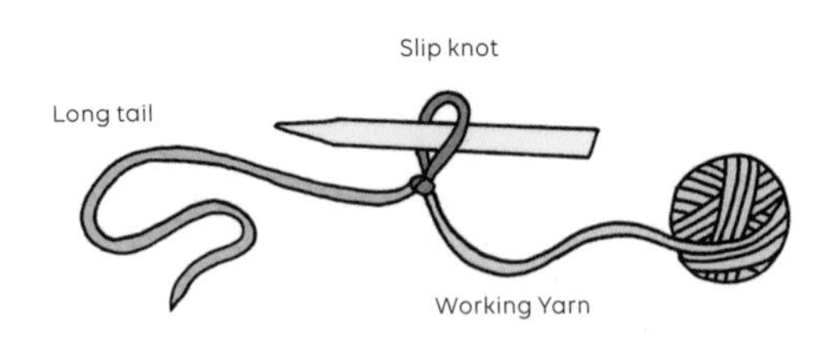

1. Make a slip knot leaving a generous tail and place on needle. Your tail will need to be at least 3 times the length of the project's finished measurement to make the required number of stitches.

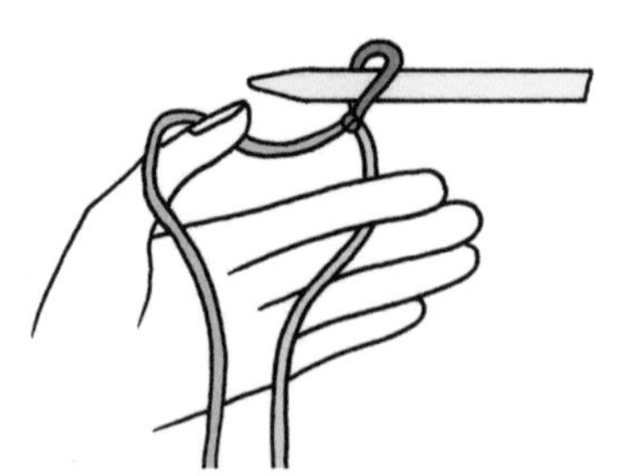

2. Arrange yarn on left hand, with the long tail over thumb and the working yarn threaded behind index finger.

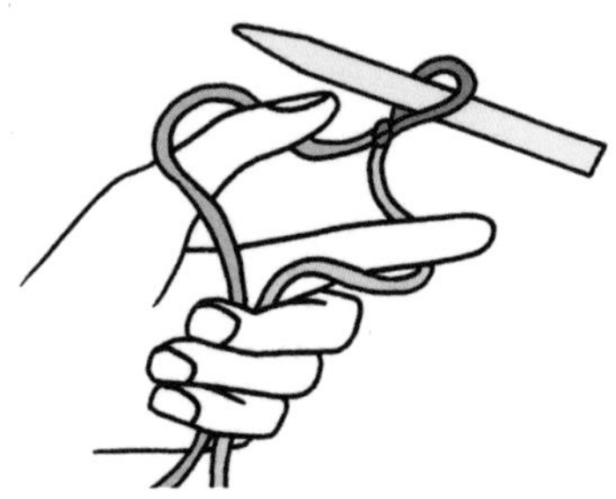

3. Bend fingers to trap the long tail and working yarn and hold secure.

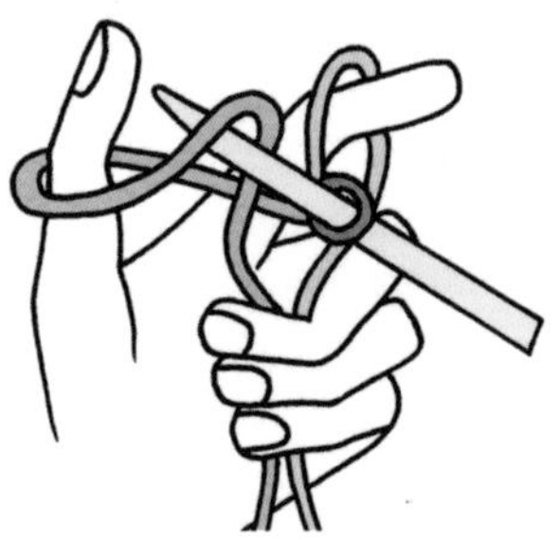

4. Scoop needle from left to right to pick up tail yarn on left side of thumb.

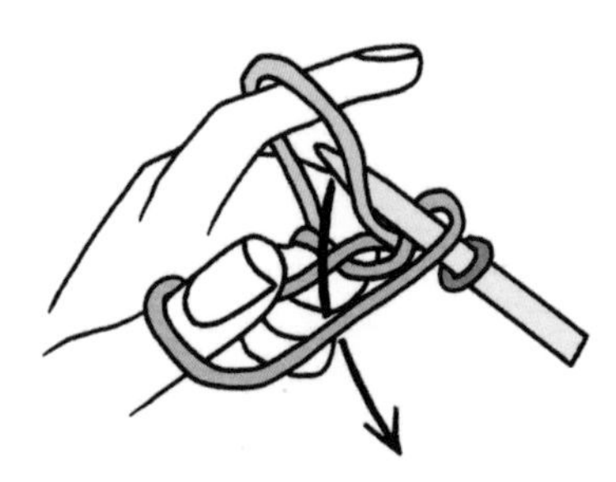

5. Lean needle to pick up working yarn looped over index finger.

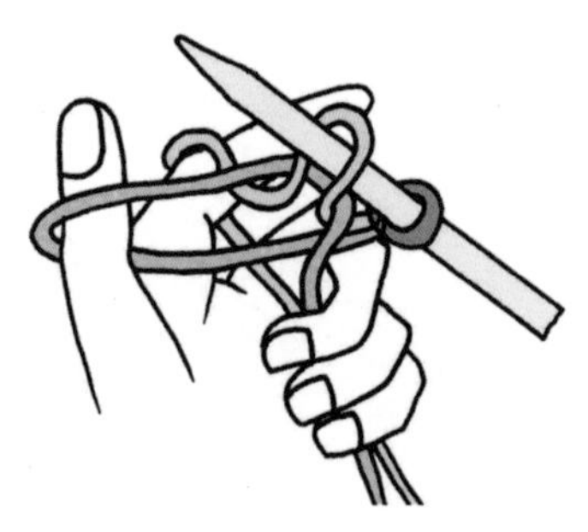

6. Draw working yarn through to create stitch on needle.

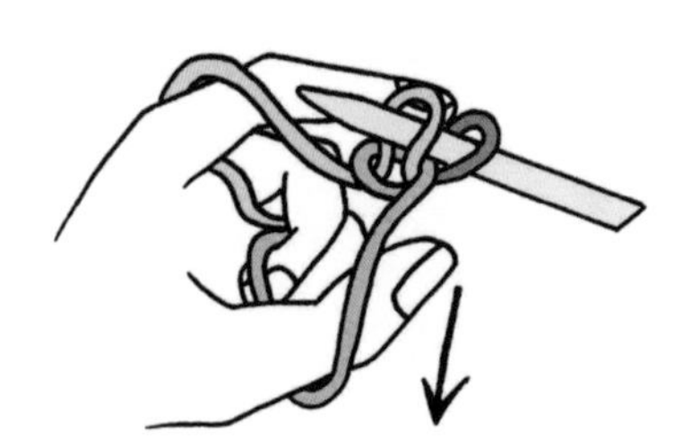

7. Make sure your new stitch is snug on the needle by gently pulling yarn tail with thumb in the direction shown. Don't pull too hard, you don't want your stitches to be too tight.

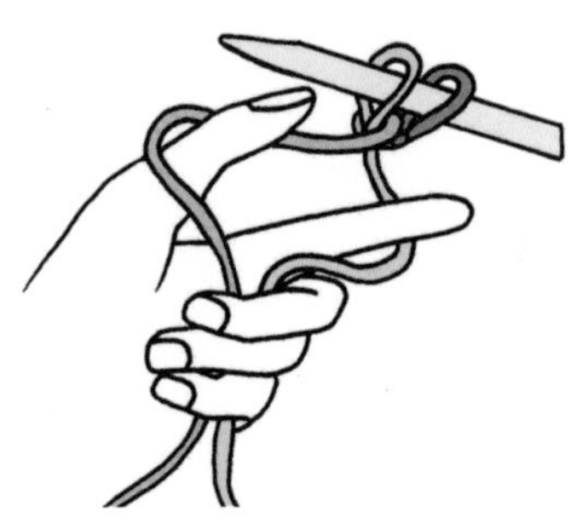

8. Ensure tail yarn and working yarn are arranged as detailed in Step 2 and repeat Steps 3 -7 to cast on required number of stitches.

GRAFTING

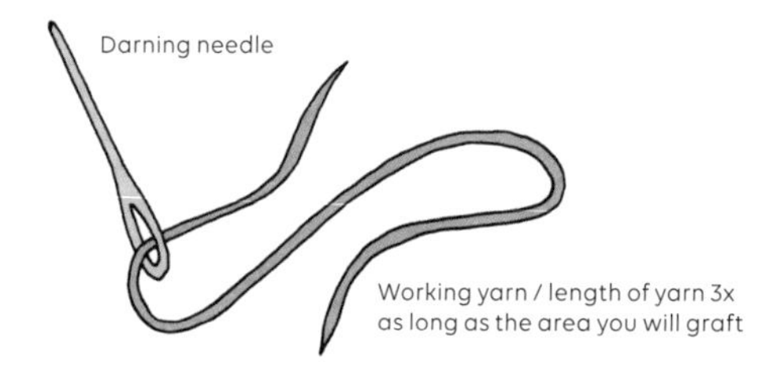

1. Thread your tapestry needle with working yarn or other length of yarn.

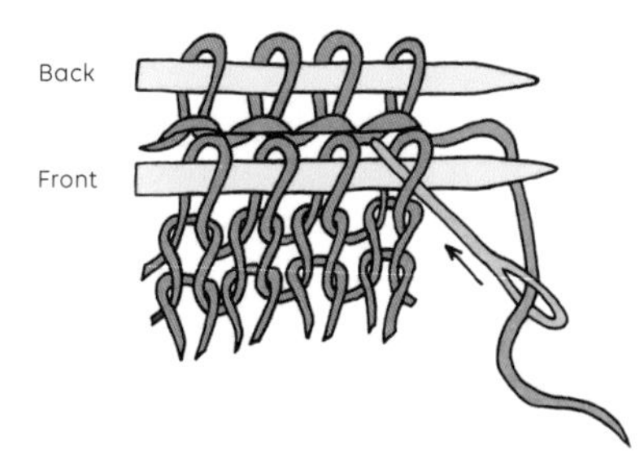

2. Arrange needles so they are parallel, with stitches at tip. Insert tapestry needle purlwise into first stitch on front needle and pull yarn through, leaving stitch on front needle.

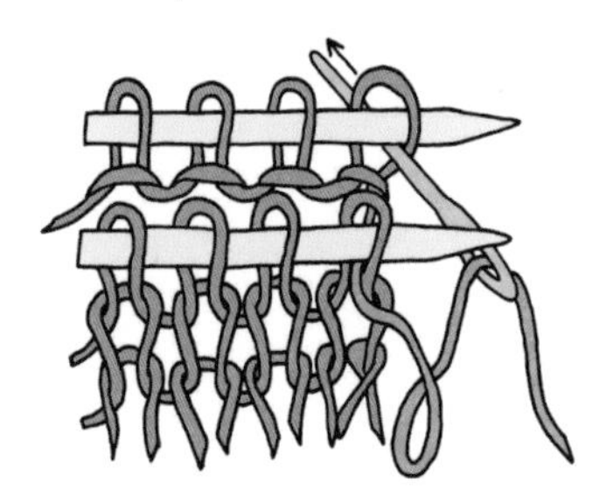

3. Insert tapestry needle knitwise into first stitch on back needle. Pull yarn through, leaving stitch on back needle.

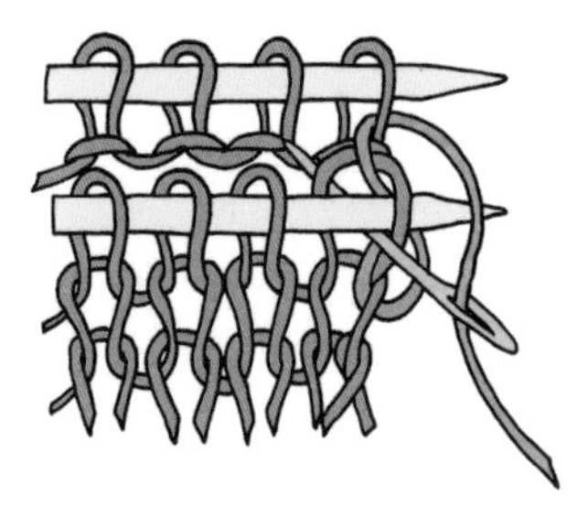

4. Insert tapestry needle knitwise into first stitch on front needle.

5. Slip this stitch off front needle. Enter next stitch purlwise and pull yarn through, leaving stitch on the front needle.

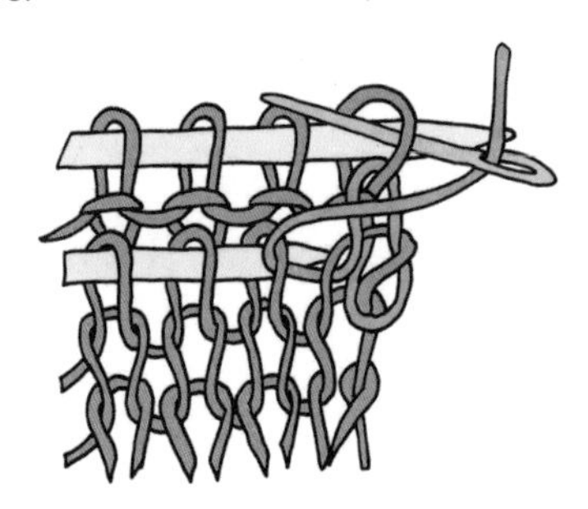

6. Insert tapestry needle purlwise into first stitch on back needle.

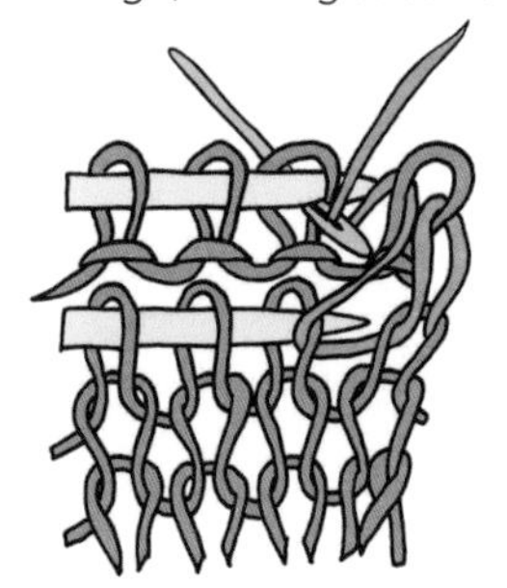

7. Slip this stitch off back needle. Enter next stitch knitwise and pull yarn through, leaving this stitch on back needle.

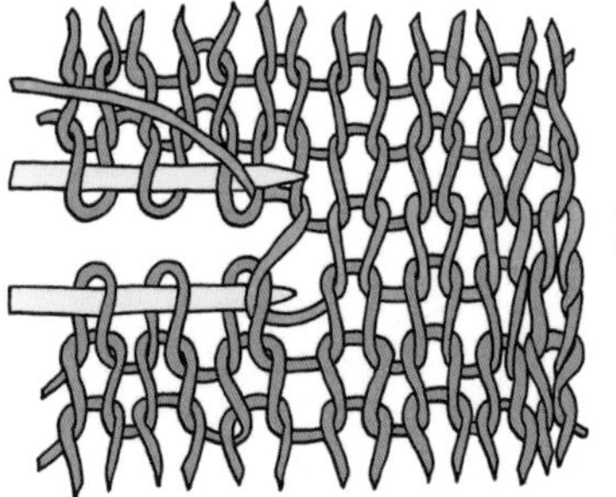

8. Repeat steps 4-7, weaving stitches together and adjusting tension as you go. Continue until one stitch is left on each needle. To finish, insert tapestry needle knitwise into stitch on front needle and slip off. Repeat purlwise on back needle and slip off. Adjust tension and weave in ends.

TYPES OF DECREASES

Slip Slip Knit (ssk) - Left-Leaning Decrease

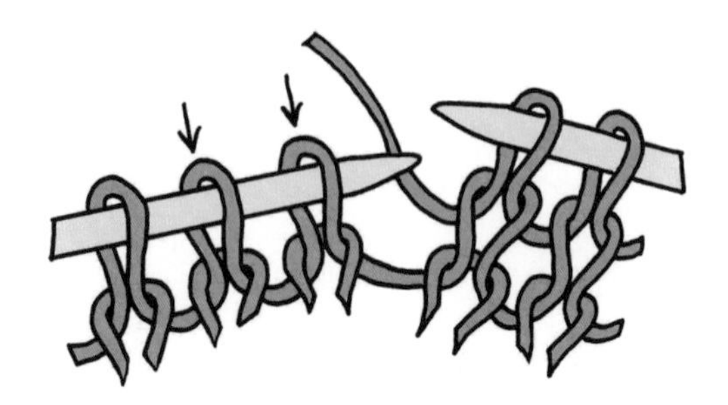

1. The arrows indicate the stitches you will work for this decrease.

2. Slip next two stitches, one after the other, from left to right needle knitwise (inserting the needle into each stitch as if to knit but passing the stitch to the right needle without knitting).

3. Now slip these stitches back onto the left needle, one at a time. They will now be twisted, as shown.

4. Knit through both stitches by inserting your needle through them from front to back, as shown. The stitches are twisted so you are knitting through the back loop.

5. Ta da!

Knit Two Together (k2tog) - Right-Leaning Decrease

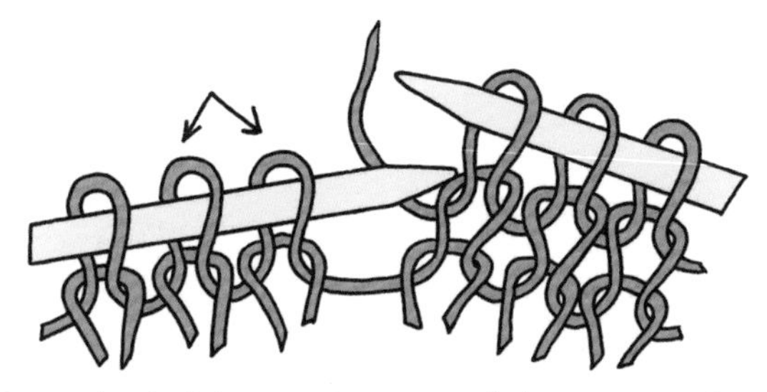

1. This method of decreasing uses all the same actions as a standard knit stitch, but the first and second stitch on your left needle are worked together.

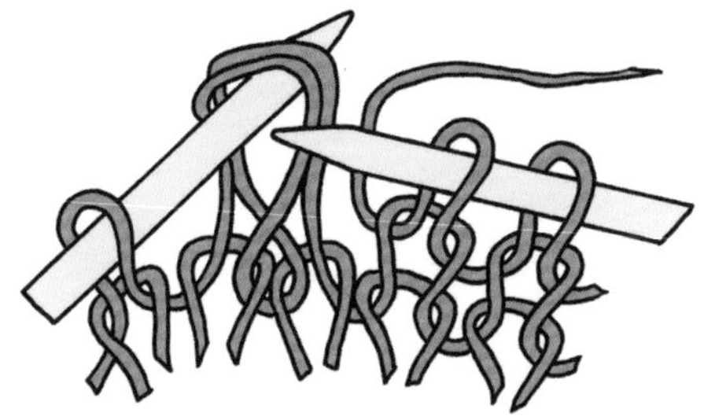

2. Insert right needle into these two stitches. First enter the second stitch from front to back, then the first in the same manner, as shown.

3. Wrap or pick yarn as you would for a knit stitch.

4. Draw the yarn through, and drop two stitches off left needle.

Purl Two Together (p2tog)

1. Insert right needle into the front of the first two stitches on left needle.

2. Wrap yarn over needle as you would for a purl stitch.

3. Draw the yarn through, and drop two stitches off left needle.

KNITTING IN THE ROUND

Joining to Work in the Round

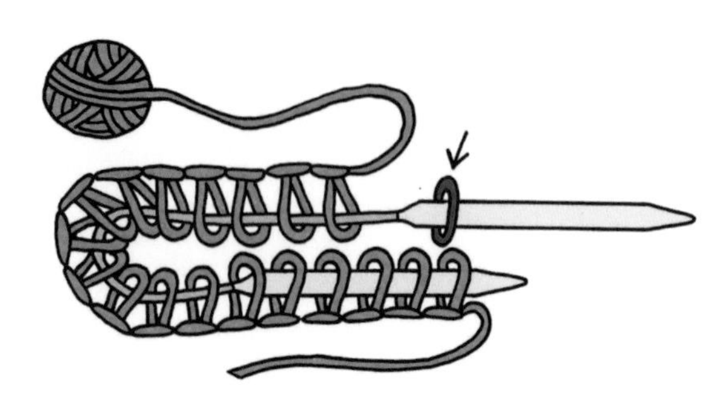

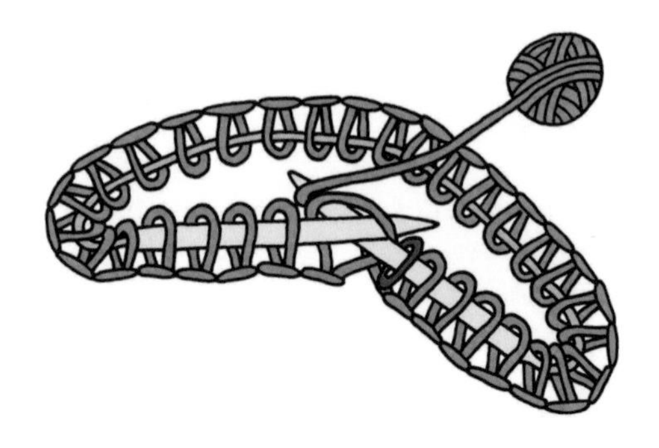

1. Cast on and ensure your stitches are not twisted. To mark the beginning of your round, place stitch marker on right needle.

2. The first stitch of the round will be the first cast-on stitch. Manoeuvre your needles so your needle with the working yarn is the right needle, and insert into first stitch to knit.

Using Magic Loop

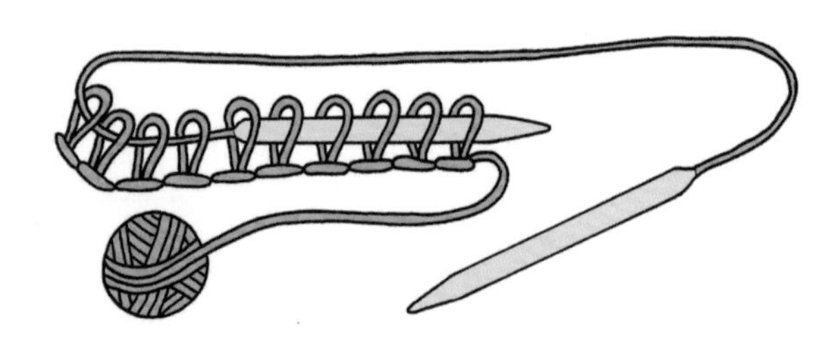

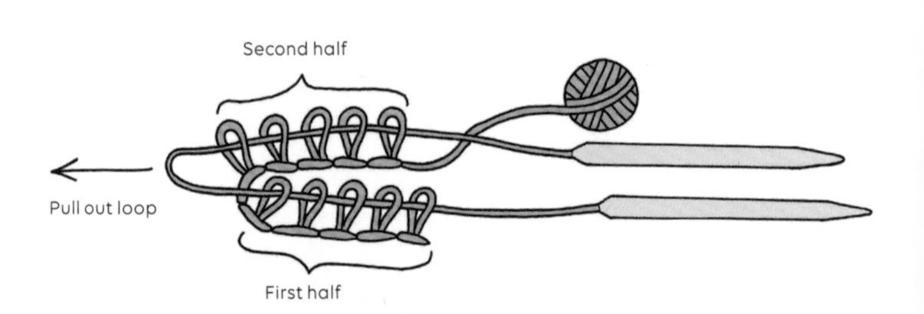

1. Cast on required number of stitches.

2. Split stitches in half and draw cord of circular needles out, creating a loop in the middle of stitches. Arrange two halves of stitches with working yarn on the second half/back needle. Be careful not to twist stitches.

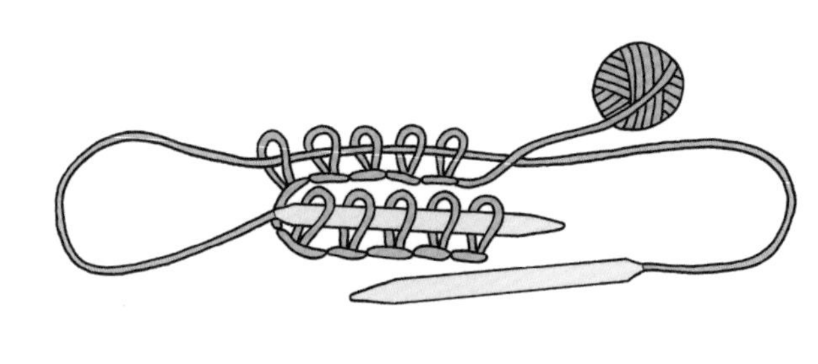

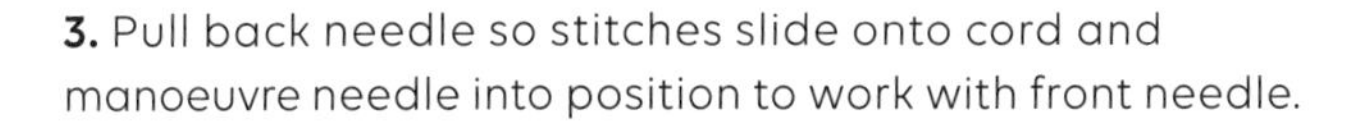

3. Pull back needle so stitches slide onto cord and manoeuvre needle into position to work with front needle.

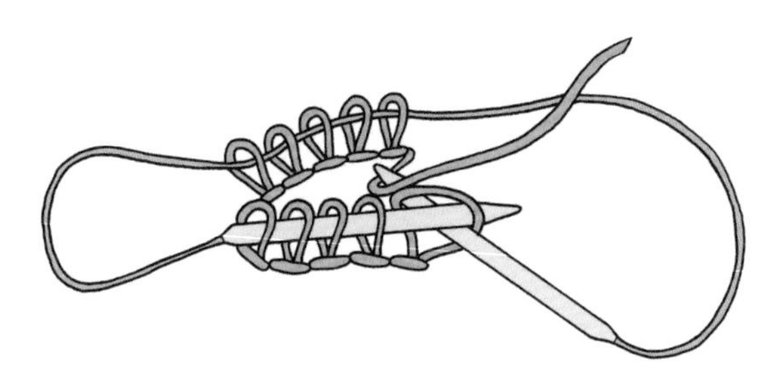

4. Knit first stitch, drawing working yarn from back needle. Pull yarn snug to avoid leaving a gap.

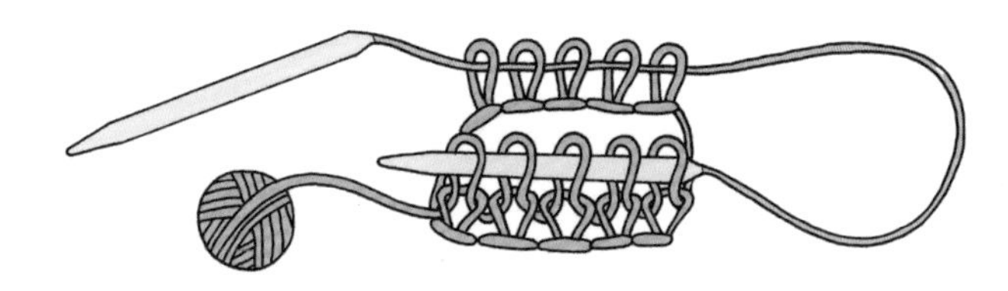

5. Knit to end.

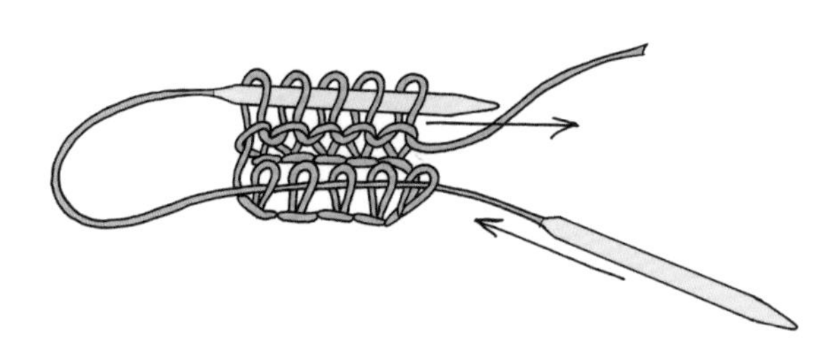

6. Turn work 180 degrees clockwise. Rearrange needles by first drawing front needle back and sliding stitches from cord onto needle. Then draw out back needle, allowing stitches just worked to slide onto cable.

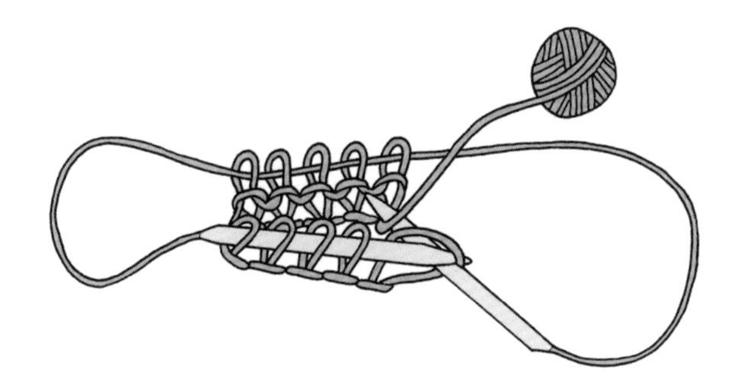

7. Knit your first stitch as shown. Pay attention to where your working yarn is; make sure it isn't looped around the cable of the circular needle or under the needle, which will create a gap. Knit all stitches to end. One round has now been worked.

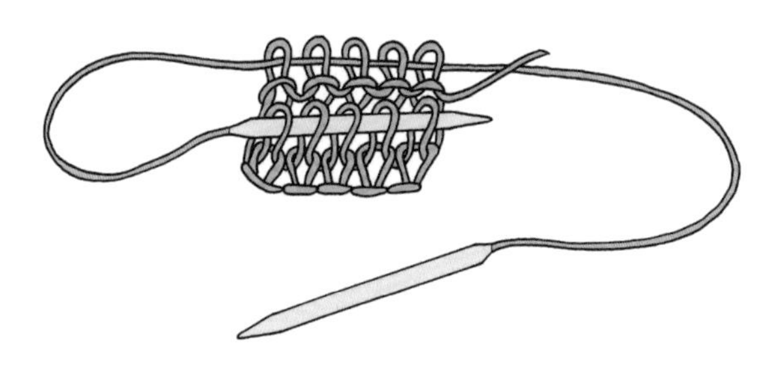

8. Repeat steps 6-7 to continue knitting in the round.

How to Knit a Small Circumference in the Round Using Double-Pointed Needles (aka DPNs)

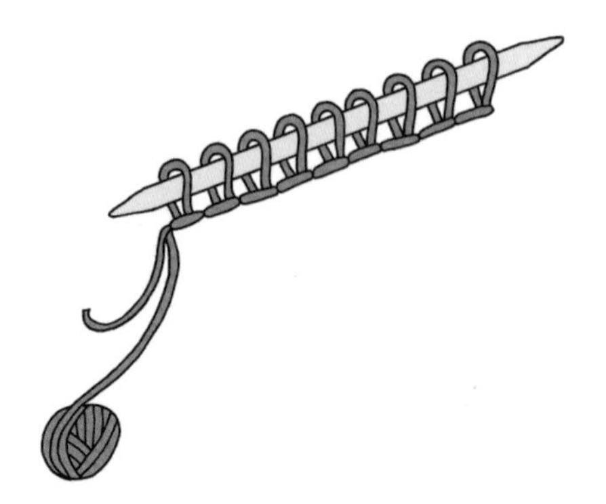

1. Cast on required number of stitches onto one DPN.

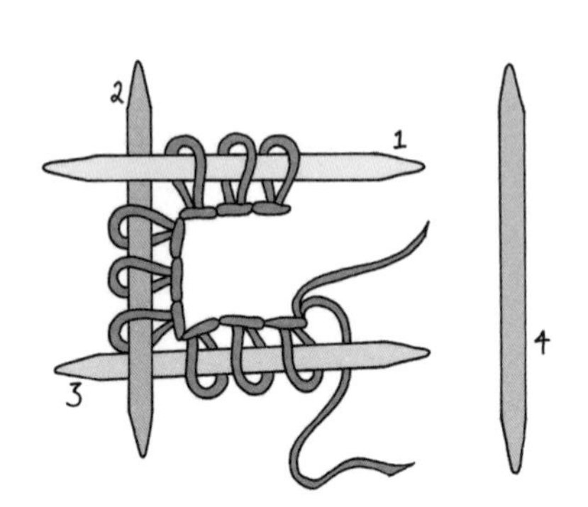

2. Redistribute stitches evenly over three DPNs by sliding purlwise, one at a time, onto needles. Arrange trio of DPNs as three sides of a square, with last cast-on stitch in the bottom right corner on DPN 3. Make sure stitches are not twisted. Fouth needle is ready for action!

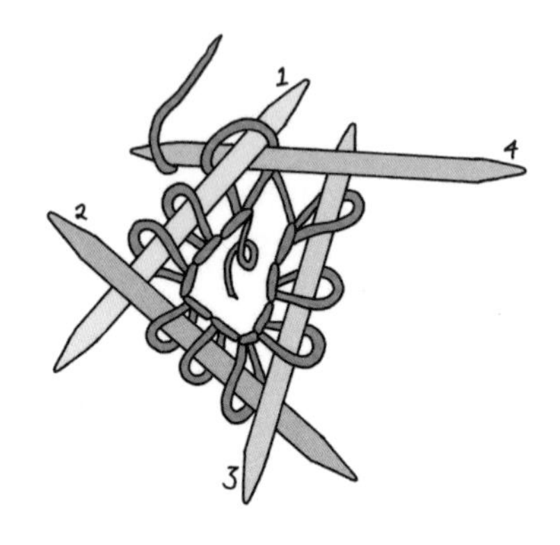

3. Bring tips of DPN 3 and 1 together to form a triangle. Insert DPN into first stitch on DPN 1 and knit this stitch. Knit across all stitches on DPN 1. DPN 4 now holds stitches and DPN 1 is empty.

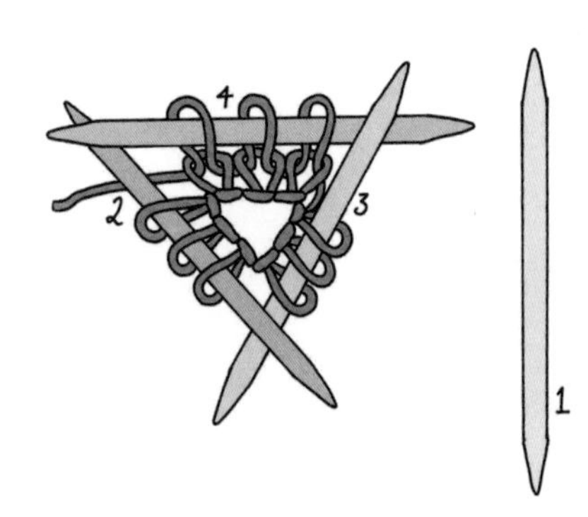

4. Now use DPN 1 to knit across stitches on DPN 2.

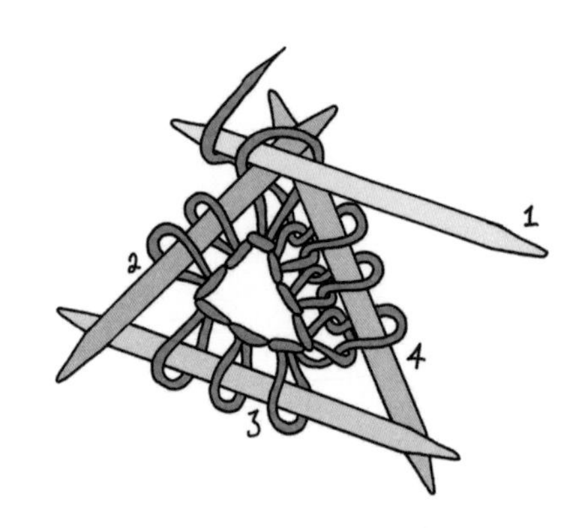

5. Continue knitting across each of the three DPNS in turn.

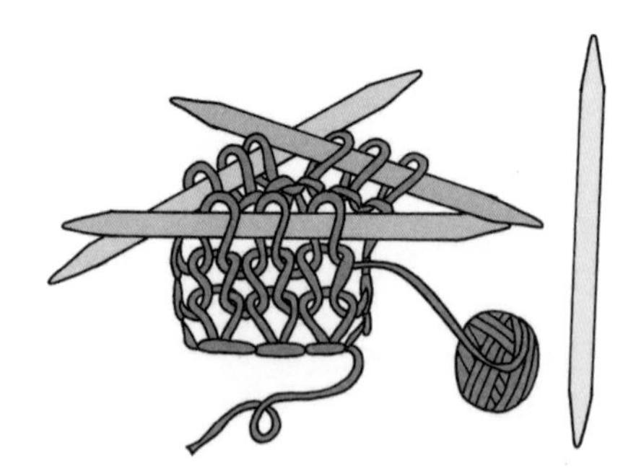

6. After a few rows, your knitting will look like this. It gets easier to work with DPNs when there's more fabric to anchor them, so your hard work will pay off!

READING FROM CHARTS

If you are relatively new to knitting, reading charts can be daunting. But, in reality, they can make your work a lot easier. And once you've learned how to read charts, it's like knowing a secret code. Chart symbols are just more simplified representations of knitting terms. So if you know that 'k' means 'knit' then go one step further and know that □ (an empty square) means 'knit' too. Likewise, 'p' means 'purl' and ⊡ is its symbol.

When you are working on a flat piece of knitting, you turn your work back and forth. When using a chart while working back and forth, you read the chart right to left on the Right Side and left to right on the Wrong Side, reversing the meaning of the symbols on the Wrong Side. Luckily for us, we're almost exclusively working in the round in the patterns for this book, so the charts are almost always read right to left (like the direction of the knitting on your needles) and there is rarely any need to reverse the meaning of the symbols.

The symbols themselves often look a lot like the stitches they represent. ⊡ is reminiscent of a purl bump, ◎ looks like the hole made by a yarn over. And ⧄ and ⧅ lean in the same direction as the decreases they depict. Every row of the chart represents a row of knitting and every column denotes a stitch.

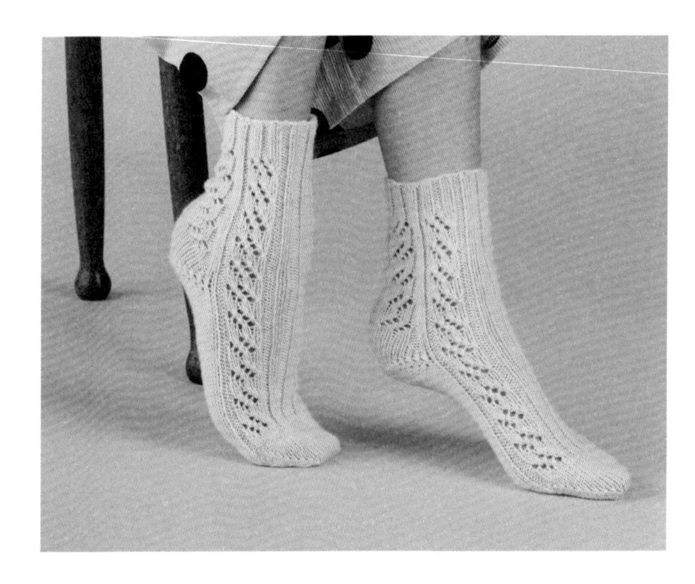

Many knitters with an initial fear of charts find them the easiest way to follow a lace or cable pattern once they jump in and try them! One of our favourite tips for keeping your place in a chart is to use removable masking tape (often called washi tape) or highlighter tape to mark which row you are working on.

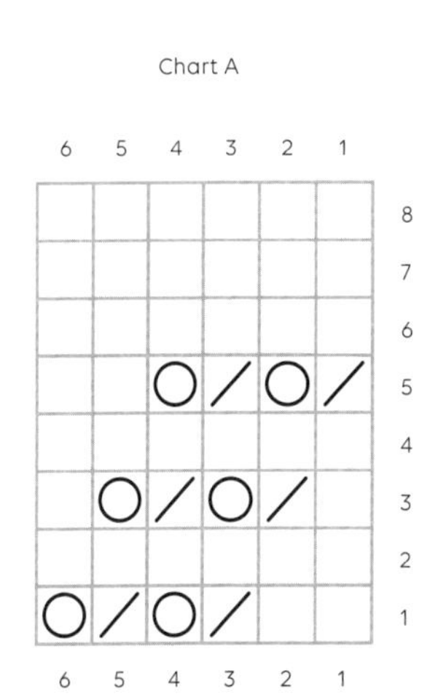

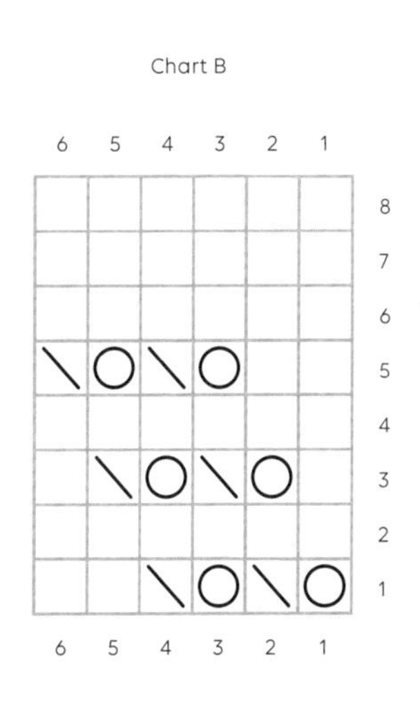

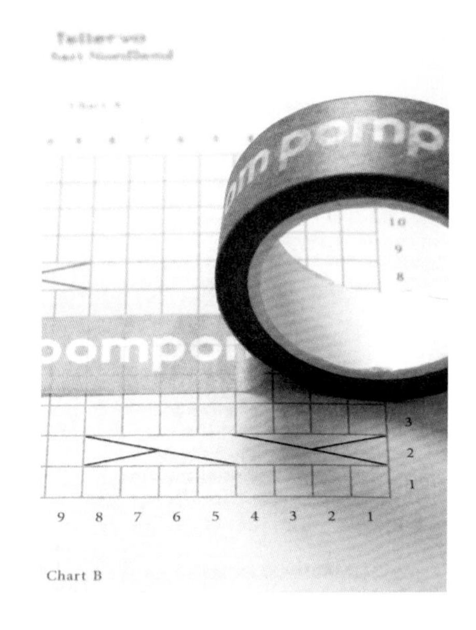

Ready Set Socks

CABLES

1x1 Cable Left Twist (1/1LC) without cable needle

1. With yarn held in back of work, slip two stitches knitwise, one at a time, from the left-hand needle onto the right-hand needle.

2. Bring the left-hand needle around to the front of your work. Place these two slipped stitches back onto your left-hand needle by initially inserting your left-hand needle into the front of the first slipped stitch, and then through the second slipped stitch.

3.Slip the two stitches off the right-hand needle onto the left-hand needle. These stitches are now twisted.

4. Knit the next stitch on your left-hand needle, make sure to knit the one that is sitting behind your work.

5. Knit the remaining twisted stitch.

1x1 Cable Right Twist (1/1RC) without cable needle

1. With yarn held in back of work, insert your right-hand needle into the next two stitches on your left-hand needle by entering the second stitch front to back, and then the first in the same manner - as if you were about to k2tog.

2. Slip the two stitches from the left-hand needle onto the right-hand needle.

3. Insert your left-hand needle into the front of the first stitch on the right-hand needle as shown.

4. Slip this stitch onto the left-hand needle.

5. Insert your left-hand needle into the front of the next stitch on the right needle as shown.

6. Slip this stitch onto the left-hand needle so both stitches are in a new twisted orientation. Knit the twisted stitches, one at a time, as normal.

2x2 Left Cable with Needle (2/2LC)

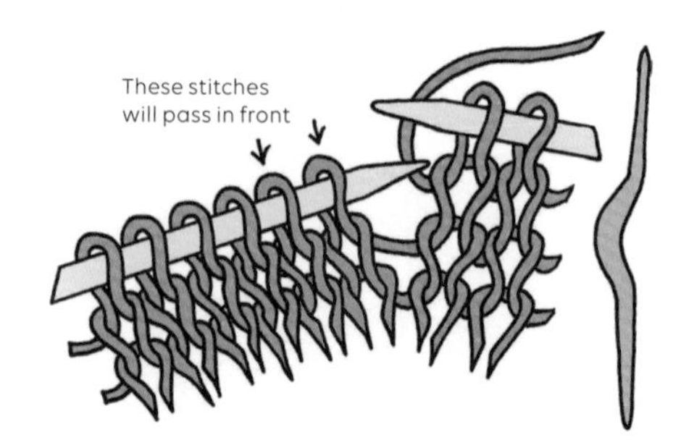

1. Work to stitches specified in pattern (shown here in pink).

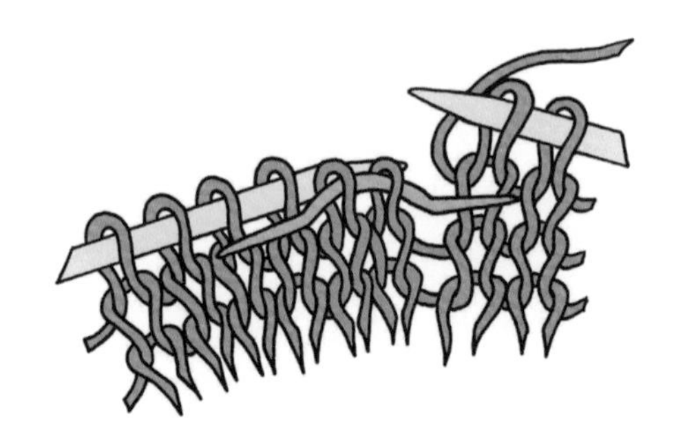

2. Slip the two stitches, one at a time, purlwise onto a cable needle. Make sure the cable needle now sits at the front of your work and leave it there for now.

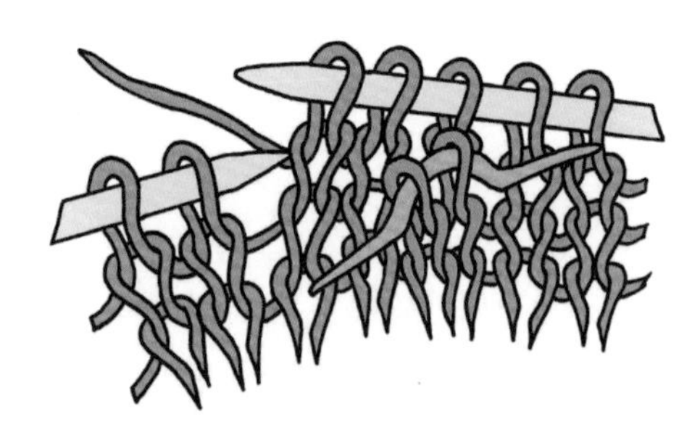

3. Knit the next two stitches on the left-hand needle, ignoring the stitches on the cable needle.

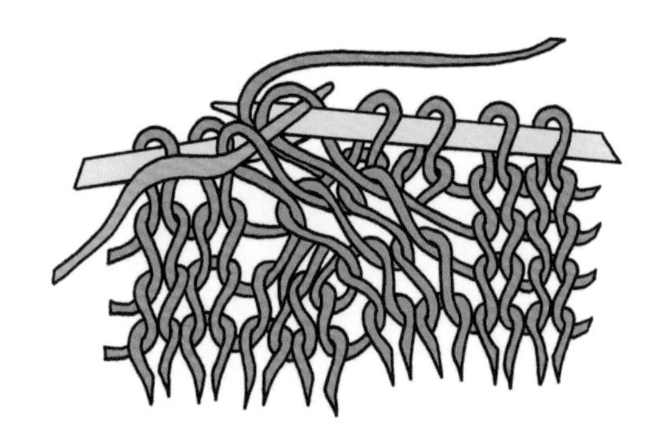

4. Manoeuvre the cable needle so it sits in place of the left-hand needle and knit the two held stitches directly off the cable needle and onto the right-hand needle.

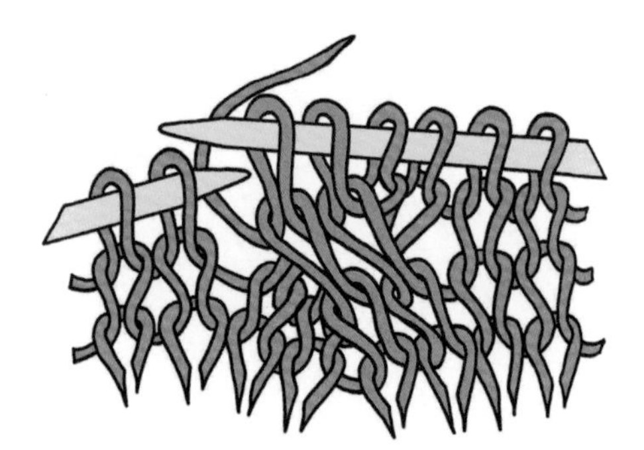

5. The cable has now been worked, you have made a left leaning cable.

Top Tip!

The steps shown here demonstrate a left leaning cable worked over 4 stitches (2/2LC), the principles of which can be applied to other cable terms. The number of stitches you put on hold (the first number in the abbreviation) plus the number of stitches worked before returning to held stitches (second number in abbreviation) will dictate the size of your cable. The direction of your cable will be determined by holding the slipped stitches in front (left-leaning, shown here) or in back (right-leaning, shown facing).

2x2 Right Cable with Needle (2/2RC)

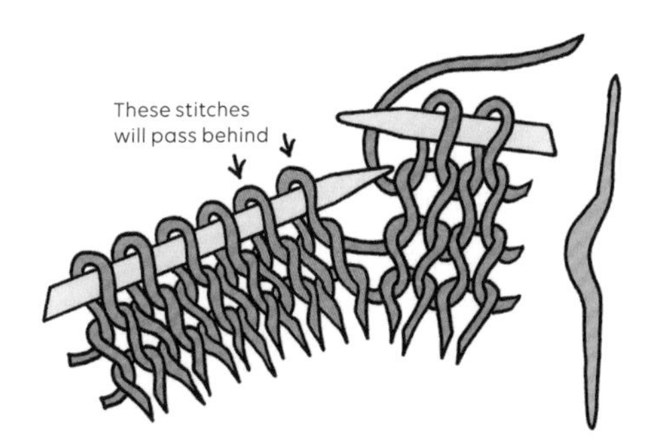

1. Work to stitches specified in pattern (shown here in pink).

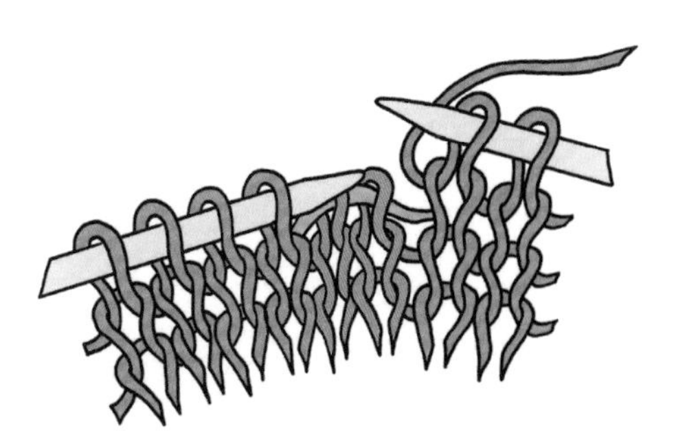

2. Slip the two stitches, one at a time, purlwise onto a cable needle. Make sure the cable needle now sits at the back of your work and leave it there for now.

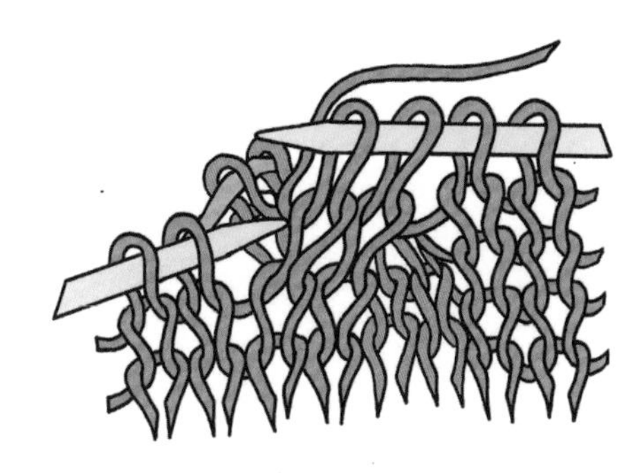

3.Knit the next two stitches on the left-hand needle, ignoring the stitches on the cable needle.

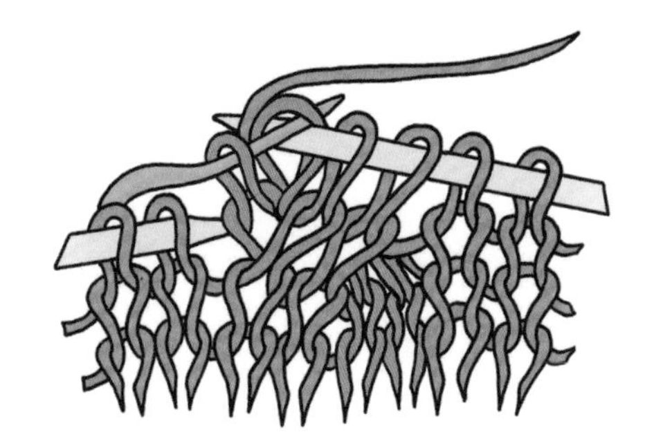

4. Manoeuvre the cable needle so it sits in place of the left-hand needle and knit the two held stitches directly off the cable needle and onto the right-hand needle.

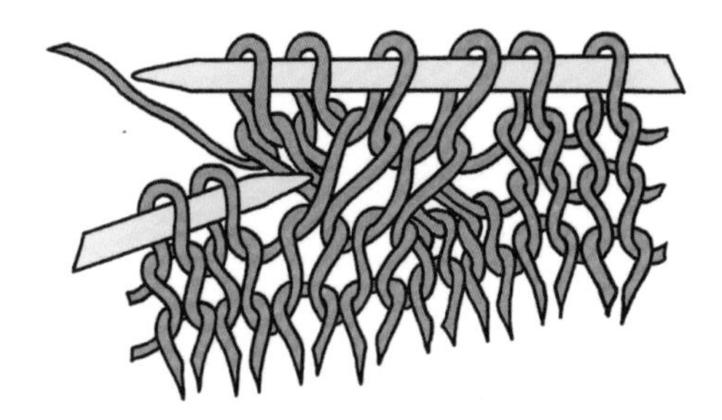

5. The cable has now been worked, you have made a right leaning cable.

ABBREVIATIONS + TECHNIQUES

beg	Beginning
cast off	Bind off
dec	Decrease
DPN(s)	Double-pointed needle(s)
foll	Follow(s)/Following
G st	Garter stitch
inc	Increase
k	Knit
k2tog	Knit 2 stitches together
LH	Left hand
patt	Pattern (i.e. work in pattern)
PM	Place marker
p	Purl
p2tog	Purl 2 stitches together
rem	Remain(s)/Remaining
rep	Repeat
RH	Right hand
RS	Right side of fabric
sl	Slip
ssk	Slip 2 stitches knitwise one at a time, knit together through the back loops
SM	Slip marker
st(s)	Stitch(es)
St st	Stocking stitch (stockinette): knit on RS rows, purl on WS rows
tbl	Through the back loop
tog	Together
wyib	With yarn held in back of work
wyif	With yarn held in front of work
w&t	Wrap and turn: On RS rows, sl st from left needle to right needle, move yarn to front, sl st from right needle to left needle, move yarn to back, turn. On WS rows, move yarn to back, sl st from left needle to right needle, move yarn to front, sl st back to left needle, turn.
WS	Wrong side of fabric
yo	Yarn over needle and into working position

Foot Length / Shoe Size Conversion

All of the patterns in *Ready Set Socks* start with the cuff and end with the toe, meaning foot length is fully adjustable. Simply knit the foot portion until it measures 0.5cm / ¼" less than actual foot length you need to ensure a perfect fit. If you are sharing the gift of handknitted socks, here is a useful reference for foot length according to shoe size, to help you get a snuggly fit for the lucky recipient!

UK Shoe Size	2	2.5	3	3.5	4	4.5	5	5.5	6	6.5	7	7.5	8	8.5	9	9.5	10	10.5	11	11.5	12
EU Shoe Size	35	35	35-36	36	36-37	37	37-38	38	38-39	39	39-40	40	40-41	41	42-43	43	43-44	44	44-45	45	46
US Shoe Size	4.5	5	5.5	6	6.5	7	7.5	8	8.5	9	9.5	10	10.5	10.5	10	10.5	11	11.5	12	12.5	13
cm	21.5	22	22.5	23	23	23.5	24	24	24.5	25	25.5	26	26.5	26.5	27	27	27.5	28	28.5	28.5	29
inches	8½	8¾	8¾	9	9	9¼	9½	9½	9¾	9¾	10	10¼	10½	10½	10¾	10¾	10¾	11	11¼	11¼	11½

YARN SUPPORT

Here's a handy list of the yarns we used in this book and where to get them. Can't find one of these yarns near you? Have a look at our substitutions advice on page 11 for help on choosing an alternative.

- Black Elephant
Sock
blackelephant.uk

- Coop Knits
Socks Yeah! / Socks Yeah! DK
coopknits.co.uk

- John Arbon Textiles
Exmoor Sock
jarbon.com

- La Bien Aimée
Merino Super Sock
labienaimee.com

- Neighborhood Fiber Co.
Studio Sock
neighborhoodfiberco.com

- Opal
Uni 4ply / Uni 6ply
woolwarehouse.co.uk

- Purl Soho
Posy
purlsoho.com

- Retrosaria Rosa Pomar
Mondim
retrosaria.rosapomar.com

- The Uncommon Thread
Tough Sock
theuncommonthread.co.uk

- The Wandering Flock
Sock
etsy.com/shop/TheWanderingFlock

- Qing Fibre
Classic Sock
qingfibre.com

- The Wool Kitchen
Sock
thewoolkitchen.com

- Vicki Brown Designs
Hand dyed DK, Hand dyed 4-ply Sock
vickibrowndesigns.com

ACKNOWLEDGEMENTS

Like everything at Pom Pom, *Ready Set Socks* is the product of a group effort and couldn't have happened any other way! Managing Editor Amy Collins is the glue that holds us all together, takes the ideas we have, and turns them into reality. Pattern designer Rachel Coopey suggested to us that one day it might be good to do a sock book in the style of our previous title, *Ready Set Raglan*. We wholeheartedly agreed and with Amy at the helm, *Ready Set Socks* is here.

We are endlessly grateful to not only Rachel and Amy, but also to Sophie Heathscott for her expert tutorial writing (she is a wonderful teacher in person, too) as well as her prowess in wrangling yarns and knitters to knit the projects for this book. Speaking of whom, we must also thank our fastidious test and sample knitters whose speed and attention to detail never fail to impress! Our words and instructions are only as good as their editing, and we have Jemima Bicknell, Laura Chau, Emi Ito, Chaitanya Muralidhara, and Annie Prime to thank for their expertise in those areas. Mary and Dan at Bless and our photographer Kendra Bellamy, as ever, make us look good and prove that, in fact, you *can* judge a book by its cover.

Much happens after the book goes to print, and that's where we are grateful to our wider Pom Pom team for their efforts in getting this book into your hands. Alice, Belinda, Francesca, Gayle, Jasmine, Noush, and Sofia are a team that are not only good at what they do, but also really care about what we do at Pom Pom - there is no substitute for their passion and we know that shines through in these pages.

Meghan + Lydia, Editors

A special thanks to the incredible dancers who inspired the pattern names for this book:

Cyd Charisse, Hollywood dance legend

Misty Copeland, first African American principal dancer with the American Ballet Theater

Savion Glover, virtuoso American tap dancer and choreographer

Sylvie Guillem, acclaimed French ballet and contemporary dancer

Gregory Hines, legendary jazz tap dancer, actor, and choreographer

Janet Jackson, American pop R&B singer and dancer

Sono Osato, first Asian American dancer to travel the world with the Russian Ballet

Debbie Reynolds, Hollywood actress, singer, and dancer

Alice Sheppard, groundbreaking British wheelchair dancer

Kenneth Shirley, dancer, filmmaker, and founder of the Indigenous Enterprise dance group